NAVAL DOCKYARDS SOCIETY
www.hants.org.uk/navaldockyar
Supported by the National Maritime Museur

The Inaugural meeting of the Naval Dockyards Society was held at the National Maritime Museum, 14 September 1996 and the Constitutional meeting held at the National Maritime Museum on 1 March 1997.

Mission

To stimulate the production and exchange of information and research into naval dockyards and associated organisations. The Society will be concerned with all aspects of naval dockyards including construction, history, workforce, technology, ongoing conservation and surrounding communities.

Aims

1. Compile and distribute a list of members and their interests.
2. Publish two newsletters a year containing information, members' reports of activities, issues and book reviews.
3. Organise meetings and other relevant activities.
4. Increase public awareness of historic dockyards and related sites.
5. Increase access to historic dockyards and related sites.
6. Create links with related organisations in Britain and abroad.
7. Coordinate and promote new research.
8. Create a database of the present status of historic dockyards and related sites worldwide.
9. Offer assistance to those establishing dockyard heritage sites.
10. Encourage the storage and collection of oral history interviews related to dockyard history.
11. Coordinate the historical, architectural and technical expertise available within the society.
12. Compile a dockyards bibliography.

Navy Board Research Project

In 1999 the Society agreed to continue a project begun as a research undertaking by Richard Saville and Susan Lumas in the 1970s to create an index and database of class ADM 106 documents at the Public Record Office (now The National Archives). This collection of Navy Board in-letters 1658-1837 comprises miscellaneous correspondence from dockyard commissioners, officers and workers, naval captains and contractors from around the world. The project will foliate letters from ADM 106 and ADM B and ADM BP at the National Maritime Museum Greenwich, list and index their contents and input data to an on-line research resource. Researchers may access and interrogate the database electronically on The National Archives' online Catalogue.

Over 100,000 letters have been completed: 24% of ADM 106 at Kew and 32% of ADM B and ADM BP at Greenwich. Years available online are 1696, 1738-1741, 1744, 1745, 1750 and 1754-1770. Some of ADM B and ADM BP (listed as ADM 354) covers 1738-1739 and 1749-1758. The gap 1741-1744 represents damaged letters which are being conserved at Kew.
Fourteen volunteers work across the two sites. Among such routine matters as stores, transports, superannuation, surveys, embezzlement and wages, are unique items such as the ropemakers' 1675 mutiny, experiments and inventions, materials and medicines, Plymouth Yard expansion in 1761 and the Surveyor General of HM Woods difficulties in America. This is an invaluable resource for international students of naval, dockyard, technological, social

and administrative history.

The Society also supports Project Dockyard 2010: The History of Simon's Town Dockyard, 1900-2010

The South Africa Naval Heritage Trust and Simon's Town Historical Society are producing a history of Simon's Town Dockyard (East Yard) in 2010 to commemorate the centenary of commissioning the Selbourne Graving Dock. A Project Officer is collecting information from retired naval officers and 'Home Agreement' men. Contact Project Officer, Project Dockyard 2010, SA Naval Museum, Private Bag X1, Simon's Town, 7995, Republic of South Africa. kemndine1@telkomsa.net   www.simonstown.com/stdc/civic/sths/dockyard2010.htm

Society Membership

Members receive a list of members' interests, two newsletters a year, with an annual conference presenting the latest research, and the opportunity to participate in the research project, the Annual General Meeting and at least one outdoor visit a year. Currently we have around 200 members throughout the world: ex-dockyard personnel, family historians and academics.

Subscription rates for 2006

> £15 *Individual Members*
> £20 *Joint Members: two people living at one address*
> £30 *Institutional Members*

Members are encouraged to pay by Standing Order. For overseas members (without a sterling bank account) to generate no exchange expenses or other deductions to the Society, the cheapest method is to pay by international money order.

2006 COMMITTEE

CONTENTS

ACKNOWLEDGEMENTS

This is the first volume of *The Naval Dockyards Society's Transactions*. Fittingly it records our most successful conference to date. The Society intends to publish as many of our previous conference papers as possible. As many members live too far away to attend our conferences, the Society undertakes to make them available to all the members and a wider audience, to show what the Society is achieving. Some have been published elsewhere, others were not made available, but it is now a condition for selecting speakers that they must offer their paper for publication.

Preparations for 'Portsmouth Dockyard in the Age of Nelson' were inextricably linked to the other events planned for 2005, a year when one could be confident that major maritime history events did not clash, thanks to two years of coordination by SeaBritain. Our preparations started in 2002, when I asked Jonathan Coad to give a paper on the Block Mills and Alan Aberg to chair the Conference. From the start English Heritage collaborated generously with us: Chairman Sir Neil Cossons, Jonathan Coad, Robert Law, Keith Falconer and Peter Guillery, all of whom have been involved in a defining architectural and documentary survey of the building. Also Tony Woolrich, who researched that defining moment when Nelson visited the Block Mills on 14 September 1805, his last day in England before the Battle of Trafalgar. During one of the local planning meetings, when participants were suffering from Nelson-fatigue, it was remarked grimly that Nelson would greatly have relished all the attention paid him.

The focus was Nelson, but the substance was the naval administration and technology produced by John Jervis/Earl St Vincent, Charles Middleton/Lord Barham, Marc Brunel, Samuel Bentham, Simon Goodrich, Benjamin and Joseph Tucker and Sir Robert Seppings. Our Trafalgar 200 sub-committee, composed of Director Campbell MacMurray, Assistant Director Colin White and Development Manager Julian Thomas from the Royal Naval Museum, and Louis Shurmer-Smith and Ray Riley from the University of Portsmouth, started meeting in March 2003. These meetings continued at roughly three-monthly intervals and I gained tremendously from the experience and insight of my colleagues. The Society is indebted to Campbell for welcoming the delegates and donating the conference facilities at the Royal Naval Museum, the superb assistance from Sue Goodger, Vicki Ingles and Matthew Sheldon and the good-natured and technical expertise of Keith Davis and Bryn Jenkyns. I am very grateful to Tim Goodhead, Head of the School of Environmental Design and Management, for the use of University of Portsmouth's conference facilities, to the audiovisual expertise of David Sherren, and to Ruth Pearson, David Sherren and Bill Johnson for designing the posters. Thanks also to Chris Arkell of the Royal Naval Museum Bookshop, who gave delegates a discount, of which I believe they took full advantage, and to Portsmouth Royal Dockyard Historical Trust Support Group whose bookstall was provided by Wally and Win Ryder.

I valued the early collaboration of Portsmouth City Museum, through Museums and Records Service Manager Paul Raymond and Local History Officer Katy Ball, who with Duncan Walker created a marvellous mini-exhibition on 'Portsmouth at the Time of Nelson' at the pre-Conference welcome evening, assisted by Lorna MacDougall and Geoff Coats.

Over the two days of the conference the most important people to thank were, of course, the speakers, Jonathan Coad, Susan Wilkin, Ray Riley, James Thomas, Matthew Sheldon, Roger Morriss, Ann Coats, Peter Goodwin and Andrew Lambert, all of whom delivered outstanding papers. Our anonymous referees ensured the quality of this publication. Sir Neil Cossons launched the conference incomparably by his outstanding grasp of technological history, before introducing Jonathan Coad's paper, which is expanded in *The Portsmouth Block*

Mills (English Heritage, 2005). Alan Aberg chaired the Conference wittily and impeccably and Charlotte Frost and John Gunn were invaluable in registering and assisting the delegates.

A treat on the first day was a tour of the Block Mills, guided by Jonathan Coad, Robert Law and Peter Guillery of English Heritage. Portsmouth Royal Dockyard Historical Trust Support Group was indispensable, providing the knowledge of Brian Patterson and Archie Malley, escorts, Brian Paterson, Archie Malley, Bob Russell, and Alan Meaby. Jacqui Shaw, Lisa Sunderland and Lucy Thomson of Flagship Portsmouth and Campbell MacMurray, Julian Thomas, Vicki Ingles, Keith Davis and Bryn Jenkyns of the Royal Naval Museum were also invaluable as escorts. Alec Barlow, who worked in the Block Mills till it closed in 1974, was also a guide, displaying his own collection of artefacts in the former Smiths' Shop. For allowing delegates to gain safe access to the Block Mills I must also thank Chief Naval Base Safety Officer Captain Andrew Kirk, Naval Base Security Officer Lt Cdr T Ford, Steve Barrow of the Customer Estates Organisation and Health and Safety Officer Andy Anderson.

Chris Muir of Terracotta Room provided delicious meals at a very reasonable price and the Conference Dinner and Trafalgar Ale were provided by the now, sadly, defunct George Gale & Co Ltd at the Old Customs House, Gunwharf Quays.

On the second day Lt Cdr Frank Nowosielski, CO HMS *Victory*, kindly give permission for the delegates to visit the *Victory* Sail exhibition in Storehouse 10. We then had a fascinating tour of the Royal Naval Academy, for which I must thank Cdr A R Trevithick (appropriately a descendant of engineer Richard Trevithick), Mess President, and Duty Officer Lt Cdr John Webb, for their generosity in welcoming and escorting the delegates.

The boat crew from Solent & Wightline Cruises handsomely transported those who remained for the tour of Portsmouth Harbour, to put the events discussed into context. To gain access to Royal Clarence Victualling Yard they were given every consideration by Andrea Parsons and Lisa Söderbaum-Beach, archaeologists at Gifford & Partners and Richard Manville of Berkeley Group. At Explosion! Peter Lawton, Bill Sainsbury and Marc Farrance organised their tour from guide Mike Hockin and they could take peaceful tea overlooking the beautiful little harbour built to serve Priddy's Hard.

Finally I must thank the seventy-seven delegates for their contributions, good humour and patience, Chairmen Roger Morriss and David Davies and the Committee for giving me a free hand, and Ray Riley for editing these *Transactions* and bringing the first volume to life.

Ann Coats, Hon.Secretary and Conference Organiser, 2 July, 2006

PREFACE

Ray Riley

Arguably Britain's most outstanding naval personality, Nelson is particularly associated with Portsmouth since the town was not only his point of departure for Trafalgar, but is also host to his flagship, HMS *Victory*. Moreover, it has recently been established that Nelson undertook a tour of the Dockyard, including a visit to the Block Mills, on his last morning ashore. The bicentennial celebration of Trafalgar in Portsmouth in June 2005 inevitably focused on matters naval, with a review of an international array of warships by the Queen, a mock battle between ships of the line and an impressive fireworks display. Far less attention was paid to the supporting infrastructure in both the Dockyard and in the town of Portsmouth where the fleet was based. To its credit, the Naval Dockyards Society rose to this challenge and held a conference in the Naval Base between 30 April and 2 May taking as its theme 'Portsmouth Dockyard in the Age of Nelson'. Nelson and Trafalgar, then as now, may have exercised the minds of the nation, but coincidentally, beneath the gingoism and heroism, lay a raft of technological change in the Yard which made an important contribution to the defeat of the French and Spanish fleets. Speakers addressed this issue from a variety of standpoints, collectively adding to knowledge of several aspects of contemporary shipbuilding, repair and fleet servicing.

It is all too easy to view Portsmouth Dockyard as a closed system, an enterprise concerned with the construction and repair of naval ships. Reality is more complex. The Yard effectively danced to the tune played by the Admiralty and to a lesser extent the Navy Board, rendering it important to examine their policies in order to understand developments at Portsmouth. Taking warship construction as his start point, Andrew Lambert demonstrates the way in which the Admiralty sought to overcome the limitations of the existing building methods by seeking the support of the Royal Society for the innovatory proposals advanced by Sir Robert Seppings. It is argued that the principal stumbling blocks were not technical, but rather political and bureaucratic. Continuing the theme of the role of influences upon the Dockyard, Roger Morriss looks at the work of Samuel Bentham who was appointed by the Admiralty as inspector General of Naval Works in 1796. Such were Bentham's innovatory qualities that it is probably simpler to consider aspects of production and support activities that he did not improve, yet despite his wide ranging reforms, Bentham himself regarded innovation as social engineering as much as technical change. Moving from top-down influences, Susan Wilkin offers a detailed statistical examination of what actually went on in Portsmouth Yard between 1793 and 1815. A rich vein of data is presented on production and refit, on changes effected to the dry docks, in metal and wood working, including the manufacture of pulley blocks, handsomely supporting the proposition that productivity in the Yard was of a high order. Focusing specifically on ship repair, Peter Goodwin describes the work carried out on HMS *Victory* at Chatham in 1800-3, and on two vessels at Plymouth. It is not unreasonable to suggest that similar repairs were undertaken on ships at Portsmouth.

Despite the innovations charted in the previous papers, it is arguable that the major technological breakthrough took place in the Portsmouth Block Mills. Here pulley block-making machinery, designed by Marc Brunel, and brought to fruition with the assistance of Bentham, Simon Goodrich and Henry Maudslay, not only reduced the cost of manufacture, but also represented the world's first metal machine tools for mass production. The latter is popularly associated with Henry Ford, but the Portsmouth machinery predates it by a century. Portsmouth's role, and indeed that of the naval dockyards, in the industrial revolution is seldom recognised, probably because historians have concentrated on private sector developments. Three papers endeavour to redress the balance. Jonathan Coad looked at the introduction of steam power in the Block Mills, together with their construction and the organisation of pulley block manufacture. Additionally, he examined the roles played by Bentham's staff, by Marc Brunel and Henry Maudslay. Coad's paper is not included in the *Transactions* since a substantially more comprehensive account, entitled *The Portsmouth Block Mills*, has been published by English Heritage. The operation of the pulley block machinery is generally regarded as the province of engineers, rendering Ray Riley's description in simple terms of how things worked a helpful exercise. However, of considerable interest is his attempt to place the machinery within the history of technology; many of the principles had been established earlier, by Leonardo da Vinci for instance, but it was Brunel's genius to bring them together. Moving away from the machinery, Ann Coats considers issues such as recruitment, rates of pay and working practices in the Block Mills. She argues that although the machines were new and the workforce recruited from outside the Yard, working practices reflected tradition, despite Bentham's efforts to the contrary.

The Block Mills, the new docks and modified shipbuilding techniques may have been at the core of innovation during the age of Nelson, but the victualling of vessels was a crucial issue, one that has attracted little research effort, despite the employment of over 500 men, more than were to be found in the largest textile mills at the time. Matthew Sheldon's paper offering an overview of the work of the Victualling Office is therefore timely, opening up an important aspect of the broader naval system. Just as the Dockyard was set within the political environment of government and Admiralty on the one hand, it was also embedded within Portsmouth's civil environment on the other. James Thomas takes up the relationship between the Yard and the town, demonstrating that the aims of the two were not always compatible, despite the symbiotic situation that obtained. Taken together, these papers unquestionably throw fresh light on the Dockyard in the age of Nelson, and should provide a fruitful platform for further research.

SCIENCE AND SEAPOWER:
THE NAVY BOARD, THE ROYAL SOCIETY AND THE STRUCTURAL REFORMS OF SIR ROBERT SEPPINGS

Andrew Lambert

Abstract

The Revolutionary and Napoleonic wars made unprecedented demands on the structure of the wooden warship, exposing the limitations of the existing system of ship construction. To solve the complex problem of design, coupled with timber supply and treatment problems, the Admiralty increasingly looked outside the existing structures, the Navy Board and the Dockyards, securing the support of the Royal Society for the radical reforms of Sir Robert Seppings. However, the main issues were political and bureaucratic rather than technical or scientific. The Admiralty used science to exert control over a recalcitrant Navy Board as the war ended, and new policies were required for the post-war reconstruction of the fleet.

Introduction

This essay examines the often difficult relationship between the Navy Board, based at Somerset House, and the Admiralty in Whitehall, through the issue of shipbuilding technology.

In the 18th century large warships spent much of their time at anchor, and many were paid off through the winter, but the Wars of the French Revolution and Empire caused a fundamental shift in strategy. In a total war the fleet had to be available year round, because the cost of failure was no longer the loss of overseas possessions, large or small, but the complete destruction of the nation's political, economic and religious systems. France employed new, terrifying methods of war, ideologically motivated mass conscript armies, supported by revolutionary fifth columns to undermine the states it attacked. To defeat the threat of invasion British fleets remained on station in all weathers, and all seasons. Admiral the Earl St. Vincent adopted this approach in 1799 off Brest, and those who came after him kept it up. This strategy crippled the French navy, denied it any opportunity to achieve significant results, and cut its supply lines.[1] At

the same time this strategy wore out the British fleet at an unprecedented rate, making ever-greater demands for timber, demands that could not be met using existing sources and methods of construction. Mounting evidence of structural weakness and the shortage of key pieces of timber prompted the development of several short term expedients, notably Gabriel Snodgrass's system of internal bracing, which was applied to older, smaller units to produce a fleet to blockade the Scheldt between 1803 and 1805, while the larger and more modern units were stationed off Brest and Toulon. Others substituted iron for key timbers, especially knees. While useful, these measures merely tinkered with the consequences of the problem, and offered no long-term solution.

One ship will stand as a metaphor for this problem. The nearly new 74 gun ship of the line HMS *Kent* served in the Mediterranean under Nelson's command between 1803 and 1805.[2] In little more than two years this ship was torn to pieces by sustained cruising in heavy weather, and as Nelson waited for fresh ships became so weak that he dared not send her home alone. By April 1804 she was reported, 'so leakey and unsafe a state to keep the sea in bad weather' that Nelson ordered a committee of Captains and carpenters to report on her hull and topsides. Their report convinced him that the *Kent* had to be sent home that summer, accompanied by a transport: 'her hull being is so bad a state makes it unsafe to trust her, even at this season of the year'.[3]

Eventually the shattered ship limped home with cables strung under her hull. Few would have expected much future service from such a wreck. Yet she would remain afloat and in service for another 80 years. When she reached Chatham dockyard she was rebuilt by the greatest innovator in the history of wooden shipbuilding, effectively laying the foundations for the modern ship.

In responding to the structural issues raised by twenty years of total war, and a shift of the strategic paradigm, British Shipwright Robert Seppings produced a series of connected developments in naval architecture between 1800 and 1820 that transformed the structural design of the wooden ship. He used an entirely evolutionary empirical approach to the problem, relying on extensive testing at sea, and the minimum of pure science.

Appointed Master Shipwright at Chatham by St. Vincent in 1804, Seppings spent the next six years refining his concept of diagonal riders by applying it to a number of old or damaged ships with highly satisfactory results. The first of these was the *Kent*, and he specifically rejected the Snodgrass method when proposing his own system. In 1806 the Navy Board gave permission for another 74 and a frigate to be repaired in the same way. Only in 1810, after extensive testing did Seppings approach the Admiralty with his concept, making a presentation supported by models and diagrams. The Admiralty recognised the importance of his work. They were also aware of the opposition of the two Surveyors of the Navy, the senior naval architects who sat at the Navy Board and exerted a powerful influence over the Controller, Captain Sir Thomas Thompson.

Seppings' work would become the *lietmotif* of post-war naval reconstruction, and a landmark in relations between the Admiralty, the Navy Board and the Royal Society. In the final half dozen paragraphs of his written submission Seppings set out his two key points: increased structural strength, which builds longer life; and improved timber usage, both in design and treatment, which reduced demand. These two concepts would solve the timber problem 'should the well grounded hopes of durability be realized, the saving of timber, and indeed of every article required for this enormous branch of the national expenditure, would be immense.'[4] Seppings' work was essentially practical, he thought in terms of real ships, real problems and effective solutions. This was the best approach to the infinitely variable fabric of the wooden warship, which could never be reduced to pure science and abstract theory.

At the Admiralty the reformers, led by the First Lord, Sir Charles Yorke (FRS) and the Second Secretary, John Barrow, (FRS 1805), saw Seppings' system as the solution to the three great problems of late war naval policy, high estimates, timber shortage and worn out ships. Along the way they could shake up the Navy Board, which had become set in its ways, relatively inefficient and increasingly minded to be independent of the Admiralty.

The System Explained

On February 5th 1810 Seppings offered his scheme for reducing timber consumption by altering the disposition of materials in the frames of ships to the Navy Board. He was invited to present his model and ideas to the Board on the 14th.[5] Two days after the presentation Seppings was still at Somerset House, writing up his concept in detail. His core argument was that the arrangement of the materials, rather than mere quantity, determined the strength of the ship. The triangular principle he employed would prevent hogging, the obvious indicator of structural weakness, by providing uniform strength throughout. In addition his complete wedged fillings in the lower would exclude rats and improve caulking. He even referred to the work of the Society for the Improvement of Naval Architecture in the 1790s. Having already submitted his idea to other shipwrights, 'sea officers and civilians of science' Seppings was confident that he had the answer to the timber problem. However, he realised that it was a bold step to propose so radical an alteration to the time-honoured system. The paper was referred for the consideration of the Surveyors.[6]

Three weeks later Seppings resumed his initiative, pointing out to the Board that in the monthly progress statement they had approved his submission to repair the 74 gun HMS *Tremendous* using his new methods. He wanted confirmation that this was what they meant. Anticipating opposition he suggested comparing her sailing qualities before and after the work, the type of wholly practical test that he always preferred when assessing his work. If successful his principle promised to save thousands of pounds and hundred of oaks.[7] Evidently the Surveyors called Seppings' bluff, reporting against his proposal. He quickly prepared a point-by-point refutation of their case, and sent it to the Admiralty, stressing that the issue was 'of considerable national importance'.[8] The destination of the paper revealed the real authority behind his otherwise astonishingly bold action in challenging his line managers at the Navy Board. A month later the Admiralty used this information, ordering the Navy Board to allow him to repair the *Tremendous* because it had, 'in our judgement in great measure removed those objections you are hereby required and directed with a view of giving Mr Seppings' Plan a fair trial'.[9]

The First Lord of the Admiralty was sufficiently impressed by Seppings' ideas to visit the *Tremendous* at Chatham once she was ready. Sir Charles Yorke was in the yard in mid October 1810, accompanied by his brother Naval Lord Admiral Sir Joseph Yorke. This gave Seppings the opportunity to show them the frame and structure before the ship's internal bulkheads were fixed.[10] The fate of the system was now overtly linked to the performance of the *Tremendous*, and when she had been at sea for close to a year the Admiralty sent a copy her Captain's highly satisfactory report to Seppings. This revealed a degree of leakage from the decks, but Seppings was able to show that this stemmed from her imperfect initial caulking, and the green timber used for her deck planking. Satisfied by his explanation the Admiralty ordered her to be re-caulked at Sheerness as soon as possible. More

significantly the paper was referred to the First Lord.[11] Although Charles Yorke only served as First Lord between May 1810 and March 1812 his interest in Seppings' work was sustained long after his term as First Lord through his active role as a Fellow of the Royal Society.

The Search for Validation

On the strength of the *Tremendous* report Yorke was prepared to go further. However, the Navy Board was still resisting change. Invited to respond to Seppings' submission, the Surveyors turned to Jean Louis Barrallier, second assistant to the Surveyors, for a report. This was highly significant: the *émigré* Frenchman Barrallier was the only member of the Surveyor's office with a theoretical education in naval architecture.[12] Having failed to win over one office in the Somerset House quadrangle the Admiralty turned to find support on another.

On November 19th 1811 the Admiralty requested a distinguished group of experts, both theoretical and practical, to attend the Admiralty for a presentation of Seppings' system. They were Sir Joseph Banks, President of the Royal Society; Doctor Thomas Young, the Foreign Secretary of the Society, and William Wollaston, Principal Secretary of the Society; John Wells EsqHuddart of the East India Company, a noted maritime innovator;

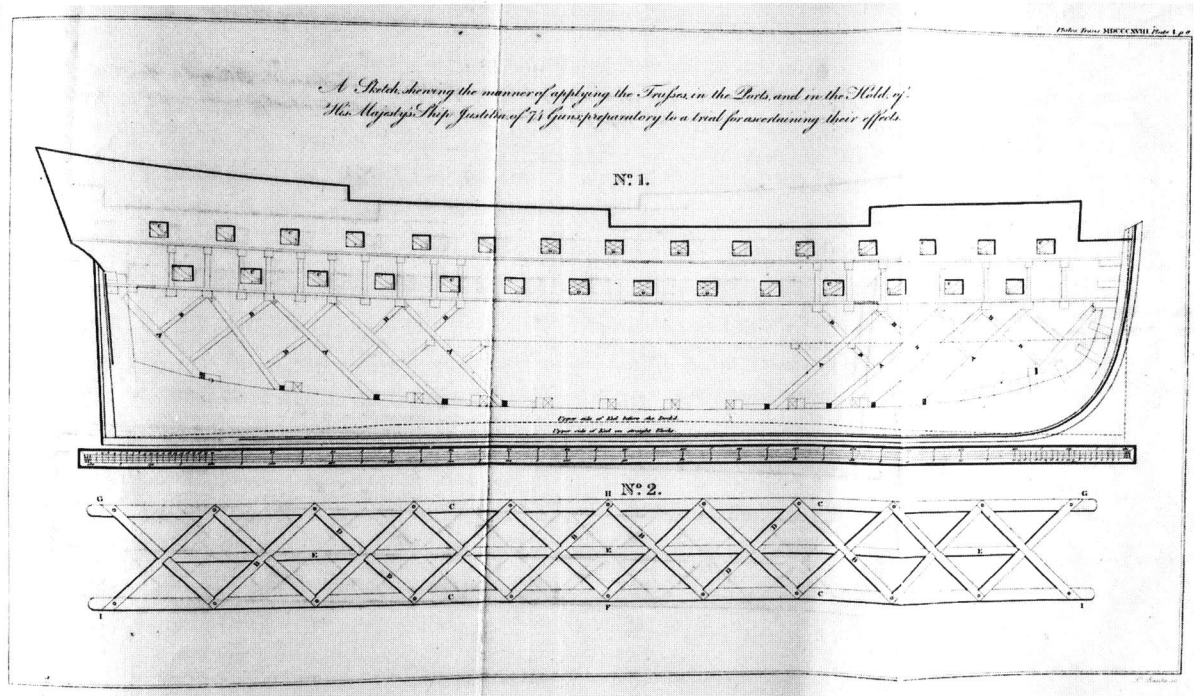

Fig. 1. Plan showing Seppings' system of triangular bracing applied to the 74-gun ship HMS *Justitia*.
Courtesy: RN Museum, Portsmouth.

Huddart of the East India Company, a noted maritime innovator; the engineer John Rennie; Mr Smart; William Allen of the Royal Institution[13] and Doctor Taylor, Secretary to the Society of Arts. Of these Wollaston and Young would produce written reports, suggesting that the other gentlemen were either content, or did not attend.[14]

While the Admiralty had found in Seppings' paper the *leitmotif* for a major policy initiative they needed to validate his concept, using another method to complement empirical observation. Here the key intermediary was John Barrow, Second Secretary to the Admiralty 1804-06 and 1807-1845. Despite the opposition of the Navy Board Barrow had persuaded Yorke as First Lord of the Admiralty to adopt Seppings' methods on an experimental basis. Barrow was also a Fellow of the Royal Society, elected in 1805 following the publication of his travels in China and South Africa. He quickly became a favourite with the authoritarian President of the Society, Sir Joseph Banks.[15] While greatly facilitated by physical proximity ever closer links between the Navy Board, the Admiralty and the Royal Society in this period reflected the growing importance of scientific enquiry, the lack of any suitable naval expertise and the willingness of the Royal Society to take up the task.[16] The President of the Society, and very much the leading figure between 1778 and 1820, was Sir Joseph Banks. Banks had accompanied Cook on his first voyage, and developed from an inspired amateur botanist into the leading spokesman of science in Britain, and an intimate of his fellow agriculturalist King George III. Banks was a leading figure in the neo-mercantilist school that grew up after the loss of America, which saw the Empire and all its resources as the basis of future prosperity and imperial self-sufficiency. This approach he applied with particular enthusiasm to any issues connected with the navy, from rope and timber, through food preservation to copper sheathing and steam engines.[17] Down to his death in 1820 Banks was the first port of call for any naval enquiry, and his location at the Royal Society, or at his home in Soho Square ensured communication was rapid. By combining his scientific interests with those of the Navy Banks created one of the key alliances that promoted the revival of the Royal Society, which had, after all, been founded by Charles II to support the state and its naval forces. It was a typically British compromise that left the provision of scientific guidance to a body that was neither controlled by, nor responsible to the state for any advice tendered.[18] Even so the value of this advice was appreciated by George III, who backed the Royal Society's request for enlarged accommodation at Somerset House.[19] In 1815 the Society was still a broad church for the advancement of knowledge, combining dilettantes and scientists, noblemen, politicians and explorers. While Banks lived the battle between pure and applied science, gentlemen and experts would be balanced to favour applied science and the contribution of gentleman. Banks controlled nominations to, and the business of the Council, and therefore ran the Society. One of his most effective lieutenants in the last decade of his Presidency was fellow traveller Barrow, a man with a talent for securing the friendship of the great.

The initial enquiry for scientific validation was sent to Banks at the Royal Society, who redirected Barrow's official approach to a number of favoured experts in science and engineering.[20] Barrow's letter to Young of November 19th 1811[21] is typical. It invited him to report on Seppings' method, but was written in language that made it quite clear the Admiralty was seeking scientific validation to counter ingrained opposition at the Navy Board. Barrow wanted a ringing endorsement for a system:

'by which it would appear that an advantage is obtained in strength and durability, while at the same time a very considerable saving of timber is effected and, my Lords having caused a ship of 74 guns to be fastened according to this new mode of construction which after a trial of many months in the North Sea has been found to answer every expectation.. and being desirous of submitting this new principle to the consideration of such men of science and practical experience as may have turned their attention to mechanics in general and more particularly to the construction and fastening of ships.'

Young and Wollaston attended the Admiralty Office on November 24th when Seppings used a model and drawings to explain his principles.[22] Once again the location was critical. Such matters would normally have been dealt with at the Navy Office, far closer to the Royal Society. Wollaston sent in a letter on the December 27th, and Young on the 30th.[23] Both were thanked for their 'interesting communication', which were then forwarded to Seppings for comment.[24] Wollaston's paper was broadly favourable, accepting the 'two leading points viz: oblique bracing and filling in between the timbers'. While he missed the point that ships are constantly faced with shifting forces, and had not understood the structural strength of the diagonal riders as fastened to the keelson and the shelf pieces, Seppings was sure Wollaston's queries would 'soon be removed' if they met.[25]

While Young's primary expertise lay in the field of mathematics, he had compiled a theoretical analysis of carpentry. He chose to view Seppings' submission as a question of the contrast between pure science and practical experience. From his discussions with Seppings he realised that the Surveyor was no mathematician, and more significantly that his ideas were opposed by almost the entire shipwright profession, especially those in high office, an allusion to Senior Surveyor Peake.[26]

Young reported within a month, his paper being dated 30 December 1811. After twenty pages of analysis and advanced mathematics he declared:

'It appears therefore to be sufficiently established, that the principle of employing oblique timbers is a good one, provided that it be so applied as to produce no practical inconvenience.'

He then questioned whether Seppings had arranged his timbers 'in a manner likely to be effectual and not liable to any material objection'. Aware that the Admiralty had already committed itself to the system, he was satisfied that he had found nothing to warrant stopping the experiments. But he was anxious to show that there were limits to the development of any new technology conducted on purely practical grounds. He concluded with a strong re-assertion of the primacy of theoretical science:

'But it must be remembered, in forming conclusions from such experiences, that when arrangement of any kind has nearly attained the maximum of its perfection, it may demonstrably be varied in a considerable degree without a proportional alteration of its effect; so that the most correct knowledge of scientific principles, and the minutest accuracy in their application, must become indispensibly necessary, in order to secure us from the introduction of material errors, derived from the latent operation of accidental causes, foreign to the immediate subjects of investigation.'[27]

While perfectly comprehensible to the scientists, this was altogether too inconclusive for Barrow's purpose, and missed the wider purpose behind the Admiralty initiative. Little wonder Young was told his science was esteemed, but too learned.[28] There was no intention of denigrating Young, or his work as was shown by his appointment to the Admiralty controlled Board of Longitude in

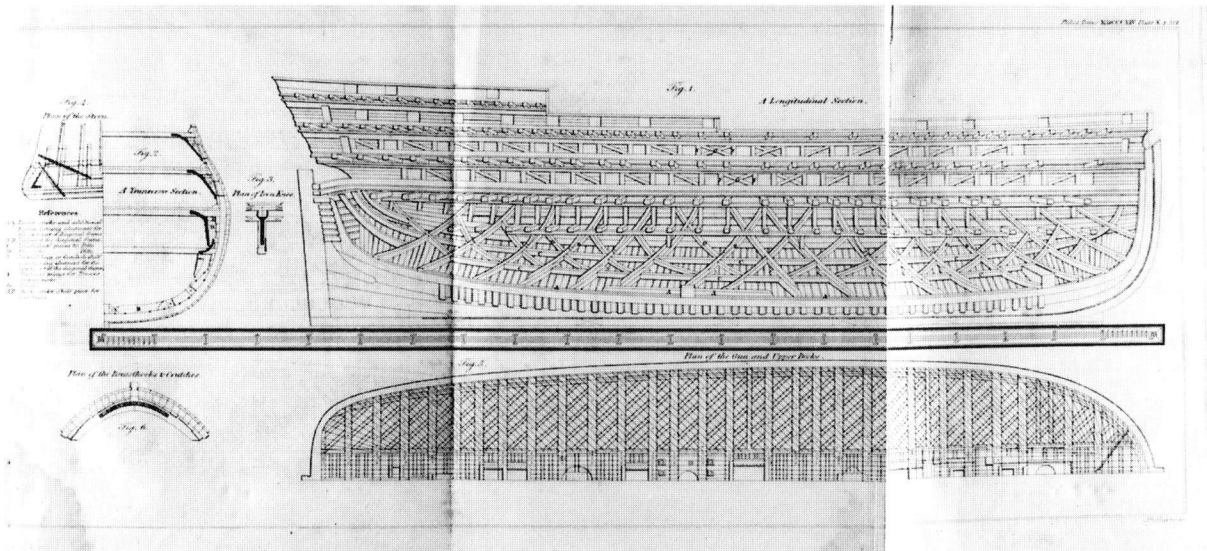

Fig. 2. Longitudinal section of a vessel showing Seppings' bracing system.
Courtesy: RN Museum, Portsmouth.

1818. In a posthumously printed Memoir of 1846 Barrow praised Young's work on the Board, but ignored his report on the Seppings' system.[29] His silence may reflect the embarrassment that Young's report would cause when it resurfaced three years later.

Quite unwittingly the Admiralty had stepped into a political minefield. Their enquiry had re-ignited the increasingly fraught struggle for control of the Royal Society agenda, giving Young an opportunity to strike a blow for pure science. The theoretical scientists were concerned to collect facts by observation or experiment, before reducing them to a theory of universal application. They did not share Banks' pragmatic agenda.[30] While Young shared the views of the pure scientists his critique was tempered by his paid appointment at the Society, and the Board of Longitude. His restraint made it possible for Banks to restore a semblance or order, and produce the necessary scientific credentials the Admiralty required.

After the failure of this initial search for scientific validation Seppings wrote directly to Yorke, with a diagram of an experiment he had conducted to meet an objection posed by Surveyor Peake.[31] When Yorke left office Seppings sent his personal notes to another supporter, Admiral Sir William Domett, one of the senior Naval Lords, while the Captain of the *Tremendous* informed Yorke that she was 'the most perfect ship in His Majesty's service' and hoped the plan would be adopted 'notwithstanding the opposition of the wooden heads'.[32] However the main lines of Admiralty policy were not altered by the new First Lord, Robert Saunders Dundas, Second Viscount Melville. Melville retained the key advisors from Yorke's board, especially Admirals Yorke and Domett.[33] When they met Seppings secured a promise that Melville would inspect the system. For this he built further models (including it appears, the comparative half section now in the National Maritime Museum collection). Melville was impressed, pointedly directing the Navy Board to order Seppings to attend the Board of Admiralty to explain his system.[34] Within a month Seppings had secured an order for the new 120 gun ship HMS *Howe* to be built at Chatham using his diagonal system.

From internal evidence it is clear that the submission (ADM 7/709) was written out in 1812, before Seppings moved to the Surveyor's Office, and may have been compiled for presentation at this appointment.[35] Seppings developed this paper from his earlier manuscripts, and it shows clear links with the submission of March 1810. The paper was bound up and placed in the Admiralty Library, itself a measure typically used by Second Secretary to the Admiralty, John Barrow, to denote the importance of the contents. Barrow also used the document as the basis for the short paper read to the Royal Society, which deleted the polemical material Seppings had included in his long footnotes, and the critical references to the Navy Board.

The fate of Seppings' system was heavily influenced by the steady improvement in the wartime situation after mid 1812. As Napoleon's defeat became inevitable the Admiralty began to consider post-war policy. Although they sought economy and efficiency the precise nature of the programmes that would achieve this remained uncertain. Melville favoured building a huge new dockyard at Northfleet, to take in and repair the existing fleet.[36] For this work Seppings, whose work had transformed the quality and quality of rebuilds, was an obvious candidate.

However, the Navy Board at Somerset House had become increasingly independent minded in matters of technical policy, where it had an undoubted advantage in expertise, and the Admiralty had not been able to exert the type of close control that would be required for such a major policy shift. Indeed the Admiralty had to push hard to secure even modest changes. As a first step toward mastering the opposition of the Navy Board, where the Controller would be guided by the Surveyors on issues of design practice, Seppings was appointed an additional Third Surveyor of the Navy on 14th June 1813. Melville (FRS 1817) took this step on the advice of Barrow. Seppings' situation cannot have been pleasant, clearly seen as an agent of the Admiralty. Fortunately he spent much of his time travelling around the major dockyards inspecting progress. His main reward for the move would be a house, No. 6 Somerset Place, but in 1814 he was still living outside the complex in Chapel Row, Bedford Street.

The appointment of Seppings prompted a crisis at the Navy Board. Recognising that wholesale change was essential to secure their economical objectives the Admiralty determined to appoint a new Controller, as soon as the war ended. Only a change at the top would overcome ingrained opposition. In late 1814 Rear Admiral Sir Thomas Byam Martin would be appointed Controller with a mandate to transform the Navy Board, to ensure Admiralty policy intended to create an economical post-war fleet of durable ships using Seppings' methods.[37]

In the interval the Navy Board had to be forced to accept the Seppings system. Recognising that the Navy Board had no answer to high profile public science, Barrow used his close relationship with Banks to get Seppings' paper read at the Royal Society on March 10th 1814. Among those in the audience were senior Naval Lord Admiral Yorke, ex-First Lord Sir Charles Yorke and Marc Brunel, the Admiralty's favoured engineer. Seppings attended the next Society meeting the following week, as Barrow's guest, to hear his paper recorded in the minutes.[38] The paper, now titled 'On a New Principle of Constructing His Majesty's Ships of War' was almost unchanged from the 1813 original, even using the same diagrams.

Evidently Barrow was unaware of the trend in Society politics, and was horrified when Young's 1811 Admiralty paper was read to the Society only a fortnight later.[39] The faint and inconclusive praise was bad enough, but its publication immediately after Seppings' paper in the first volume of *Philosophical Transactions*[40] for 1814 alarmed Barrow. He struck back quickly, securing Seppings' nomination for the Fellowship, and publishing a severe critique of Young's report in the highly influential Tory *Quarterly Review*. This reflected the importance the Admiralty attached to Seppings' work, and the weight of Young's opinion, if not the rather opaque nature of his paper. Barrow needed to refute Young's equivocal paper, but he could not do so in the Society's publication, where he lacked the scientific standing. This task he left to Seppings, who would have to work round his limited maths to make a better case. Instead Barrow sought a far wider audience in the pages of the *Quarterly Review*.[41] Here Barrow was on home ground, and anonymous. With Admiralty First Secretary John Wilson Croker he was one of the three core contributors to John Murray's powerful journal, and had his pick of subjects to discuss.

The review was restricted to two texts; Young's paper as printed in *Philosophical Transactions* and Seppings' response, his published pamphlet with its rich haul of empirical appendices. After a historical discourse Barrow[42] largely repeated Seppings' explanation, and then attacked Young, accusing him of 'damning with faint praise'. His key argument was the limited relevance of 'abstract science'. He stressed that 'science will not enable a man to become a shipwright.'[43] This line was developed through the review, notably when he stated that Young had no business calling into question Seppings' claims for savings in timber.[44] He also condemned Young's attempt to show that the French had adopted a diagonal system, by the practical test of referring to an example, captured in 1806, which had broken her sheer by feet, rather than the inches normally found on a standard British ship.[45] There were also opportunities to laugh at Young's obscure language, Barrow inviting his tory audience to join him in laughing at passages 'beyond any endeavour of ours to comprehend'.[46] Finally Barrow trumpeted Seppings' preferred test for his system, the one he must have been confident it would pass. Observing that the new 120 gun first rate *Nelson* had broken eight inches in launching, he predicted that her diagonal built sister ship HMS *Howe* would break less than three inches.[47] The paper is littered throughout with evidence from dockyards and ships, which must have been collated by Seppings.

Banks's response to the minor crisis in Admiralty/Society relations was to nominate Barrow for a seat on the Council of the Society. Once on the Council he would serve five years, down to the death of his patron, and he was joined by First Secretary John Croker. With powerful London based naval figures on the Council, the interests of the Navy could not be ignored by the Society. Barrow always stressed the key importance of the connection, approving Banks' remark that one of the Admiralty Secretaries should always be a member of the Council.[48]

Barrow was the prime mover in Seppings being proposed for the Fellowship of the Royal Society. He had the contacts to assemble the eminent list of Admiralty and practical men. Charles Yorke, First Secretary Croker, James Watt, John Rennie, Young and Barrow all signed a citation which declared Seppings to be 'well versed in various branches of natural Knowledge and particularly in the Science and practice of Naval Architecture', and 'likely to become a valuable and useful member'. The election required the notice to be hung in the meeting room for ten weeks.[49] He was elected on November 11th 1814,[50] which dates his proposal back to mid August. His fellow new boys were Captain the Hon. Courtenay Boyle, later to be a Commissioner at the Navy Board, and Captain Francis Beaufort, later Hydrographer of the Navy. All three paid £50 for entry and compounded annual fees.[51]

Shortly after he had been nominated for the Fellowship, Seppings' system was adopted as standard design practice for the Navy, by Admiralty Order of October 1814.[52] The first new ship ordered to this design was the 74 *Malabar*, built in Bombay by the East India Company. With the end of the war the demand for new ships had almost collapsed, and there would be time to reconsider which types and classes to construct, but for the interval the yard at Bombay required work.[53]

Seppings' response to Young's objections was defiantly empirical, continuing the theme of practice versus theory. The first initiative was to reprint his Royal Society Paper as a pamphlet in 1815, accompanied by a mass of empirical data drawn from ships at sea. Given the source of the additional evidence, and the importance of the paper to Admiralty plans it is likely that Barrow had a hand in funding and possibly editing a publication which he would use to great effect in his review article. In a second Royal Society paper, 'On the Great Strength given to Ships of War by the application of Diagonal Braces' Seppings provided a more calculated response to Young, and his other critics.[54] It took the form of a report on 'a practical experiment' carried out on the old, and greatly deformed ex Danish battleship *Justitia*. Having docked the ship at Portsmouth, Seppings straightened her wracked hull using simple diagonals, installed sights to record her shape and removed the braces. Seppings established his empirical credentials on the first page, stressing that he had only brought his ideas to the Society after the 'utility of the experiment had been fully established in the opinion of most naval officers'. He then challenged anyone to show that it had ever been 'applied' elsewhere. To show that his system was on an altogether larger scale he cited the inspiration drawn from 'the plans and drawings of the celebrated bridge at Schäffhausen[55], and from no other source.' By the use of quickly applied diagonal braces, a dry dock and accurate sighting instruments Seppings was able to measure the impact of his diagonal principle on a seriously deformed ship. He also secured reports from the dockyard officers, including Simon Goodrich, the Navy Board engineer.[56] These allowed him to take a well-merited swipe at Young. The experiments had shown exactly what had been predicted. Seppings concluded on a triumphant note, reporting that the 120 gun ship *Howe* had broken little more than three inches in launching, in contrast to more than nine in her regular built sisters *St. Vincent* and *Nelson*. This was, unsurprisingly, the test that Barrow had set out for the system in his *Quarterly Review* article. In addition Admiral Sir George Cockburn, who would join the Admiralty Board in a few months, contributed his praise on the partial application of the system to HMS *Northumberland,* which he had used to carry Bonaparte to St. Helena.

The whole paper was neatly constructed, clear, and overwhelmingly impressive. However, it contained not one word that would have been recognised a pure science, and very little that passed muster as applied science. Only the rigorous sightings on the *Justitia* showed scientific enquiry. In selecting the Schäffhausen bridge as an inspiration, Seppings demonstrated his preference for craft tradition, the bridge design being triumph of Swiss practical carpentry, not theory.[57]

The Triumph of Seppings' system

The award of the Copley Gold Medal of the Royal Society in 1818 recognised the national importance of Seppings' work and, according to the most acute critic of the Society, was itself a highly symbolic gesture.[58] That the award was made by a Council led by Banks, and including Barrow and Croker, should make the purpose clear. Largely through their efforts to secure scientific validation for Seppings' system the Admiralty had acquired an unprecedented degree of influence in the affairs of the Society.[59] Although no scientist, Seppings did not disgrace the Society, being one of only 51 members then living to have published three or more papers in 1830. He would serve on the Council for one year, and took an active part in Society affairs.[60]

The final piece of the Admiralty initiative was the installation of the new Controller, Admiral Sir Thomas Byam Martin. Martin would work closely with Seppings over the next fifteen years, adopting the 1814 paper as the basic document on which the policy of the Navy Board would be based. Although Peake and Tucker continued to resist the system, Seppings could rely on Byam Martin and, if necessary, Melville to force his views on his colleagues. When Peake retired in 1822, Seppings' position became far stronger. By 1818 Martin was so far convinced of the merits of his chief coadjudicator that he recommended him for a major financial reward on basis of the savings secured by his work. In 1819 Seppings was knighted through the agency of Croker, despite the disquiet of Melville, then absent in Scotland.[61]

However, the Admiralty's influence in the Royal Society came at a price. At the end of the war Banks, aided by Barrow, urged the use of naval vessels for exploration and surveying, reviving initiatives Banks had been pushing since his heroic days sailing with Cook. When Barrow prompted the Admiralty to send a steam vessel to explore the Congo River, Banks was consulted. On the basis of his own experience as a mine owner, and his close connection with leading practical scientists at the Royal Society, he recommended an engine from Boulton & Watt, installed by John Rennie. Seppings designed the vessel, HMS *Congo*, and she was successfully driven by her paddle wheels, but the engine was too heavy for a sea passage and had to be removed. Even so her legacy was important, for the choice of engines, ship design and engineering expertise were to dominate the first generation of Royal Navy steamships, which the Navy Board had designed by

Seppings, built by his pupil Oliver Lang at Woolwich, only a short barge journey down river, and fitted with Boulton & Watt engines.

Seppings' third Royal Society paper 'On a New Principle of Constructing Ships in the Mercantile Navy' of 1820 served many agendas. Although an obvious reform for a maritime commercial nation the last paragraph continued the response to Young, although there were other targets. The criticism of merchant shipbuilding practice justified the post-war decision not to build warships in merchant yards, and represented a lecture on how to do better in future, when the country has need of these resources again. Once again Barrow sent the paper direct to the President, the ailing Sir Joseph Banks. In requesting that it be read he stressed its importance, and the fact that it came from 'our active and intelligent surveyor'.[62] It was duly delivered on March 2nd and 9th; although members were advised that 'several drawings accompany this paper, the inspection of which is requisite to render the further details which it contains intelligible.'[63]

By this stage the Navy Board was also closely linked to the Royal Society across the courtyard at Somerset House. Commissioners Courtenay Boyle, and Robert Barlow joined the list of naval FRS, while John Knowles, Chief Clerk of the Surveyors Office was elected FRS in 1822 for his pamphlet *The Elements and Practice of Naval Architecture*, a robust defence of Seppings' system. Needless to say Seppings was one of his proposers, along with Marc Brunel, Plymouth breakwater constructor Joseph Whidbey, and Admiral Barlow, the Navy Board Commissioner at Chatham. Knowles' pamphlet was quickly taken up by the historian William James, who used it to complete his entirely favourable discussion of the system.[64] This was unsurprising, given his links with the Admiralty.

Key Admiralty policy-makers were also strongly represented in the Royal Society, Admiral Sir George Cockburn (FRS 1820), Sir George Clerk, First Sea Lord Sir William Johnstone Hope, Lord Melville's Private Secretary Robert Hay, Hydrographer Horsborough, William Marsden, Basil Hall, Thomas Frankland, Earl Spencer, Joseph Whidbey and Charles Yorke ensuring that the Admiralty was strongly represented on the

Society's ruling Council almost continuously from 1800 to 1820. After the death of Banks in 1820 the increasing specialisation of Royal Society reduced the Admiralty's interest. The abolition of the Navy Board in 1832 greatly reduced the input of Somerset House into naval policy, shifting all policy decisions to Whitehall. Even so the Royal Society was still seen as an important validator of shipbuilding development after the reforms. Although Seppings was dismissed in 1832, chief constructor John Edye and the new Surveyor Captain Sir William Symonds were both FRS, along with Sir William Burnett, the Director of Medical Services and proposer of a standard prophylactic for dry rot.

After 1815 the Royal Society took an increasing role in applied science and mathematics, but not all naval/scientific collaboration was successful. After assuming the Presidency of the Royal Society in 1820 Humphry Davy continued the connection with the Navy. He devoted two years to pioneering work on electricity based protection systems to slow down the erosion of the copper sheathing on ships' hulls.[65] Adopted after insufficient sea-going experience this pioneering example of electro-chemical science was a complete failure, reminding naval administrators that the gulf between practical science and real ships was a great as it had been with Seppings. The relationship between naval need and scientific provision would have to be re-thought.[66] This process began with the establishment of a standing Admiralty Committee in 1829, to advise 'on all questions of discoveries, inventions, calculations and other scientific subjects'. The fee of £100 for each of the three members was no small incentive.[67] Michael Faraday continued the connection down to the 1850s.[68] Both Navy and Science were in transition, recognising mutual interest, but increasingly diverging as the Royal Society emphasised pure science, losing touch with the needs of the navy, which began to develop its own scientific expertise.[69]

Conclusion

The adoption of Seppings' structural engineering reforms, the key to an effective post 1815 naval policy, exposed the complex relationship between the Admiralty and the Navy Board, forcing the Admiralty to call on new allies to force the system onto the nominally subordinate board. The Royal Society provided vital scientific validation for the policy change, despite the faint praise of Thomas Young, and in return secured the support of the Admiralty for post-war exploration missions. That the first of these combined Banks' and Barrow's African interests, Seppings' structure and his sponsor James Watt's engine, demonstrated how the process served all those who participated. Defeated and forced to follow Seppings' methods under post-war Controller Byam Martin the Navy Board was ripe for the radical reform that Melville had planned and Graham carried out in 1832, that is, total abolition. Once the entire policy-making process had been taken to Whitehall the Royal Society ceased to be an important player in the Navy's internal debates.

Seppings' system enabled the wooden warship to grow by over 50%, and bear the weight and vibration of early steam engines. It provided the wooden ship with another forty years of pre-eminence, and spanning the age that separated *Victory* from *Warrior*. The role of the Royal Society in securing the adoption of the system demonstrated the importance of the improved ships to the state, rather than the scientific basis of Seppings' ideas. In any choice between pure science and empirical knowledge, early 19th century policy-makers would always trust their own eyes.

References

1   Arthur, C.B., *The Remaking of the English Navy by Admiral St. Vincent – Key to the victory over Napoleon. The great unclaimed naval revolution (1795-1805)*, Boston, University Press of America, 1986.
    Morriss, R. ed. *The Channel Fleet and the Blockade of Brest 1793-1801*, Aldershot, Navy Records Society, 2001.

2   Built 1795-8 by Perry of Blackwall. Fitted with Seppings' diagonal riders in 1805. Rebuilt with a round stern in 1816. Broken up in 1881 after long service as a sheer hulk at Chatham.

3   Nelson to Admiralty Secretary William Marsden 25.4.1804: White C. ed. *Nelson: The New Letters*. Boydell Woodbridge 2005 342
    Nelson disposition of Fleet 21.6.1804: Nicolas, H.N. ed. *Letters and Dispatches of Lord Nelson, Vol. VI*, London, 1846, 81.

4   See 17 of the 1814 pamphlet version of 'On a New Principle of Constructing His Majesty's Ships of War'.

5   Seppings to Navy Board 5.2.1810 & endorsement: ADM 1/5019 S290.

6   Seppings to Navy Board 16.2.1810: *ibid*.

7   Seppings to Navy Board 6.3.1810: *ibid*.

8   Seppings to Croker 27.3.1810: *ibid*.

9   Croker draft letter to Navy Board 30.4.1810: *ibid*.

10   Admiral Sir Robert Barlow (Commissioner at Chatham, later FRS and a correspondent of Banks.) to Yorke 4.10.1810: YOR/2 Yorke MSS NMM.

11   Seppings to Barrow 24.10.1811 & endorsement: ADM 1/5019 S1838

12   Barrow to Barrallier 16.12.1811: ADM 2/903 250

13   William Allen (1770-1843) a Quaker philanthropist and pharmacist who lectured at the Royal Institution. I am indebted to Dr Frank James of the Royal Institution for this information.

14   Barrow to Banks et.al. 19.11.1811: ADM 2/903 102.

15   Gascoigne, J. *Science in the Service of Empire: Joseph Banks, the British State and the Uses of Science in the Age of Revolution.* Cambridge UP 1998 126-7

16   Hall, M. B., *All Scientist now: The Royal Society in the Nineteenth Century,* Cambridge UP, 1984, 4-5.

17   Gascoigne: *Neo-mercantilism* 81-107, Navy 93-8, 124-7

18   Gascoigne, 30

19   Gascoigne, 32

20   *ibid.* 29

21   Barrow to Young 19.11.1811 ADM 2/903/101: cited in Wood, A. & Oldham, F. *Thomas Young, Natural Philosopher, 1773-1829,* Cambridge, 1954, 294-7. While quoting two Admiralty letters, Wood and Oldham rely largely on Peacock's 1855 biography noted below, which is not wholly convincing on this issue, and introduce new errors.

22   Young to Barrow 22.11.1811 ADM 1/509 also in Wood & Oldham

23   Barrow to Wollaston 30.12.1811 & Barrow – Young 9.1.1812: ADM 2/903 f 335, 388.

24   Barrow to Seppings 30.12.1811: ADM 2/903 333-4

25   Seppings to Barrow 1.1.1812: ADM 1/5020 S32

26   Peacock, G, *Memoir of Thomas Young,* London, 1855, 347

27   Young, T. 'Remarks on the employment of Oblique Riders, and on other alterations in the construction of Ships. Being the substance of a Report presented to the Board of Admiralty, with additional demonstrations and illustrations.' *Philosophical Transactions,* 1814 303-336 at 324 & 336

28   Peacock, 349

29   Barrow, J. „*Sketches of the Royal Society and Royal Society Dining Club,* London, 1846

30   James, F A J L, 'Davy in the Dockyard: Humphry Davy, the Royal Society and the electro-Chemical Protection of the Copper Sheeting of His Majesty's Ships in the mid 1820s.' *Physis: Rivista Internatzionale ds Storia della Scienza,* Vol. XXIX, 1992, 205-25 at 206-07.

31   Seppings to Yorke 20.1.1812: ADM 1/5020 S65a

32   Seppings to Domett 7.4.1812: ADM 1/5020 S333 Captain Robert Campbell to Yorke 26.2. (1812?) YOR/3.

33   Melville to Yorke 3.3.1812: YOR/11

34   Seppings to Melville 4.8.1812: ADM 1/5020 S774

35   Seppings submission the Admiralty: ADM 7/709.

36   Lambert, A.D., *The Last Sailing Battlefleet: Maintaining Naval Mastery 1815-1850,* London, Conway Press, 1991, 18.

37   *Ibid.,* 18-22.

38   *Royal Society Copy Book,* Vol. XLI 1813-17, 116-120. Meetings of 10 and 17.3.1814.

39   *Ibid.,* 125 for 24.3.1814.

40   Seppings' paper ends on 302, Young's begins on 303.

41   Shine, H. & Shine, H. C., *The Quarterly Review under Gifford: Identification of Contributor,.* Chapel Hill North Carolina, 1949.

42   *Ibid.,* 44. It was the first article in the issue.

43   Barrow, J. (although printed unsigned as was the custom at the time, it was not difficult to penetrate the anonymity.) Seppings *Improvements in Shipbuilding & Young Remarks on the Employment of Oblique Riders. Quarterly Review,* January 1815, Vol XII no. xxiv, 444-466. At 456.

44   *Ibid.,* 462

45   *Ibid.,* 457-8.

46   *Ibid.,* 460.

47   *Ibid.,* 465-6.

48   Barrow, J., *Sketches of the Royal Society and Royal Society Dining Club,* London, 1846, 6.

49   Babbage, C., *Reflections on the Decline of Science in England,* London, 1831, 50-1.

50   RS Journal Copy Book XLI 10.11.1814 182

51   Babbage, 43.

52   Navy Board – Admiralty 27.10.1814: 106/2265 Admiralty to Navy Board 18.2.1815: ADM 83/1

53   Admiralty to Navy Board 7.3.1815: ADM A/3106

54   Read, 27 November 1817: *Philosophical Transactions,* 1817 2-8.

55   Singer, C. et. al., *History of Technology: 1500-1750. Vol. III,.* Oxford, 1957, pp.427-8. The bridge was built by Hans Ulrich Grubenmann in 1757, using a framework of struts to span two sections 172 and 193 feet across. It was burnt during the French Revolutionary War

56   The mechanist at the Block Mills, Simon Goodrich, was involved in the experiment, which occurred just outside his workplace, and recorded his own set of data. Simon Goodrich notebooks 10.2.1817: Science Museum Box 5.

57   Ruddock, T. *Arch Bridges and their Builders, 1735-1835,* Cambridge, 1979, 134-8.

58   Babbage, *Reflections on the Decline of Science in England,* London, 1830 130 et. seq.

59   Babbage, 66-7.

60   Seppings to Babbage 23.6.1820: Add. Ms. 37,182 f.269

61   Morriss, R., *Naval Power and British Culture, 1760-1850: Public Trust and Government Ideology.* Aldershot, Ashgate Press, 2004, p.193. Melville's concerns would appear to reflect the complex politics of the post-war Tory government, with the powerful Grenville faction supporting Seppings' rival Surveyor Joseph Tucker. Melville's support did not waver.

62   Philosophical Transactions, MS ,1820, Barrow to Banks 1.2.1820: This letter accompanied the original ms. of the paper, which is marked by the inky fingers of the printers.

63   *Royal Society Journal Book,* XLII 1817-1822 2 & 9.3.,1820, 332, 334.

64   James, W., *Naval History of Great Britain,* Vol. VI, London, 1826, 417.

65   Knight, D., *Humphry Davy: Science & Power,* Cambridge, 1992, 145

66   James 'Davy in the Dockyard', *Physis,* 225.

67   Hall, 43

68   Cantor, G. *Michael Faraday: Sandemanian and Scientist,* Cambridge, 1991, 154-5

69   Hylton, B., *Charles Babbage: Pioneer of the Computer,* Princeton, 1982, 47-55 et. seq.

Professor Andrew Lambert *is at the War Department, King's College, London.*

THE OFFICE OF THE INSPECTOR GENERAL OF NAVAL WORKS AND TECHNOLOGICAL INNOVATION IN THE ROYAL DOCKYARDS

Roger Morriss

Abstract

This paper considers what Samuel Bentham, the Inspector General, himself claimed to have contributed by way improvement in the 'manufactures requisite in naval arsenals' and in the 'formation of naval arsenals'. Within manufactures he recognised 9 headings: steam engines, saw mills, system of machinery, new tools, system of manufacturing establishments, millwrights shop, wood mills, metal mills, rope and sail cloth manufactories. Within 'formation' he recognised 16 headings, including docks, dams, timber seasoning, fireproof buildings, mud barges, roman cement milling, and space saving. Bentham was aware that he dealt in ideas as well as tangibles. It is demonstrated that Bentham saw technological innovation as a matter of social engineering as much as technical engineering.

The office of Inspector General of Naval Works was established at the Admiralty in March 1796. The Inspector General was directed to consider all matters which related to ...

'the improvement of the building, fitting out and arming of... ships and vessels as well as what may conduce to the better navigating and victualling of them; the construction of docks, slips, basins, jetties and other works subservient to the construction and equipment of the ships and vessels; togther with the due choice, preservation and economical employment of the several stores and provisions made use of in the navy.'[1]

The post was held by Samuel Bentham, brother of Jeremy Bentham, the writer on jurisprudence whose writings also encompassed ethics, logic and political economy. Samuel had previously risen to become a colonel in the service of Catherine the Great of Russia and termed himself in England Brigadier-General. For this reason, and perhaps because he held the title of Inspector General, Samuel was sometimes known as General Bentham. Between 1796 and 1807 Bentham managed a department at the Admiralty which included an architect/engineer, a mechanist, chemist, secretary, draughtsman and three clerks. In 1800, when the Admiralty Office, excluding the Admiralty Court, comprised 55 people, the Inspector General's department formed one sixth of that establishment. It then contained, respectively, Samuel Bunce, Simon Goodrich, James Sadler, James Peake, and James Burr. The office was transferred to the Navy Board in October 1807, when it was renamed that of the Civil Architect and Engineer of the Navy. This post was then abolished by the order in council of 28 November 1812.[2]

After Bentham's second office was abolished in 1812, Samuel Bentham wrote a series of papers entitled 'Statements of Services'. The statements were printed in 1813, and survive in that form in the British Library.[3] The original manuscript versions survive in the miscellaneous letters received by the Admiralty Secretary.[4] The statements provide a good summary of what Samuel Bentham himself claimed to have contributed in the way of improvements to dockyard operations. They indicate that he was concerned with naval technology on a wide front, and supply some insight into Bentham's thinking in 1813 concerning the work he performed, which at many points involved technological innovation.

Two of the statements seem particularly relevant. His 'Statement of Services relative to the Improvement of Manufactures requisite in Naval Arsenals' proceeds under nine headings: steam engines, saw mills, system of machinery, new tools, system of manufacturing establishments, millwrights shop, wood mills, metal mills, ropery and sail cloth manufactory. His 'Statement of Services relative to the Improvement and Formation of Naval Arsenals' has sixteen headings: accommodations for fitting out and storing, shallow docks, increased use to works, floating dams, covered docks, timber seasoning house, wells, water works and fire extinguishing, lamps, fire proof buildings, mortar mill, roman cement mill, digging engine, mud barges, moveable steam engines, dams, foundation masses, repair of old works, saving of space, new naval arsenal, desiderata in an arsenal.

This formidable list, given in the order Bentham himself presented it, permits us to make a number of observations about Bentham's thinking. We should begin by noticing that Bentham dealt in ideas. The list of his projects includes use of space, desiderata, as well as more formal organisations and structures. He was imaginative, a lateral thinker and developed philosophical principles for the management of industrial organisations as well as directing the actual works and production lines which might now be called civil engineering and manufacturing. His managerial ideas have a particular resonance with the new processes of mass production being developed using the division of labour. They included the ideas of individual responsibility, the classification of labour, education to facilitate mobility between classes, and central financial control.[5]

We should go no further without recognising that, given Bentham's propensity for using his imagination, his statements are a subjective and highly partial source. Samuel Bentham wrote his statements to do two things: as a matter of pride, he was offering a vindication of his role between 1796 and 1812; and as a matter of necessity, he was preparing the way for claims on the public purse for sustained superannuation. To the credit of Bentham, in relation to every one of his claims he provided marginal references to the dates of official letters. This of course was because he expected the Navy Board and Admiralty in 1813 to question his claims. The references have the benefit now of providing guidance to those who might wish to trace the history of the proposals Bentham made.

At this conference we have been focussing in particular on what is now termed the block mills, and it may be worth noticing that Bentham appreciated the attention these received even in his own time as a naval administrator. He observed in 1813:

'the block making business... seems to have given as much, if not more, general gratification than any other improvement in... which I have been instrumental'.

Although Marc Isambard Brunel now receives the credit for the milling machinery, Bentham emphasised that it was he who recognised the value of the machines of which Brunel showed him drawings; and that he recognised the soundness and extent of Brunel's mechanical knowledge. As we shall see, the block machinery was of type that fit well with the wood-working machinery Bentham had already established in Portsmouth yard. However Bentham did ackowledge that he only directed Brunel to apply to the Admiralty and that, although when asked for his opinion he recommended the adoption of the machinery, the decision for its adoption was that of the Admiralty. At the same time Bentham also recognised that the navy was fortunate in the subsequent development of the block-making production line to have Brunel fully entered into the spirit of what Bentham wanted. Brunel is credited with the perfection of the machinery and for helping to train the work people – 'even giving those who showed particular instances of desire to acquire dexterity, or who were remarkable for industry, some little reward out of his own pocket'. Contrary to what has been suggested, there is no evidence that the navy was ever in danger of being starved of blocks had it continued to remain dependent on contractors, but in 1813 Bentham maintained the mills made the blocks better than before, and that their milling at Portsmouth saved the public £16,621-8-10d a year.[6]

With regard to the block making process, Bentham's observations indicate that he regarded himself as a facilitator. As head of an Admiralty department, his was the political job of getting sanction and funding for others to develop and operate the new facilities. Yet he suggests this was not his most difficult task. As a political administrator, he indicates that his greatest challenge was to overcome, or rather to under-mine, resistance to the introduction of new technology. This is demonstrated with regard to his discussion of the introduction of steam engines. They already existed outside the dockyards, so the Inspector General was not concerned with a new invention. His achievement, in his view, was to propose how they could be used, to overcome arguments against their use, and to undertake their installation and application. The task of undermining resistence he presented as one of social engineering.

So far as contemporary technology was concerned, from the vantage point of 1813 Bentham regarded the royal dockyards in the 1790s as 'undeveloped'. This lack of development he put down to a lack of leadership and passive submission to the concerns of artificers. This he recognised was no more than what was happening outside the dockyards:

'when (with leave of absence from the Russian service) in the year 1791, I made a tour in this country, visiting the principal manufactories, I found 'tis true steam engines extensively employed for giving motion to pumps for raising water from mines, to machinery for working cotton, and to mills for rolling and for some other work in metal: but in regard to the working of wood, steam engines had not been applied to this purpose: no machines or engines, other than turning lathes, had, so far as I learned, as yet been introduced for the working of this material; excepting that some circular and reciprocating saws and boring tools had been applied to the purpose of block making by the contractors who supplied blocks to the navy; even saw mills for slitting timber, though in very extensive use abroad, were not to be found in this country – an attempt indeed had been made to introduce a saw mill in the neighbourhood of London, but the destruction of it by the machinations of sawyers seemed to have prevented any further attempts at innovations of this nature.'[7]

Likewise within the dockyards, the Navy Board opposed steam engines from fear of deranging established practice and of arousing the opposition of artificers; from fear of fire and from an apparent lack of efficiency on the part of the engines. We should recall that in 1756 and 1775, at the outbreak of previous wars, the shipwrights had not scrupled to oppose and strike against Admiralty policies for the termination of chip-taking and the introduction of piecework.

Bentham claimed he undermined this opposition by degrees. In 1795 he had been permitted to order a steam engine for use at Redbridge, Hampshire, where the Admiralty had commissioned him to build some ships of his own design. The engine was not completed in time for this use but, shortly afterwards, motive power being needed to drive some new pumps for the docks in Portsmouth dockyard, Bentham took the opportunity to propose the engine for that use, in which neither the danger of fire and nor the opposition of artificers were feared. However, once this use was accepted, as the engine was not used for pumping for much of the time, Bentham proposed the engine drive machinery, which was accordingly introduced. Later he proclaimed that

'by degrees the advantages of this premium mobile in pumping up water were seen and acknowledged; by degrees other and larger steam engines have been introduced, and their use has been by my means extended gradually to other purposes, as prejudices could be removed, till now, at length, I have the satisfaction of seeing the objections to the use of steam engines and machinery in His Majesty's Naval Arsenals entirely done away'.[8]

As with steam engines, so with regard to other types of machinery. That which the first steam engine was used to drive was the product of Bentham's own making, for which he has been described as an ingenious mechanic.[9] In Russia Bentham had made some machinery for working in wood. In the early 1790s, while at his brother's house in Queen Square Place, London, he developed more, aiming to give employment to 'some thousands of untaught hands in a public establishment' – probably the projected panopticon prison in which he and his brother were trying to interest the government.[10] He claimed to have made machines by which 'the need of skill and dexterity in the workman was done away'. He had machines for planing, rebateing, morticing, and sawing in curved, winding and transverse directions. To demonstrate their utility he developed an apparatus for preparing all the parts of a window sash, and an ornamental carriage wheel, which had only to be assembled. The machines became a popular attraction in Westminster, significantly even attracting people like Henry Dundas, Secretary of State, Chairman of the Board of Control for India, and close friend of William Pitt. The machines could be driven from a rotating shaft, and thus by a steam engine. Later he claimed to have realised that

> 'the introduction of them into His Majesty's dock yards would be one of the applications of machinery to the working in wood, which would be found least obnoxious, I accordingly very early proposed, and received authority for, the introduction of a saw mill into Portsmouth dockyard. Saws of various descriptions were accordingly provided for that yard, and amongst them were some of the identical saws which had... been at work at my brother's residence; and which have since been in constant use in the wood mills for such purposes as slitting and edging deals; for cutting wood for blocks etc. Reciprocating saws have likewise been erected there for cutting timber into plank'.

By 1813 additional saws in the wood mill permitted cutting at the rate of 9-10,000 foot of timber each week, the timber being of different descriptions, including four and five inch plank. Bentham took particular pride in the claim that 'of late' joiners in Portsmouth dockyard had expressed discontent when given deals slit by sawyers and not by machinery.'[11]

Bentham suggests that he further undermined prejudice with machine tools that were small and apparently non-threatening. These included his own inventions

> 'for rebating, cutting dove-tails and tenons, boring and cutting mortices and for forming mouldings'.[12]

Others of his own device included ...

> 'coque sinking tools; guides for boring holes accurately in point of direction; tools for mooting treenails with single and double drift;[13] augurs for boring single and double drift holes for treenails; rotating tools for forming the heads and points of treenails; punches for driving treenails...; augur shanks with universal joints by which holes can be bored... in situations where there is not room for turning the handle of an ordinary augur; apparatus for preparing

nuts and screw points to copper bolts'.[14]

Success in managing innovation on a small scale led to the challenge of managing the new technology on a large scale. At Portsmouth he proposed the institution of three new departments – the wood mills, the metal mills, and a millwrights departments[15] – each with its own master craftsman and specialist artificers. Because the Navy Board and dockyard officers declared themselves incapable of managing these new departments, Bentham was given their management. He then attempted to use the new departments 'as standards and examples', to exhibit the efficiency of that kind of management which in Bentham's opinion was best suited to naval arsenals. Bentham had been apprenticed in the dockyards, and was aware of the working practices that would be inconsistent with the efficiency of operation of his new departments. From the beginning, uneconomic customs common in private yards were barred. He refused to allow the millwrights higher rates of pay for work at night; paid them by classified degree of skill; insisted they be assisted by labourers; and teach other artificers like carpenters and joiners who were apprenticed as millwrights and would thus become 'double-handed' men.[16]

The Millwrights department at Portsmouth made machine-tools (like coqueing tools) for use in the other dockyards. The department helped to fit and improve articles used on board ships like pumps and steering apparatus. It advised on better or cheaper ways of performing existing tasks, like the use of boring 'engines' (turned by men) to bore holes in iron knees in the Smiths shop. Above all it maintained

> 'the whole system of water works for raising and supplying fresh water, for pumping water into or out of all the docks, basins and reservoirs, of all the steam engines, as also of the whole extensive works... for extinguishing fire'. This fire extinguishing system, installed at Bentham's suggestion, was 'kept constantly in complete order for immediate use'.[17]

In the Wood Mills, Bentham brought together all work in wood that could be 'advantageously executed by machinery'. He classed the operations by the saws needed for them. Large, strong saws cut rough timber; slighter saws slit deals into lengths; cross- and diagonal-cutting saws cut to length; circular and reciprocating saws cut to fixed depths as for rebateing, tonguing, grooving, and cutting tenons. Connected to each batch of saws were 'wood millers', who specialised according to the 'division of labour' in the work of those saws and the use of appropriate tools to finish the work. There was no apprenticeship, and the mills had their own working hours and recompense.[18] The Wood Mills at Portsmouth served as a model for mills elsewhere. By 1813 (at Bentham's suggestion of July 1811) the Wood Mill at Chatham was being erected to operate in conjunction with water and fire-extinguishing works. He had 'no doubt' that 'there, as well as progressively at all the other dock-yards, establishments of the same nature will be productive of very extensive benefit'.[19]

The Metal Mills were founded in 1803. Like the Wood Mills, the Metal Mills at Portsmouth owed their success in Bentham's view to his management: to the 'due choice and arrangement of machinery, from the selection of persons possessed of appropriate skills..., and from a mode of management calculated to call forth their best exertions'. With the installation of equipment to smelt, cast and roll metal, by 1812 the Metal Mills were manufacturing articles of cast iron, mixed metals and copper sheathing. The efficiency with which the daily business of the mills was conducted owed a great deal to the Master of the Mills, W.E. Sheffield, recruited from private industry. But Bentham had more in mind than manufacture on established principles. He aimed to improve quality and economy of production, for which experiments to ascertain the strength of different metals had begun in the office of the Inspector General in 1798.

The first objective was to re-process old copper sheathing. For this, furnaces had to be erected in the other dockyards to smelt the old copper into parcels for shipment to Portsmouth. Difficulties were encountered because, owing to the retention of this copper in the dockyards, the private manufacturers were deprived of that supply and, so they claimed, consequently prevented from fulfilling their contracts to supply the navy.[20] Nevertheless by 1813 Bentham could claim that the copper sheathing 'has been for some time manufactured to a sufficient extent for... sheathing the whole of His Majesty's Navy and has been found on experience to be of superior quality to that heretofore supplied by contract'. Improvements had also been made in the quality of mixed metals for use in the sheaves and coques of blocks, for pintles and braces, and for bolts and nails. Indeed by 1813, through experimentation, the Mills provided specifications of mixtures to private manufacturers to permit them to fulfil their contracts for items of mixed metal.[21]

At the time the former Inspector General was writing, the savings to the public from the Metal Mills amounted to £40,950-12-8d a year. Bentham anticipated their further development, for he considered they would be needed to extend the uses to which metal were put in ships. He looked forward to the use of metal chains for cables, to metal standing rigging (suggested by John Peake), and to metal as a substitute for timber. He was particularly keen on the greater use of mixed metals. His tests had demonstrated that hammered Swedish iron broke under a strain of seven and a half tons, rolled English copper sustained six tons, while mixed metal could support five and half tons. At a time when iron anchors were very expensive, Bentham thought that mixed metal might be used instead of iron.[22]

In 1804 the Inspector General also had a Ropery and Sail Cloth Manufactory sanctioned by an order in council. Yet, as Bentham claimed, it was subject to the 'implied objections, concealed influence, unfair experiments, and partial statements' of 'interested persons', all of which he was about to counter when in 1805 he was sent to Russia. Nevertheless in the eight preceding years the Inspector General's innovations of a manufacturing nature had been significant. According to Bentham in 1813 the Millwrights department, the Wood Mills, and the Metal Mills at Portsmouth were performing work worth in labour and materials over a million pounds.[23]

These new departments were thus

financially as well as technologically important. But at a time of war, the Inspector General's primary task was to enhance the operational efficiency of the dockyards. Bentham was not a sea officer; but he was imaginative and aimed to use technology to promote naval efficiency.

From this naval point of view, Bentham claimed he was the first to propose fitting and storing naval vessels within the boundary of a dockyard, rather than by small craft at moorings or an anchorage in harbour. At Portsmouth his work on the basin and docks was intended to permit even ships of the line to dock for refitting without the removal of their guns and stores. It entailed halving the length of the existing double dock, deepening and enlarging the basin, and increasing the number of docks leading from it by the construction of two new deep docks.[24] Not only was the yard's dock capacity increased, in theory time, trouble and thus money was saved because, in Bentham's view, ships did not have to be dismantled for docking and later re-equipped; the use of steam power to maintain appropriate levels of water in the docks meant that four ships could be docked or undocked either from or into the basin regardless of the tide; the docks could be used more frequently; and ships were removed from their operational duties for less time. Research suggests that in practice few ship returned to sea 'in as few days as the weeks that were requisite before these accommodations were provided' – some 74s and frigates between 1801 and 1805. Even so, these few were important – for example before Trafalgar[25] – and the Inspector General was able to demonstrate what was potentially possible in the subsequent construction of docks and basin.[26]

The idea of artificially increasing the depth of the older, shallow docks off the basin at Portsmouth by raising their water level was not perhaps technological innovation, even though Bentham claimed that by this means docks designed for frigates were made to accommodate ships of the line. Nor was the idea of converting the Boat Pond at Portsmouth into a basin, and the North Camber or channel into a double dock, all of which were capable of accommodating frigates. Nevertheless the use of caissons or floating dams to serve as gates was technological innovation. The first was contrived for closing the large basin at Portsmouth. According to Bentham, the caissons were cheaper than gates, occupied less space, were more easily repaired, could be opened and closed with less labour, and one caisson could serve at various places, for example to divide the North Camber into different lengths sufficient for one, two or three vessels.[27]

Incidentally, it is evident that where different water levels were required within different parts of the same channel or double dock, the pumping could be conveniently performed by moveable steam engines. They were mounted on wheels and the first was developed for use at Portsmouth for pumping docks or working cranes. By their means, Bentham claimed, ships of any draught could be floated on to blocks of any height within any dock.[28]

The idea of covering docks and slips was not new: Bentham traced it as far back as 1776. But the Inspector General proposed enclosure as well, provision for heating, lighting and ventilation, and sufficient space within the covered area for the conduct of related shipwrights' work. His ideas for such enclosures were promoted by his inspection of the covered docks at Karlscrona, Sweden, on his way back from Russia in 1807. These coverings had been 'spoken of as being perfect'. But Bentham found the docks covered by 'nothing more than a shed-like roof, supported by piers of masonry'. Bentham only put forward formal plans in late 1811/early 1812, when slip number one at Chatham had to be renewed. But he noticed the Navy Board recommended covering docks and slips 'very extensively' from that time.[29]

The covering of docks and slips was related to the Inspector General's plans for a seasoning house. Seasoning sheds had been established in the 1770s by Lord Sandwich. However Bentham was concerned to experiment with the numerous different methods of seasoning and different substances that had been proposed for impregnation in timber. Indeed before he was sent to Russia he began a course of experiments in 'one of the cellars allotted to the use of the Wood Mills in Portsmouth Dock Yard'. These were not resumed after 1807 but Bentham did review 'such facts as seemed worthy of consideration with a view to experiment'. None of this was ground-breaking. What was new, however, was the Inspector General's proposed scientific approach. He had no doubt

'that whenever the conduct of a well digested series of comparative experiments on this subject shall have been entrusted to some one person possessed of chemical and other appropriate scientific knowledge, acquainted with the history of what has already been done, his mind at the same time free from bias as to any particular mode, the advantages that will result from such experiments will be that, in as far as regards timber, the durability of our ships may be secured for a period two or three times as long as they usually last at present'.[30]

Of more immediate benefit was the introduction of water piping and pumping into the dockyards. Amazingly, before 1797 neither Portsmouth, Plymouth nor Sheerness had natural supplies of water, their respective requirements being shipped from Southampton Water, Southdown and Chatham. At Plymouth the navy became dependent on a private company for a supply of water from Dartmoor. At Portsmouth and Sheerness, however, the Inspector General had wells sunk. At Portsmouth water was raised to an elevated reservoir by the steam engines connected with the Wood Mills, and distributed through the yard by a system of cast iron pipes passing close to all the principal buildings, and by the sides of the docks and jetties. To prevent inconvenience from blockage or bursting, two adjacent pipe courses were installed, with means to add branch pipes and fire hose. In case of fire, the steam engines could raise and pump fresh or sea water into the first floors of buildings and over ships lying within the dockyard.[31]

The fear of fire, so much dreaded in eighteenth century dockyards, was spur to two further innovations. Instead of candles, lamps enclosed in glass were used in the Wood Mills at Portsmouth. And Bentham proposed the construction of buildings made of non-combustible materials. In 1794 he 'had

devised and caused the iron work to be cast for a very extensive building for the Public Service' – the panoptican prison project. Within the dockyards, he proposed fire-proof construction for a ropery at Woolwich, in particular the tarring tower. Later, the cash and record rooms at Sheerness, Portsmouth and Plymouth were built fire-proof according to his plans.[32]

It might be argued that the dockyards were ripe for improvements of this nature. More demanding of the imagination perhaps was Bentham's claim to have made a 'saving of space'. This, he maintained, could be seen 'in the arch work thrown over the reservoir in Portsmouth dock yard'.

'In the state in which I found it, it was a square excavation occupying about 3/4 of an acre, lined with masonry to the depth of above 30 feet below the level of the yard; the only use this reservoir was designed for, or ever put to, was that of receiving the water when let run into it out of the docks, so that there was only a height of 5 or 6 feet from the bottom occasionally employed; but the four or five and twenty feet above that, up to the level of the yard and all above, were constantly useless. At my suggestion the useful part of this reservoir has been arched over, and above that cellars have been constructed, some of which are used as storehouses, others as workshops for smiths work, one for seasoning wood by artificial means. Over a part of this cellaring the Wood Mills have been erected, but the greater part still remains unbuilt upon, ready to be appropriated for the farther extension of buildings for this establishment, or any other purposes; and in the mean time it is employed for spreading timber, plank,etc.[33] *to the amount of 3/4 of an acre, and being in the very centre of the yard it cannot but be considered as of very considerable value.'*[34]

Around the water boundaries of the dockyards, the Inspector General demonstrated the cost of only working between tides to strengthen embankments and quays, then introduced the use of coffer dams. Bentham cited the saving achieved by the use of a coffer dam on the embankment in the northern part of the Portsmouth dockyard. One was also used when strengthening the river wall at Sheerness. Here, in places where the ground seemed unlikely to hold a coffer dam, Bentham developed what he called 'foundation masses' upon which masonry could be built. To support the bottoms of docks he also laid claim to the introduction of 'inverted arches of masonry'.[35]

For the vast quantities of mortar needed for these works, the Inspector General first devised a mill for grinding and mixing calcareous cements. This was horse driven but was nevertheless, according to Bentham, copied by private architects and engineers. Later, at Sheerness, he established a mill for making roman cement, a commodity which apparently was 'particularly liable to imperfection in the manufacture, and to injury in the package, carriage, and keeping of it'.[36]

Off-shore, where dockyards demanded the excavation of greater depth, the Inspector General early designed the first dredger driven by steam engine. Hitherto virtual hand digging at low water had made such excavations so tedious and difficult as to preclude extensive improvements to harbours. Bentham's bucket ladder steam-dredgers, however, made the work easier and faster. The first was completed at Portsmouth in 1802 and could raise 80 tons an hour. A second dredger was completed for work in the Thames and could raise 60 tons of shingle or 90 tons of mud an hour. These dredgers worked at 14 foot and 21 foot respectively; by 1812 steam dredging had reached 26 foot below low water. Associated were mud barges designed to receive the dredged material. One type had scuttles in the bottom to permit deposition under water; another delivered soil from the side to make or raise new ground.[37]

What emerges from this survey of innovations claimed by the Inspector General? What does it show about Bentham's thinking? To my mind, seven things stand out.

1. Firstly, Bentham used his imagination to reconcile contemporary technology and dockyard opportunities. He consciously dealt in ideas: in his view, systems and desiderata were as worthy of pursuit as structures like docks, dams and foundation masses. He thought laterally, justifying facilities in terms of several purposes.

2. Secondly, Bentham regarded himself as a facilitator, to work at a political level to achieve sanction and funding for the technology he recognised and advocated as valuable.

3. Thirdly, he consciously strived to undermine resistance to new technology. In the educational process, he was aware that it was important for the artificers to accept the machine tools made by the Millwrights department and that it was an ideological achievement to have artificers want machine milled timber to work with rather than that cut by hand.

4. Fourthly, he used the management of new dockyard departments to establish labour practices which broke with traditional labour culture and prepared the way for further change in this area.

5. Fifthly, he addressed the operational, wartime needs of the navy by enlarging the dock and basin capacity of Portsmouth dockyard and contributed to an ability at Portsmouth occasionally to dock ships for short periods without completely unloading them.

6. Sixthly, at the Metal Mills and in his attitude to timber seasoning Bentham used the thinking of a scientist to improve the nature of the materials available to the navy, and to demonstrate good practice.

7. Finally, it is clear that Samuel Bentham had a goal which was to shift thinking in the royal dockyards to a new level of technological performance. It is my opinion of this that this goal was achieved and that Samuel Bentham as Inspector General of Naval Works played a major role in that achievement.

References

1. *17th Report of the Select Committee on Finance,*, Appendix G5, 43, in *Reports of Committees of the House of Commons, 1797-1803*, 1st series, xii, 342.

2. J. C. Sainty, *Admiralty Officials 1660-1870*, London, 1975, 91; J.M. Collinge, *Navy Board Officials 1660-1832* ,London, 1978, 19-20.

3. British Library, 1414. d.3 (1),(2) and (3). This paper examines the content of the last two; the first is entitled 'Services rendered in the Civil Department of the Navy in investigating and bring to official notice abuses and imperfections in and in effecting improvements in relation to the system of management'.

4. National Maritime Museum, ADM. BP/33B, 21, 30 April 1813.

5. Roger Morriss, *Naval Power and British Culture 1760-1850. Public Trust and Government Ideology*, Aldershot, 2004.

6. 'Statement of Services relative to the Improvement of Manufactures requisite in Naval Arsenals', ff. 21-25.

7.   'Improvement of Manufactures', ff. 1-2.

8.   'Improvement of Manufactures', f. 5.

9.   *Selectiions from the Coirrespondence of Admiral John Markham, 1801-4 and 1806-7,,* ed. Sir C. Markham, Navy Records Society, 1904, 342.

10. J. Dinwiddy, *Bentham,*Oxford, 1989, 7-10, 16-17. Jeremy Bentham's 'panopticon' was based on Samuel's idea for a prison, factory or workhouse constructed on a circular plan with a central observation point from which a supervisor could keep the whole establishment under observation.

11. 'Improvement of Manufactures', f. 6.

12. Though small, Bentham maintained that these pieces of machinery saved money. For example, about 1,600 small deal tables were needed by the navy each year and, while previously they had cost twenty shillings each, his machinery produced them for ten shillings and six pence each, a saving so he maintained of £700 a year. 'Improvement of Manufactures', f. 8.

13. For note and possible association with the machine for turning treenails currently in the block mills.

14. 'Improvement of Manufactures', f. 8.

15. For erecting and repair of machinery.

16. 'Improvement of Manufactures', ff. 10-11, 13-14.

17. 'Improvement of Manufactures', ff. 15-16.

18. In the development of this establishment, Bentham gives credit to James Burr who, as well as being draughtsman in the office of the Inspector General, was appointed Master of the Wood Mills, and to Mr Kingston, the Master Millwright. 'Improvement of Manufactures', ff. 19-21, 28-9.

19. 'Improvement of Manufactures', f. 29.

20. Roger Morriss, *The Royal Dockyards during the Revolutionary and Napoleonic Wars*, Leicester, 1983, 50-52.

21. 'Improvement of Manufactures', ff. 29-30.

22. 'Improvement of Manufactures', ff. 31-34.

23. 'Improvement of Manufactures', ff. 35, 37, 40.

24. For assistance in planning and supervising the execution of these works, Bentham recorded his debt to Henry Peake, a shipwright officer in Portsmouth dockyard who was placed under the Inspector General. Subsequently Peake served as Surveyor of the Navy 1806-1822.

25. For example, the *Defence* and *Agamemnon*, which were docked for one and four days respectively in July and September 1805. NMM, copies of Admiralty progress books.

26. 'Statement of Services relative to the Improvement & Formation of Naval Arsenals', ff. 1-3; Morriss, *Royal Dockyards*, 20-1, 48-9.

27. 'Formation of Naval Arsenals', ff. 4-5.

28. 'Formation of Naval Arsenals', f. 17.

29. 'Formation of naval Arsenals', ff. 5-8.

30. 'Formation of Naval Arsenals', ff. 8-10.

31. For the later extension of fire-extinguishing systems to the other dockyards, Bentham acknowledged the help of his assistant, Simon Goodrich. 'Formation of Naval Arsenals', ff. 11-12.

32. 'Formation of Naval Arsenals', ff. 12-14.

33. This observation is of current interest in view of the use by the Mary Rose Trust of the space to store some of the *Mary Rose*'s timbers.

34. 'Formation of Naval Arsenals', ff. 20-22.

35. 'Formation of Naval Arsenals', ff. 17-19; Morriss, *Royal Dockyards*, 56.

36. 'Formation of Naval Arsenals', ff. 14.

37. 'Formation of Naval Arsenals', ff. 15-16; Morriss, *Royal Dockyards*, 54.

Dr. Roger Morriss *lectures at the Universities of Bristol, Exeter and Greenwich.*

PREPARING HMS *VICTORY* AND THE SHIPS FOR TRAFALGAR

Peter Goodwin

Abstract

This paper examines the preparation of some of those warships which were to participate in the Trafalgar campaign. HMS Victory's great repair at Chatham 1800-3 is described. Attention is then turned to work undertaken at Plymouth, very fully documented by Master Shipwright Joseph Tucker, whose papers have survived. The kind of work carried out at Plymouth, and arguably at other Dockyards, is presented on a deck by deck basis, but for two ships of different sizes a complete inventory of tasks completed is offered.

At the time of the signing of the Treaty of Amiens on 27 March 1802 *Victory*, later to become Nelson's flagship, was already in dock at Chatham undergoing what had started in late 1800 as a middling repair costing £23,500. A second survey revealed that parts of her hull needed rebuilding, that 60% of her wooden knees needed refastening or replacing, and that many of her port lids needed renewing. As a consequence the work became a larger and more costly repair.

During this refit she was altered to comply with new construction practices. Her elaborate stern with open galleries at upper and quarter deck level were rebuilt as what was termed a closed stern, that is, completely flat without galleries. This modification, made in compliance with an Admiralty order of 1798, was effected to eliminate structural problems inherent in some 160 ships, *Victory* included. Concurrently her stern davits were removed in order to prevent swinging boats smashing the glazed windows which had formerly been open galleries. She was also fitted with two additional gun ports at the fore end of the lower gun deck, although no extra guns were mounted at these positions.

Victory's bulwarks running the length of her quarter deck and forecastle were raised and built up to provide better protection in battle. The hammock cranes running along the length of the poop had already been barricaded on the outboard sides with 1½ inch thick boards. The purpose of the boarding was to protect the hammock and netting from muzzle flashback common to carronades. It is planned to fit this feature to *Victory* in 2005. Internally her magazine was rebuilt in compliance with new regulations, utilising copper and lead sheeting and lining bulkheads with lathes and mortar plaster as an anti-flash precaution against fire. During the refit *Victory's* old ornate figurehead was replaced with one of simpler design reflecting the recent Admiralty restriction on carved work to effect financial and material savings.

With the high possibility that war with France would soon reopen, new orders were sent to Chatham on 15 March 1803 requiring *Victory* to be prepared for sea service. On 9 April she was re-commissioned under a new commander, Captain Samuel Sutton. Undocked on 11 April, *Victory's* great repair had cost £70,933. Once afloat she received her masts and rigging. It is doubtful whether all her rigging blocks were made in the Portsmouth block mills, but this was dependent on size. Sailmakers would have been busy making new sails in the sail loft at Chatham. A full suit of 37 sails is estimated to have taken 20 men 83 days to produce. Her sides were repainted with the now standardised black and yellow bands; her gun port lids however may not have been so painted until Nelson finally entered the ship on 31 July 1803. What other work was undertaken? Unfortunately no detailed shipwrights' accounts concerning the works in Chatham and Portsmouth and Chatham have yet come to light.

However, because the method of fitting ships very much followed a standard practice repeated in all the royal dockyards, comparisons can be made between the *Victory* and other ships preparing for the restart of war in 1803. For this we may analyse the dockyard papers held in the Royal Naval Museum, Portsmouth, compiled by Joseph Tucker, the Master Shipwright at Plymouth.[1] The document provides a highly detailed record of the amount of work undertaken in, and the quantity of materials used in refitting individual ships. The document covers a host of ships including the 112 gun *San Josef* captured by Nelson at the battle of Cape St Vincent, and the 80 gun *Foudroyant,* his flagship 1799-1800. More importantly it covers 12 of the ships present at Trafalgar. They are: the 98 gun ships *Neptune Prince* and *Temeraire,* the 80 gun, formerly French ship, *Tonnant,* the 74 gun ships *Conqueror, Mars, Minotaur, Spartiate* (formerly French), and *Thunderer,* the 38 gun frigate *Naiad,* the 36 gun frigate *Sirius,* and the armed schooner *Pickle.* Tucker also lists the wages expended for each ship. Thus: *Neptune* £948 19s 3d, *Prince* £556 15s 0d, *Temeraire* £954 6s 0d, *Tonnant* £377 0s 10d, *Conqueror* £303 3s 9d, *Mars* £272 2s 1d, *Minotaur* not recorded, *Spartiate* £365 12s 1d, *Thunderer* £10 15s 1d, *Naiad* £32 10s 8d, *Sirius* £48 5s 11d, and *Pickle* £139 5s 4d.

The document is important because although we can obtain much information from many ship plans held at the National Maritime Museum, they do not detail the finer points of fitting out; nor were they meant to. What was being sought from Tucker's document was a trend from which it is possible to understand what exactly was going on in each ship, and how this trend reflects how ships were actually fitted out for war; that is, what innovations were being introduced. The typical work undertaken on a deck by deck basisis as follows:

Hold

The construction and fitting out of the magazines is universal; considerable mention is made of the use of lining boards, copper sheathing, lead work, tin plate work, and plaster work. All magazine racks have drawers to collect loose powder. The fitting of covers and sashes is also common. Tin plate is used to line breadroom bulkheads to ensure a dry environment.

Orlop Deck

Lead is laid in the magazine and lightroom passages. Leaded cisterns are fitted around the foremast to hold water to flood the powder bin in the magazine. Cisterns for paint are fitted, and the storeroom bulkheads are lined with tin plate.

Lower Gun Deck

Breadth riders are refastened, gun room cupboards are rebuilt, an engine is used to fit up wooden and iron knees, and an armourer's bench is made.

Middle Gun Deck

Two iron staircases are fitted and cooks' lockers and tables with cranks are built.

Upper Gun Deck

Ordinary galleys and their bulkheads are taken down, original galleys are refitted, cooks' lockers and tables with cranks are built, tinplates presumably around the galley are fitted, moulds are made for an iron staircase which is fitted, riders are refastened and fitted, shot lockers to the foremast are built (these are not to be confused with racks and garlands which are equally mentioned), and in the case of *Conqueror* carronade chocks are fitted.

Quarter Deck and Forecastle

Copper voice pipes are fitted, an iron staircase and hammock boards are refitted, moulds for iron stanchions are made and the latter fitted, and in the case of *Spartiate* carronade chocks are fitted.

Without Board

Copper sheathing is shifted, the number of pieces cut out and replaced in the ship are listed, anchor linings and billboards are fitted, the ordinary crane and housings are taken down, iron stanchions are fitted, steeping cisterns are fitted, and in the case of *Conqueror* there is mention of 6 water tables.

Without going into the host of work related, for instance, to gun port lid planking, port rope pipes, repairing gratings, ladders and doors, and the quantities of items or material involved, the final point to be gleaned from the document, is what happens to a ship going into ordinary. Internal planking is replaced to close in the sides and is also replaced at the bulkheads, all of which had to be removed to permit the ship's structure to be well ventilated when laid up to prevent rotting and damp.

In order to provide fuller details of work undertaken on ships of different sizes, an inventory of tasks competed on the 74 gun *Conqueror* and on the schooner *Pickle is* set out in full.

Conqueror[2]

Conqueror 74 Guns: Hold; Trimd & fastend cieling (thickstuff) 704 feet shut in openings in bulkheads 480 feet lined bulkhead &c. 1906 feet, refitted timberboards 52 feet –

Magazines Hackt off bolts & refitted & bolted 8 pallating beams, took up & refitted 28 carlings & 24 scuttles, refitted & fastend 6 wing panels, 2 cisterns 24 chocks fitted & fixed the lanthorns; refitted drawers, ballins racks &c, fitted & naild 94 tin plates & 9 sheets of copper.

Orlop & Platforms: trimd & plasterd cieling 46 feet, refitted & fastend plank on the flat 266 feet, trimd & set up 2 stantions, trimd rabbetted and fasten'd board to bulkheads 320 feet, trimd and fastend lining 268 feet shut in openings to bulkheads 796 feet & refitted & fastend lining 1769 feet refitted 10 scuttles, refitted & hung 4 wing doors, refitted & fastend cistern to the foremast & leaded the same, took down refitted & fastend the cheese racks; refitted 11 hatch bars examined & easd down 8 gratings & 4 hatches naild 42 tin plates to bulkheads; made & hung one door made and grating & desk & took down guarding stantions &c.

Gundeck: took up deck flat 104 feet trimd & fastend waterways 20 feet, flat 199 feet jirrings on lodging knees 76 feet & shut in the openings on the flat 892 feet, refitted got in place & fastend waterways 248 feet – took down refitted & set up manger stantions & chocks, refayd & fastend manger boards & cants, refitted bucklers, bars & rollers & unbolted 2 bolsters on the hawse hook – let out & trimd 12 scuppers, refitted & fixed 3 shot lockers, unshipt refitted & reshipt the cross pieces; took down refitted & set up 16 pillars; refitted & bolted shot racks 115 feet made drawers to and refitted armourers bench, refitted Ironwork to 6 port cants – trimd & fastend cants for & refitted 30 washboards to the ports, trimd & fastend 2 conductors for tiller ropes; trimd & fitted with Ironwork 6 rollers; drove out 56 plugs from port rope holes; bored holes & drove 4 ring bolts & built 2 cupboards refitted 3 cap scuttles & repaired 4 gratings, took down guarding stantions &c.

Upper Deck Fayd & bolted 7 Iron stantions, trimd & fastend shot garlands 148 feet flat of the deck 21 feet cabin cants 48 feet, hammock racks 437 feet & belaying racks 25 feet; unbolted took up & rebolted 12 head ledges & combing 97 feet, trimd & bolted 12 head ledges & combings 97 feet & trimd & let down 4 ledges & one hatchway carlingtook down bulkheads of the ordinary galley & fireheath & leaded the flat 152 feet took down refitted & set up galley stantions & jambs, trimd & fastend cants bolted the fireheath, built cupboards & refitted cooks tablestrimd & fitted with Ironwork a tiller, refitted & fastend deck flat 58 feet & cabin cants 91 feet; refitted 2 rother chocks & 2 sampsons posts; refitted & bolted 4 cheek blocks; cut out openings in clamp 132 feet built shot locker to the foremast; trimd and fayd 54 chocks under shot garlands; ript up shot cants 148 feet & cabin cants 129 feet-trimd let up & bolted 4 cap carlings, trimd & set up 2 refitted & set up 6 pillars; shut in openings in the sides 85 feet and fitted battins for gunners stores 78 feet – made molds for & fitted an Iron staircase & bolted Iron plates to hatchways trimd & bolted 2 ranges & eased in the tiller rope — drove out and redrove 22 eyebolts made 3 gratings & one half port; repaired 4 ladders & 10 gratings & cut holes in 40 half ports — bored holes & drove 12 bolts in showels 6 eyebolts, one tyebolt to the bitts & 20 belaying pins.

Forecastle Waiste Quarterdeck & roundhouse: Took off housing from the gear & unbolted awning stanchions – trimd & bolted 16 carronade chocks with cants & bored holes thro & let in 16 Iron plates – trimed and got in place 4 short timbers & 48 fillings, trimed & fastend birthing plank 540 feet, quickwork 56 feet cabin cants 80 feet rubbing pieces to beams 38 feet, 10 bulls eyes & 2 face pieces to drifts – unbolted & rebolted mizen topsail sheet bitts & crosspiece & shifted flat 18 feet – cut openings in the clamps 132 feet; dubbed of the molding on the plansheer 332 feet & hackt of 17 bolts – refitted 8 Iron stanchions & roughtreerail 48 feet – trimed & bolted 8 & refayd 7 blocks & 2belaying racks-refittedn & fastend cabin cants 87 feet, trimd and fitted 2 sampsons posts; bored holes & let out 10 lead pipes; fitted Ironwork for & hung the bell fitted 6 half ports made 2 gratings; bored holes for & drove 22 bolts in timbers, 2 long tye bolts & 125 ring & eyebolts.

Withoutboard: Took of housing &c & took the ordinary crane shoots &c &c – unbolted harbour bolsters, refayd & bolted hawse and anchor bolsters, filling & washboards – made molds for & bolted 2 Iron knees to catheads, trimed & fitted 2 chocks & let in & bolted 4 Iron plates between cathead & headrail – took off the Channelrails, got up 44 deadeyes with channel plates drove out & redrove 14 preventer bolts, & refitted 44 preventer plates with washers; – refitted & bolted 4 goosenecks & fastend the channel rails – made molds for & fitted 8 & refitted 66 Iron stantions, trimed & fitted hammock board 184 feet & refitted 744 feet – made & fastend 14 shoots to the sides & made molds for & hung 2 Iron plates over pumpdale scuppers – refitted & bolted bumpkins, chock of the bowsprit accommodation stantion & carlings chesstrees & bolsters for main Jack – refitted & fastend 2 rubbing pieces to the roundhouses 2 billboards, 2 trunks to the roundhouses & lining of the anchor 30 feet – trimd & bolted 4 boat davits, trimd & fitted 2 billboards with Iron plates & 2 rollers for main sheets – unhung the bridle ports, trimed & fastend 4 steps, 18 port wriggles & eased in 28 scuttle lids, made & repaired one long trunk in the head & secured the same with Iron straps – drove out & redrove Eyebolts took down, refitted & fastend 30 balusters shifted lead 98 feet refitted & fastend 6 water tables, 2 console brackets, 3 stiles, birthing 48 feet & pallating 31 feet; refitted stools bored holes & fitted cranks & stays & refitted & fixed stern lanthorns made stages for performing the above works - cut out and put in 31 pieces in different parts of the ship and performed works incident to rigging.

Schooner Pickle[3]

Pickle. Hold. Trimd & bolted a piece of apron; bored for & drove 14 bolts in the keelson & crutches cut & set up 6 well stanchions, trimd & fastened 5 pallating beams, flat 50 feet bulkhead to well & coalhole 118 feet & shifted

jambs round the foremast: – Platform fitted & bolted 2 Iron breasthooks, trimd & fastend one beam, shifted platform 46 feet bulkheads to storeroom 181 feet & unhung & rehung 2 doors made one scuttle lid repaired 2 hatches & fitted & fastend lead copper & tin in the galley.

Upper deck: Got in place bored off & bolted 14 Iron hanging knees, trimd & bolted 6 carronade chocks & one lodging knee; shifted the hawse pieces, drove out & redrove 22 ring bolts; split down a knee, unbolted trimd over & rebolted a crosspiece to the bitts & 3 ranges – took off refitted & fastend birthing 104 feet trimed & let down 14 port sills made molds for & fitted 7 and refitted 34 hammock stantions, trimd & fitted 2 short timbers, hammock board 127 feet & a wood lock to the rother; cleard & took off plansheer & trimd & bolted 6 arch pieces over the ports, built a case to the rother, repaired the roundhouse; refitted hammock board 24 feet & fitted & fastened lead on the flat 32 feet – made 6 half ports; one cap scuttle & one ladder; repaired 13 scuttle lids & 2 ladders.

Withoutboard: Grounded & lifted the schooner in the mast pond, took off the copper & dubbed the bottom, split out 7 blocks shifted staples & coppered the false keel, bolted & leaded the gripe punched up & plugg'd 3112 nails & bored for & drove 3112 nails & squared & coppered the bottom; unhung took ashore & shifted the main piece of the rother & unbolted took off refitted & rebolted. the pintles – trimd & bolted the hawse bolster & cheeks to the head & trimd & fastend the counter & quarter rails shifted wale 14 feet birthing 168 feet & rebolted the plansheers; took off refitted & fastend birthing 148 feet & made & hung 2 rowport lids – got up & let in 3 deadeyes; drove out & redrove 17 chain plate bolts & 2 ring bolts & fitted & fasten'd 4 Iron plates to channels – Made stages for the above works; cut out & put in 19 pieces and performed works incident to rigging.

References

1. Joseph Tucker, 'Account of the works performed by the Shipwrights on the Hulls of His Majesty's Ships, at the Port of Plymouth from the 11th of March (being the commencement of the equipment) to the 30th of September', RN Museum, Portsmouth, Admiralty Library Portfolio 1(3).

2. *Ibid.*, 14

3. *Ibid.*, 24

Peter Goodwin *is curator of HMS* Victory.

A TALE OF TWO CITIES: THE FACILITIES, WORK AND IMPACT OF THE VICTUALLING OFFICE IN PORTSMOUTH, 1793-1815

Matthew Sheldon

Abstract

Victualling the ships that used Portsmouth Dockyard and Harbour during the wars with France was a huge undertaking which had a significant impact on the town. At its height in 1800 the Victualling Office in Portsmouth controlled a workforce of over 570 men, yet this is a part of naval and urban history which has been little researched. This paper provides an overview of the work of the Office including the size of its task, its place in naval administration, local office holders, workforce, buildings and facilities.

Introduction

'I must further beg leave to state that the accommodation for the Victualling Department seems so inadequate to the keeping pace with the business of the Dockyard on the occasion of a sudden outfit of the fleet that I have been led to suppose that some new and extensive arrangement ... will at a future time be deemed expedient ...' [1]

Samuel Bentham, the first holder of the recently created post of Inspector General of Naval Works, wrote this letter to the Admiralty in 1799. As his letter suggests the inadequacy of the facilities for victualling in Portsmouth had long been recognised, and his was just the latest in a long line of requests for investment. In the year he wrote the local Victualling Office was busier than ever before, and provided an estimated 32,000 men with provisions. Yet it was not until 1828 that the 'new and extensive arrangement' which he anticipated was actually made and an integrated site was created, on the western side of the harbour at Weevill, to replace facilities split between the two towns of Portsmouth and Gosport.

This paper will examine a period when the Navy grew ever larger[2] and demonstrate that for the Victualling Office in Portsmouth, perhaps even more than elsewhere in the naval estate, 'growth in logistics had left the facilities behind.'[3] It will look in detail at the facilities, and the workforce, controlled by the Office and show how the lack of investment, which Samuel Bentham recognised, affected its day-to-day work. It will show how little development occurred during the wars, and suggest the particular local difficulties that prevented development. At its peak during these wars with France more than 600 men were directly employed in victualling, and £38,000 a year was paid in wages to local households; the impact of the Office on the local economy was therefore significant, but the paper will show that the precise impact it had was shaped by the lack of development. Ultimately, the local victualling service emerges, as a well-supervised, well-administered, operation which, with the usual number of complaints and periodic crises, successfully supplied the changing demands of the Channel Fleet. However, this success came at some cost and the system was slower and more expensive than it might have been.

The Victualling Facilities in 1793

At the start of the war the victualling facilities for ships at Portsmouth were split between both sides of the harbour. They were fragmented, often in poor repair, and with insufficient capacity for the fleet that used Portsmouth (see fig. 1).

The centre of facilities on the Portsmouth side was in St. Mary's Street (highlighted as 1 on fig. 1) where there were the offices of the Agent, Storekeeper and Clerk of the Checque. The Agent's residence, 'calculated for the occupation of a highly respectable family, and inferior to few others in the Town of Portsmouth'[4], was nearby in St. Thomas Street. Round the corner in King Street was the site of a bakehouse built in 1740 (highlighted as 2 on fig. 1), described by the Board in 1793 as, 'very old ... and contains but six ovens, and being situated in the Town as well as being in part surrounded by other victualling premises affords cause for great apprehension of danger by accident from fire'.[5] Directly opposite were the principal storehouses for dry provisions; one was built in 1740, and another large 3 storey building was added in 1782 (see fig. 2), but described by a visitation just before the wars as, 'so very defective as to admit the Rain in various places by which the Bread stored therein has frequently been subjected to injury'.[6]

These stores were some distance from the Victualling Wharf, through the Quay Gate in the fortifications, built on land bought from the Corporation in c.1730 (highlighted as 3 on fig. 1). The storehouses 'being situated within the Garrison' caused problems and made it, 'necessary to convey every kind of provision ... by means of drays and wagons, which very frequently, but particularly in the winter season, when the days are short, occasions considerable delays to the loading of the Craft'.[7] The victualling wharf was 440 feet long and fitted with four cranes – two for loading hoys with supplies for vessels at anchor, and two for off-loading stores received from Deptford and the other victualling yards or contractors – but was still described as 'extremely confined', and could only be used for a brief period either side of high tide.[8]

At the other side of the town, the Office used the Square Tower as a store, having built a slaughterhouse on adjoining land in 1779[9] (highlighted as 4 on fig. 1). This caused its own problems because, when the wind blew between the south-east and the south-west, the boats crews sent ashore for fresh meat could not embark with their supplies. Instead, to much local complaint, they would carry the carcasses on their backs all the way down to the Point Beach.[10]

Outside the fortifications there was a tidal mill which had been built for the Victualling Board in 1746 and expanded with an additional set of stones in 1757 (highlighted as 5 on fig. 1). This could grind 'only 200 quarters' a week, and there were again significant difficulties with access, ' the creek leading from this mill ... will admit of but one vessel at a time, and the rise of the tides ... is frequently so small as not to admit a vessel of any magnitude coming up for several days together'.[11] The mill also stood on the

bridge on the main road connecting Portsmouth and Portsea, and in 1812 the citizens of Portsmouth sought to demolish the mill so that the road could be widened.[12]

On the Gosport side of the harbour facilities were more concentrated, and were at least enclosed by a yard wall. The Victualling Board had developed the site of an old private brewery on the Weevil estate which it bought in 1752 (see fig. 3). Here there were two brewhouses (one built in 1758 and one in 1782), the associated pumphouse and reservoir, storehouses, a rolling way to take casks out to hoys, and residences for the Master Cooper and Master Brewer, etc. Weevil was also the main site for watering, but experience showed that, 'it has frequently occurred ... that the quantity of water produced (after supplying the Brewery at that place) has been found very inadequate ... and consequently the watering of a large fleet became a work of much time.'[13] The cooperage had been moved here from Portsmouth in 1766, and included a large number of coopers' sheds for dressing casks.

The Weevil site had been identified with the potential for an integrated victualling site since at least the American War. In August 1793, just six months after the start of the wars, the Board wrote:

'The business of the Victualling Department at Portsmouth has long been subjected to the most serious inconveniences, especially in times of public exigency from the detached situation of the Bakehouse and Mill and from their inability to comply with the wants of the Service... [and] it has been the agitation ever since the year 1782 to erect buildings at Weevil... conformable to their Lordships order ... of that year'.[14]

The Development of Facilities, 1793-1815.

However, no improvements were actually made at Weevil following the Admiralty order of 1782, and few alterations were made between 1793 and 1815 which fundamentally improved these deficiencies. The problems with access to the victualling wharf were partially addressed when the Commander-in-Chief agreed to station the Ildefonso, the Spanish two-decker captured at Trafalgar, as a depot for stores out at Spithead.[15] Plans were also laid in 1801 to speed up watering the fleet by piping water to Watering Island from the well in the Dockyard.[16] However, these were on a small scale and the question remains: why was the general rearrangement, so clearly recognized as necessary, not implemented?

Some of the reasons are set out by Samuel Bentham, who wrote in July 1799 of the situation in Portsmouth (my emphasis):

'the improvements proposed ... have turned out to be so intimately connected with further improvements which are requisite with regard to the Victualling Department *as well as with what may relate to* other branches of the Naval Service *in general that I have not yet been able to draw up any report ...I have accordingly intended to prepare some plans ... but as such works could not (should they be approved) be completed in any short period and as* this does not seem to be a time the most favourable for beginning ... *I have wished to keep my plan back ...'.*[17]

His letter hints at some of the general difficulties facing the victualling service. The victualling yards at Deptford and Plymouth worked as part of a single system with Portsmouth and, as all suffered from lack of investment, thoroughgoing reform of the whole was required. The wars were not the ideal time for reform of the system, or for major developments, but this should not necessarily have presented insurmountable problems. It has already been demonstrated that Portsmouth's new bakehouse, mill and brewhouse were built either during the War of the Austrian Succession or the Seven Years War. Similarly the building programme in the Dockyard of the late 1790s, which included the enlargement of the Great Basin and additional dry docks, took place in Portsmouth's busiest period.[18]

However, in Portsmouth there were also particular local problems with the Ordnance Board, and the limited progress that Bentham made illustrates the difficulty of improving facilities in a cramped garrison town where there was competition for land. Bentham's interim proposal in 1799 to tackle the problems of the location of the Office's storehouses, was to create new stores. A temporary wooden store, some 200 feet long and 40 feet wide, was built on the victualling wharf between 1800-1801; this required a piece of land from the Ordnance Board and the overcoming of their objections that it would obstruct the defences by masking Legg's Demi-Bastion. This meant stores would at least not be left on the wharf exposed to weather, but it did not improve access for hoys, and during the wars matters only got worse for the Victualling Office. The development of the Ordnance Board's New Gun Wharf from 1799 made access to the quay so difficult that in 1811 the Victualling Board was forced to protest. At which point the Ordnance Board made a particularly handsome offer - the Victualling Board could have space on Gun Wharf, and all the superior access to the harbour it provided, if they paid the cost of building a new store for the Ordnance Board. This was an significant improvement and the Office got the use of an existing 2 storey ordnance storehouse with a wharf at the west end on the New Gun Wharf. However, it was an extremely expensive way of making improvements: the Ordnance Board's 'Grand Storehouse', which the Victualling Board paid, for cost an amazing £29,700.[19] The store was only ever used for two years of war, and the cost should be contrasted with the entire cost of the integrated Yard at Weevil, with all its steam machinery, etc of £71,000.[20] These issues with the Ordnance Board were only finally settled in 1828 with the construction of the new Royal Clarence Yard victualling facilities on the Weevil site. The settlement included a transfer of 3½ acres at Weevil from the Ordnance Board to the Victualling Board, with land in Portsmouth at Gun Wharf and the site of the old Mill passing the other way.

This lack of coherent development made victualling a fleet at Portsmouth slower and more expensive, and management much harder, than it might have been. But it also meant it was impossible to make use of the efficiencies of new technology in the way that Bentham pioneered in the dockyard, and was gradually being applied in other victualling establishments.[21] The various facilities split between sites created problems; it was hard to restrain pilfering without a walled

Fig. 1. The location of victualling facilities on the Portsmouth side of the harbour in 1793. 1: St. Mary's Street with offices (precise location unknown). 2: Bakehouse with storehouses opposite. 3: Victualling Quay. 4: Slaughterhouse and Meat Store. 5: Mill.

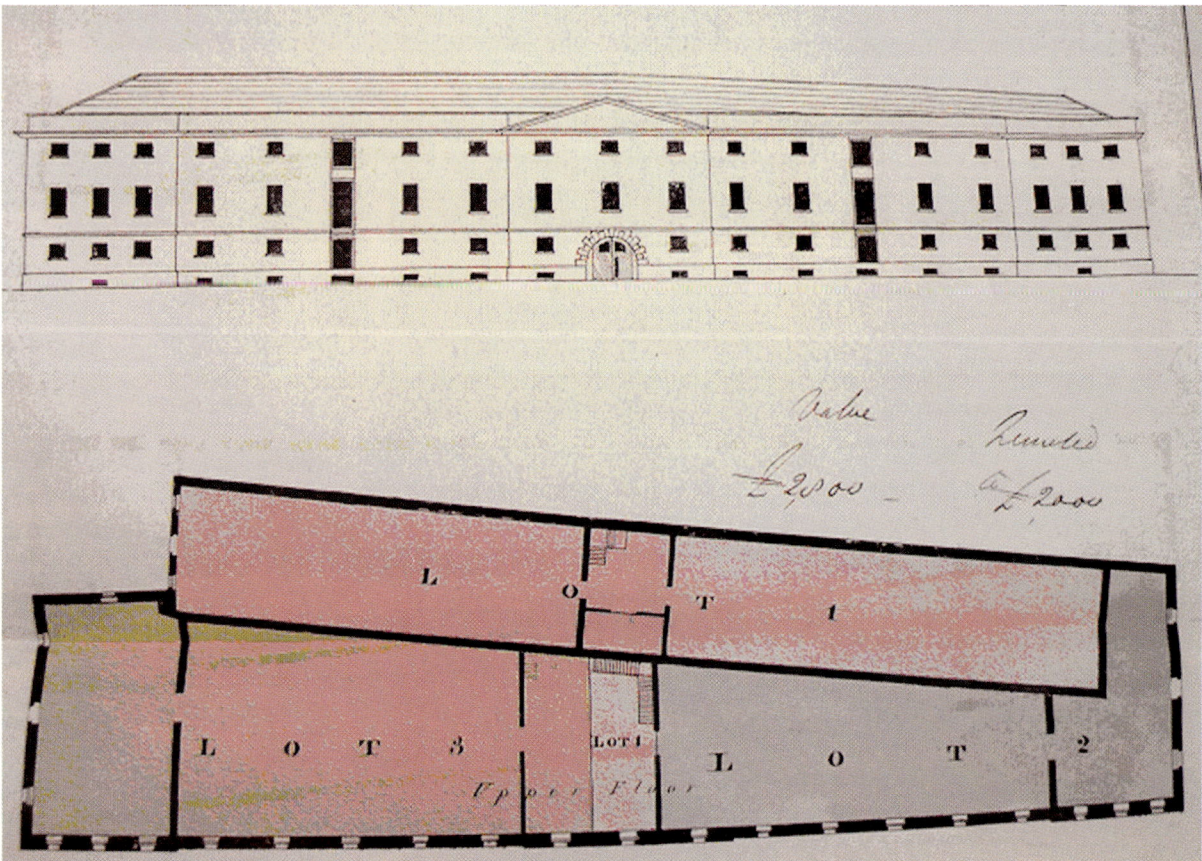

Fig. 2. Elevation and plan of the Victualling Office's Stores in Kings' Street, built in 1782 for £8,600. This illustration is from the sale partiulars of 1828; the building was to be taken down and these advertise the separate lots of scrap building materials. (TNA, ADM114/42).

Fig. 3. Plan of Weevil Yard with existing buildings and proposed extensions c.1782. The proposed Mill and Bakehouse, which were never built, are shown at 'M' – nearest the creek on the left hand side. (TNA, MP1-154a).

victualling yard in a dockyard town where 'theft was part of community culture.'[22] Supervision was difficult as, increasingly, senior officers were on the Portsmouth side of the harbour, and a majority of the work force on the Gosport side. At a minor level this meant a man like John Meredith, Second Clerk to the Checque, had his salary increased from the usual £80 to £100 because he worked at Weevil, whereas his superior, the Clerk of the Checque Thomas Pitt, was based in Portsmouth. More significantly it could lead to serious problems. Between 1808 and 1809 there was a bitter dispute at the Weevil site between Lieutenant Benamor, appointed to a new post to superintend hoys, and the Master Cooper. This was over the former's interpretation of his new duties, severely disrupted the site in 1808-1809, and ultimately led to an enquiry by the Admiralty. With a unified site it seems unlikely the dispute would have been able to fester out of sight of the Agent.

The Role of the Victualling Office, 1793-1815

Despite these problems Portsmouth supplied more men, and more ships, per year in these wars than in any earlier conflict. The Agent appears to have overcome local difficulties with great efficiency.

At the commencement of war the Agent in Portsmouth was responsible for actively supplying a larger fleet than anyone else. [23] Portsmouth's early primacy was shown in 1796 when, 'in consequence of Portsmouth being the general rendezvous of the Fleet, and of the extraordinary exertions of our Agent',[24] the Agent's salary was increased above that of the Agents at Plymouth, Dover and Chatham.

Neither the Agent in Portsmouth, nor the Board in London, appear ever to have kept a precise record of the numbers of men supplied locally. Approximate figures appear in the victualling predictions made each autumn for the following year, and the peak for these wars predicts that in 1801 35,000 men will be supplied from Portsmouth. The annual demand came principally from the Channel Fleet, which at the start of the war was based in Portsmouth. For most of the 1790s ships of the line in the Fleet did not try to keep the sea throughout the year, and this meant heavy demand on the Victualling Office for fresh meat, fresh bread and water when the ships were at anchor.[25] The fleet wintered at Spithead throughout the 1790s - not sailing for instance until May in 1794 and 1797 (admittedly after a month's delay caused by the Mutiny), and until April in 1799. However, the fleet might still need to be

victualled for sea at very short notice, as in December 1796 when Bridport was ordered to 'proceed down Channel with all possible despatch' with twenty-two ships to search for the fleet commanded by Vice-Admiral Morard-de-Galles that had broken out of Brest.[26]

This seasonal pattern changed as the war progressed, and an observer wrote in 1806, 'there was an instance in the early part of the late war of a great part of the Channel Fleet remaining at Spithead five months at one time, and now ... [ships] return into a King's port but twice a year except when driven in by stress of weather'.[27]

Further significant demands came because Portsmouth was the assembly point for the departure of military expeditions. Such expeditions were a key part of naval strategy and the Victualling Office supplied not only the escorting naval ships, but also the troops carried in transports. This could place a heavy, occasional demand on the Office; as an example the expedition to the West Indies which sailed in November 1795 contained 18,740 troops in 200 transports, and a naval force of 21 ships.[28] Admiral Hugh Christian who led the naval escort, betrayed his nervousness when he wrote that the task, ' ... appeared to me of such magnitude that I hesitated whether it might be prudent to hazard St. Helens as a rendezvous ...'.[29] However, his fears were groundless and such was his praise for the Agent's efficiency that it led directly to the increase in salary mentioned above.

The demand on the Portsmouth Office changed as the war progressed, figure 4 compares the predictions, made by the Victualling Board in the autumn of every year, for the likely numbers of men to be supplied at each out-port in the following twelve months. These show Portsmouth averaging over 27,500 men between 1794 and 1802, but just 20,300 men between 1804 and 1806, and 24,000 between 1807 and 1814. Portsmouth's relative importance in victualling compared with Plymouth, the only other out-port of significance, changes even more dramatically. From 1794 to 1799 Portsmouth was clearly expected to supply more men than Plymouth, there was no clear leader from 1800 to 1802,

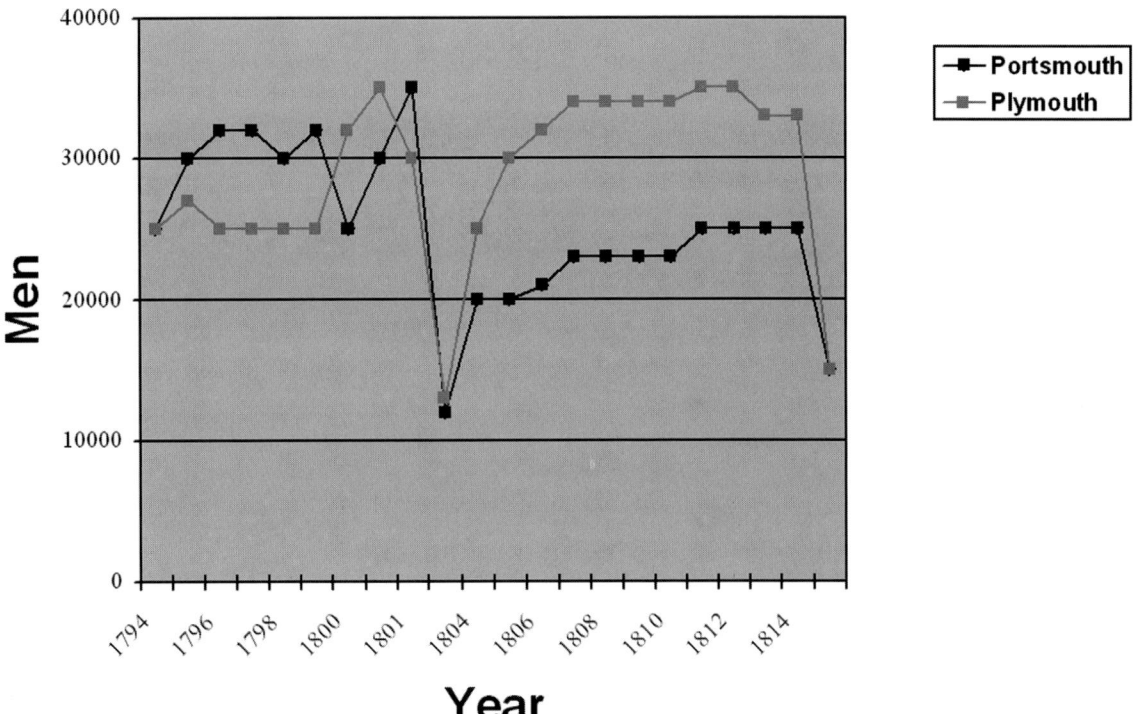

Year

Fig. 4. Comparison of Portsmouth and Plymouth victualling, 1794-1815. Totals taken from the 'victualling predictions' in the Victualling Board's out letter books. (TNA, ADM110). The predictions appear in autumn letters to the Navy Board.

but Plymouth is consistently predicted to supply between 5,000 and 10,000 more men between 1803 and 1815. The shift in importance was symbolized when in 1803 the officers of the Victualling Office in Plymouth petitioned for equal pay with their Portsmouth counter-parts, and had this plea supported by the Victualling Board.[30]

This shift in workload falling on Portsmouth reflects a different disposition for the Channel Fleet. It also illustrates an expertise that developed in keeping that Fleet at sea year round, keeping its crews healthy, and of sending provisions out to a fleet on blockade. From 1798, as the importance of maintaining a blockade on the French fleet in Brest increased, the Channel Fleet used Torbay as an anchorage and was principally supplied from the Victualling Office in Plymouth. This lessened demands on Portsmouth, though the Agent contributed by also sending supplies to Torbay – for example over the course of 1799 he hired 53 vessels to carry 'bread and beer to ships at Torbay and stores at Plymouth'.[31]

Portsmouth dockyard's advantage over Plymouth in docking facilities meant that demands also continued from ships returned for refit, and supplies were sent out to ships on station. One example is an order from the

Board to the Agent on 20th September 1805 to supply two transports with 'potatoes, carrots, onions, parsnips, and other vegetables' for Nelson's fleet off Cadiz.[32]

Whilst the demands on Portsmouth were lower in the second half of the war, they still represented a great effort, and are significantly above the totals for victualling predictions in any preceding conflicts. During the Seven Years' War the peak demand was 15,000 men in 1760, and during the American War the peak was 20,000. On balance the local Victualling Office met these changing demands efficiently, and between 1793 and 1815 there were no major problems. It is never hard to find evidence of sea officers at Portsmouth grumbling to the Admiralty about particular requests for victualling not being complied with – whether it is supplies of essence of malt as an anti-scorbutic, or substitutions of rice and sugar for butter and cheese. However, where the Agent had been unhelpful it was almost always that he had stuck rigidly to standing Admiralty orders about the scale of provisions, which ships were entitled to particular provisions, or whether provisions were just for the sick or the whole crew.

More serious complaints were rare. There was one complaint in 1805 about the Portsmouth Office's efficiency in loading provisions when Admiral Montagu writes of, 'the great delay which the King's Service suffers from the Hoys not furnishing the ships at Spithead with Water and Provisions when the Wind is Easterly'. On this occasion the Victualling Board admitted this had occurred, but blamed the contractor for hoys who had refused the Agent's request to put to sea in rough weather. In 1808, after Lord Castlereagh, Secretary of State, complained that the expedition under Major General Spencer had been delayed, 'for want of water and provisions'[33], the Admiralty ordered a general investigation into the levels of stores at all victualling ports. This found that the greatest problems have been at Portsmouth where, 'sudden demands [from] 100 sail of transport from the Baltic, and 16 sail of the line, sloops, frigates, etc. – combined with a long continuance of westerly winds attended with tempestuous weather having prevented the arrival of scarcely any supplies from the eastward'.[34]

However, these grumbles and complaints were balanced by testimonials to the Agent's work; Admiral Christian wrote in 1795 of the, 'perfect intention on the part of your Agent at this Port, to make every possible exertion',[35] whilst when visiting Commissioners of Victualling consulted the Port Admiral in 1803 he spoke of his 'entire approbation'.[36] One reason for the efficiency was that the agent was responsive, and was

an active part of the wider naval administration. In 1794 when there were complaints about ships' boats collecting fresh beef, the Agent met with a visiting member of the Victualling Board, the Port Admiral and other flag officers, conveniently assembled for a court martial, to work out a better system. Similarly in 1795-6 when the Admiralty wished to test the idea of supplying potatoes in lieu of bread and flour, they turn to the Agent who reported the views of several Admirals and Captains. With such careful monitoring and frequent communication it was hard for problems to continue.

The Local Impact of the Victualling Office, 1793-1815

During the wars the Victualling Office in Portsmouth was a major employer in both Portsmouth and Gosport, and made a considerable contribution to the local economy. Victualling contracts also had a significant impact, but this impact was shaped by the capacity of the facilities in Portsmouth.

Short of laboriously counting the men listed in the quarterly pay-lists of the office there is no easy way of showing the exact numbers of men employed, but the totals of wages paid in each quarter give a good indication of the pattern of employment (see fig. 5). This graph clearly does not give an exact match for numbers employed. It shows wages paid, rather than the men working at any one time, and these varied with the length of the day worked. Wages also reflect the

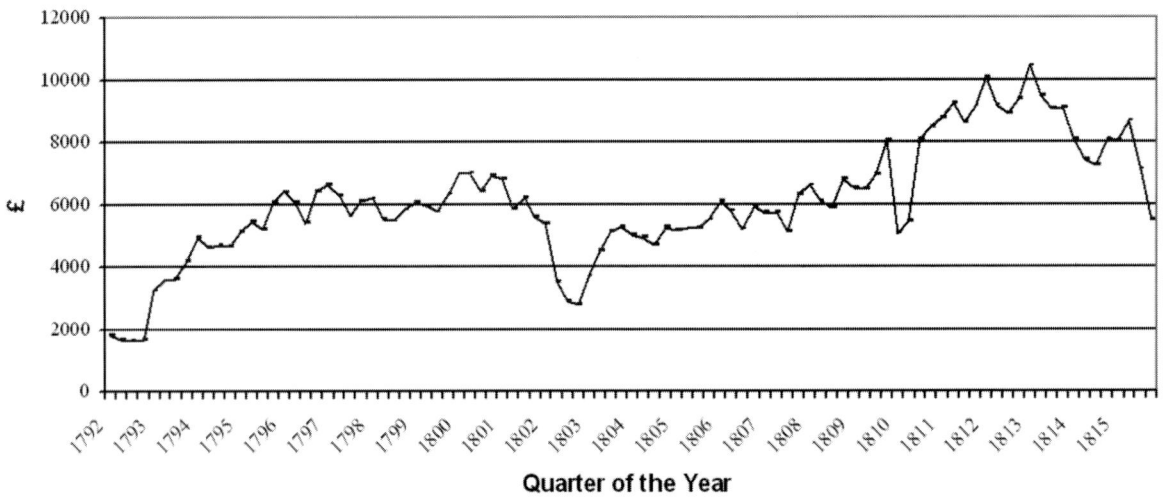

Fig. 5. Wages paid by Victualling Office, 1792-1815. Totals drawn from the quarterly pay books at TNA, ADM 113.

seasonal nature of victualling work; the 3rd quarter is usually quietest because of the lack of brewing and the absence of the Fleet. Across the period there are also significant changes in the salaries paid to office-holders, particularly from 1800 as a result of the implementation of the findings of the Commission on Fees.[37]

However, taking these distortions into account, the graph shows the impact of these wages on the local economy which were £38,019 at their peak in 1813, and the payments broadly match the pattern of activity in Portsmouth derived from fig. 4. In Portsmouth's busy period of the Revolutionary War 553 men were employed in the first Quarter of 1797, and 570 in the second Quarter of 1800. In 1803 the Board recommended a peace workforce of 192 plus the victualling officers, but observed that the returns of casks from ships would require considerable numbers of labourers and coopers for some time to come. Employment in the Napoleonic Wars was initially at a lower level, but peaked in the first Quarter of 1813 with 616 men directly employed. By this date the majority were working on the Gosport side of the harbour with the posts split as follows: 'Officers Clerks and Other Persons having fixed salaries (42),'Artificers, Labourers, &c' at Portsmouth (158), 'Hoymen' (60), 'Artificers, Labourers, &c at Weevill' (356). This figure of 616 men represented an increase of 60% from the previous peak of 387 in 1781.[38]

This paper has shown that during the wars the Fleet's demand for food increased and the Office's workforce expanded dramatically. Yet a survey of facilities has shown that Portsmouth's capacity to process food for the Navy did not develop. To be clear: between 1793 and 1815 the Office could bake no more biscuits and bread than in the War of Austrian Succession: it could mill no more grain to make biscuit meal and flour than in the Seven Years' War: it could brew no more beer than in the American War. This raises a number of questions. How was the expanded fleet supplied, what were all these extra men who were employed doing, and what were the implications for the local economy?

The first two questions have relatively simple answers, but the implications for the local economy are more complex. The extra provisions for an expanded fleet were either transferred from another victualling yard - usually Deptford - or delivered by private contractors. The extra men were that part of the workforce, largely the unskilled labourers and coopers, responsible for handling and packaging provisions. There were huge sums of money at stake in victualling contracts, but this money was not necessarily made in the Portsmouth area, and that the implications for the local economy are not straightforward. A study of two examples will illustrate how the pattern varies.

Research here is difficult. Figures for the actual quantities of food processed in Portsmouth, were not recorded, and the Victualling Board's records do not give details of precisely where private contractors delivered their supplies. However, unusually, in the case of biscuit it is possible to trace the local contracts placed by the Agent which show the gap left by inadequate facilities. In 1806 the Agent in Portsmouth made contracts with private bakers for 4,000,000 lbs of biscuit, and in addition he also issued 616,000 lbs of biscuit meal from the Office's Mill to be baked into biscuit.[39] In total this is sufficient to supply over 12,500 men for the year,[40] and the contracts were worth over £45,000. The bakers appear to have been local – some were based in Portsea, others were from Cowes and Southampton – and if one combines their contracts for biscuit meal, fuel, sacks, freight and cartage the economic impact is significant.

A contrasting example is shown in terms of supply of beer and wine. Here, unusually, figures for the quantities brewed in Portsmouth do survive over a long period and are shown in figure 6.[41] The peak year for brewing was 1796 when 23,763 tuns were brewed – enough to supply 14,000 men with their gallon of beer a day.[42] What is interesting is how brewing declined so that in 1808 there were just 8,033 tuns brewed – enough for just 4,753 men at a time when we know Portsmouth was predicted to supply 24,000 men that year. This occured not because beer was being shipped from elsewhere (it was too bulky to move economically), or because local private brewers were awarded contracts, but because wine was increasingly substituted.[43] From 1802 there were a number of Admiralty orders to suspend brewings of beer and issue wine instead. This is significant in terms of impact on the local economy because whilst brewing activity was high the Agent in Portsmouth placed some local contracts for malt, and for coals for the brewhouse. However, when the substitution occurred all the contracts for wine or spirits were settled by the Victualling Board in London for quantities to be delivered direct to the stores in Portsmouth. In this example there was no benefit to the local economy.

Conclusion

This paper has looked at the realities of victualling from one, albeit very significant base. I hope I have shown that in the case of the Portsmouth Victualling Office there was little investment, and little use of new technology. This presents a real contrast with what we have heard of the dockyard where processes like block-making and copper sheathing were taken away from contractors and placed in the dockyard's direct control.

However, it is important to note that developments in victualling elsewhere – at the Victualling Board in London, its premises in Deptford, Plymouth, or overseas – have never been studied in detail in this period. I should like to end with some questions. Is the pattern of development seen in the Victualling Office in Portsmouth typical of what happened elsewhere? Was the Board as a whole becoming more reliant on private contractors in these wars with France, and if so who was making all the money?

References

1 The National Archives (TNA), ADM 224/72. Letter from Samuel Bentham, Inspector General of Naval Works to the Admiralty, 12th July 1799

2 For the numbers of men to be fed see Nicholas Rodger, *The Command of the Ocean; A Naval History of Great Britain*, Allen Lane, 2005, 636-639. At one point in 1794 73,835 men were actually mustered on board ship, in 1812 at one point there were 138,204.

3 Roger Morriss, *Naval Power and British Culture, 1760-1850*, Ashgate Publishing, 2004, 27.

4 TNA, ADM 114/42. Letter from John Hulbert, recent purchaser of the house, 24th September 1828.

5 TNA, ADM110/39. Letter from Victualling Board to the Admiralty, 7th August 1793.

6 TNA, ADM 110/38. Letter from Victualling Board to Admiralty, 23rd August 1792.

7 TNA, ADM 110/45. Letter from Victualling Board to Admiralty, 25th November 1799.

8 TNA, ADM 110/56. Letter from Victualling Board to Admiralty, 6th January 1808.

9 Henry Slight, *The Royal Port, Garrison, Dock-Yard, and Borough of*

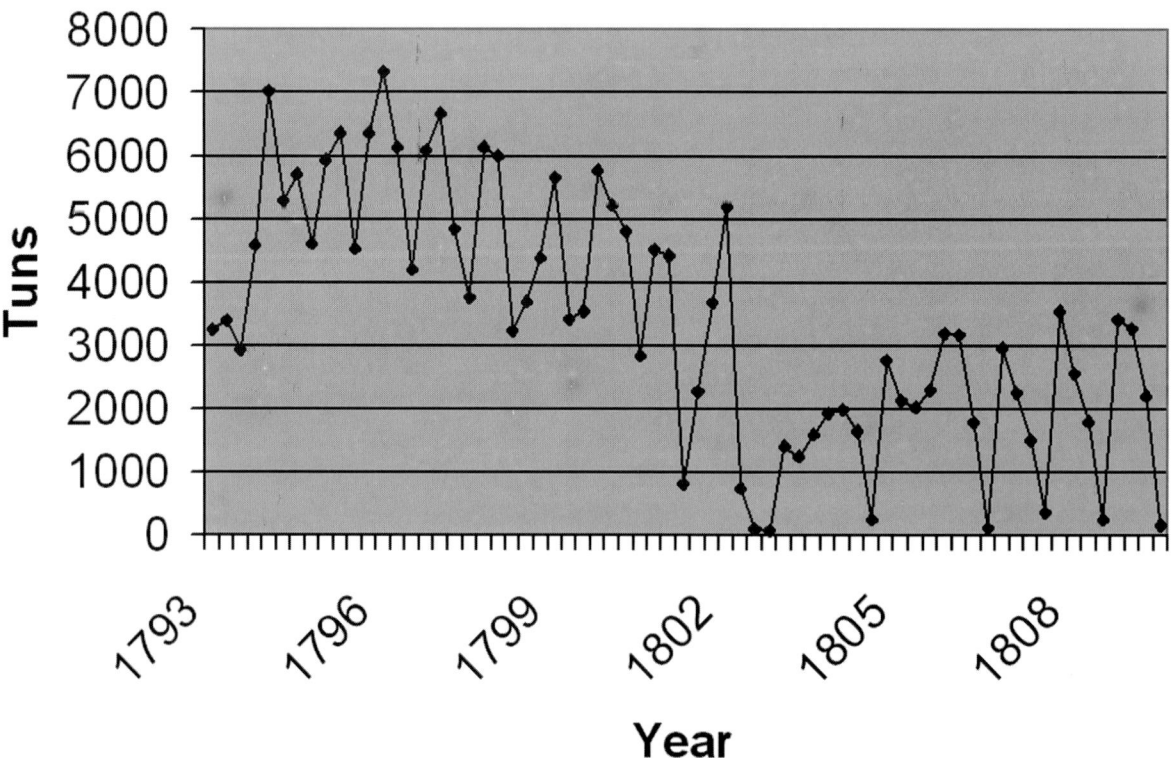

Fig. 6. Tuns of beer brewed at Portsmouth, 1793-1809. Totals drawn from quarterly pay books at TNA, ADM 113.

Portsmouth, 3rd edition, undated, 9.

10 TNA, ADM 110/39. Letter from Victualling Board to Admiralty, 1st March 1794.

11 TNA, ADM 110/39. Letter from Victualling Board to the Admiralty, 7th August 1793.

12 TNA, ADM 110/66. Letter from Victualling Board to Admiralty, 9th November 1812.

13 TNA, ADM 110/47. Letter from the Victualling Board to the Admiralty, 11th December 1801.

14 TNA, ADM 110/39. Letter from the Victualling Board to the Admiralty, 7th August 1793.

15 TNA, ADM 11056. Letter from Victualling Board to Admiralty, 6th January 1808

16 TNA, ADM 110/47. Letter from the Victualling Board to the Admiralty, 11th December 1801. This showed the benefits of the sort of joined up thinking which came from a post like Bentham's. He was responsible to the Admiralty, but was charged with making changes in the facilities controlled by the Navy Board and the Victualling Board. This new watering capacity was a spin off from Bentham's plans for piping and drainage within the Dockyard.

17 TNA, ADM 224/72. Letter from Samuel Bentham, Inspector General of Naval Works to the Admiralty, 12th July 1799.

18 Roger Morriss, *The Royal Dockyards during thr Revolutionary and Napoleonic Wars*, 1983, 48.

19 TNA, ADM 110/67. Letter from Victualling Board to Admiralty, 24th April 1813.

20 Henry Slight, *op. cit.*, 2.

21 As one example in 1807 Brunel proposed erecting at Deptford 2 steam driven circular saws for cutting staves for casks, and the Victualling Board demonstrated the annual saving on coopers' wages. TNA, ADM 110/56. Letter from Victualling Board to Admiralty, 3rd September 1807.

22 Roger Morriss, *op. cit.*, 32.

23 The headquarters at Deptford certainly processed more food, but the facilities here were under the shared control of the Board at Somerset House, and Deptford was less actively involved in supplying a fleet. Its provisions were shipped out to supply stores at other out-ports and to the Mediterranean.

24 TNA, ADM 110/41. Letter from Victualling Board to Admiralty, 14th December 1795.

25 A sense of the scale of the operations is given from the scanty references to quantities of supplies actually issued. Thus, in Portsmouth in 1796 5,782,239 lbs of fresh beef were issued. From TNA, ADM 224/72. Promiscuous letter book.

26 Roger Morriss (ed.), *The Channel Fleet and the Blockade of Brest, 1793-1801*, Navy Records Society, 2001, 169.

27 *Ibid*, 20.

28 Edwina Boult, *Christian's Fleet: A Dorset Shipping Tragedy*, 2003, 130-134.

29 TNA, ADM 110/41. Letter from Victualling Board to Admiralty, 14th December 1795. (St. Helen's is an anchorage further out than Spithead).

30 TNA, ADM 110/48. Letter from the Victualling Board to the Admiralty, 11th February 1803. It was not only the Agent at Portsmouth who was better paid, but also the Storekeeper, Clerk of the Checque and their clerks.

31 TNA, ADM 224/72. Promiscuous letter book.

32 TNA, ADM 110/53. Letter from Victualling Board to the Admiralty, 20th September 1805.

33 TNA, ADM 110/56. Letter from Victualling Board to the Admiralty, 11th January 1808.

34 TNA, ADM 110/57. Letter from Victualling Board to the Admiralty, 1st February 1808.

35 TNA, ADM 110/41. Letter from Victualling Board to the Admiralty, 14th December 1795.

36 TNA, ADM 111/69. Minutes of Victualling Board, 8th October 1803.

37 For example the salaries of major office-holders were increased as follows from 1st January 1800: Agent £300 to £500, Storekeeper £80 to £300, Clerk of the Checque £80 to £300.

38 TNA, ADM 113/230. Paybook for Portsmouth Victualling Office.

39 TNA, ADM 112/192. Contract book.

40 Seamen were entitled to 1lb of biscuit per day: 4,616,000 lbs / 365 days = 12,646 seamen for a year.

41 This is because the expense of keeping a team of horses to raise water for the brewhouses fell to the Master Brewer, and his compensation at 9d per tun appear in the quarterly paylists until 1809.

42 Seamen were entitled to 8 pints or 1 gallon of beer a day. With 216 gallons to a tun the calculations are: 23,763 x 216 = 5,132,808 gallons / 365 days = 14,062 men for a year.

43 Among the reasons for the substitution were 'the practical difficulties of embarking and stowing beer, during a war at which ships were spending very long periods at sea with only brief visits to port'. N.A.M. Rodger, *The Command of the Ocean: a Naval History of Britain, 1649-1815*, 495-496.

Matthew Sheldon *is head of research collections at the Royal Naval Museum, Portsmouth.*

THE CONTRIBUTION OF PORTSMOUTH ROYAL DOCKYARD TO THE SUCCESS OF THE ROYAL NAVY IN THE NAPOLEONIC WAR 1793-1815

F. S. Wilkin

Abstract

Through the use of a wide range of detailed statistical material, most of which is presented graphically, an attempt is made to demonstrate the work of Portsmouth Dockyard during the Napoleonic wars. There are three parts. Firstly, operational data for the fleet as a whole are examined; no less than half the 482 losses were due to the weather. Secondly, data for production, repair and refit work, including the calculation of ton dock days as a measure of productivity, are advanced for Portsmouth yard. Thirdly, there is a review of changes in the dry docks, in metal working, in the use of fibres, and in wood working, including the manufacture of pulley blocks. It is argued that Portsmouth's contribution, and by implication, the other royal dockyards, is inadequately recognised.

For much of the last three hundred years there has been a widespread tendency to summarise the Royal Dockyards' performance as corrupt, inefficient and incompetent. Undoubtedly, particularly in times of peace, there was "no smoke without fire" but equally it is impossible to avoid the fact that between 1793 and 1815 those Dockyards managed to keep over 500 ships at sea in an operational state. By any standards this was no mean achievement and to Portsmouth, which was responsible for more than a third of the fleet's refits, should go very considerable credit. This paper attempts to illustrate the nature and scale of Portsmouth Dockyard's contribution to the Royal Navy's successes across the wars and to do this, in the space available, it presents a series of interrelated numerical and diagrammatic graphics from which the reader is invited to draw conclusions on how great that Yard's contribution was and on what developments within its boundaries that depended.

The conduct of the war at sea across the period changed significantly with the passage of time and the changing political priorities.

Whilst the Royal Navy unquestionably defeated the maritime aims of France and her allies, victory came at a cost. That, as Figure I.I[1] shows, amounted to the loss of no less than 482 ships, against the 414 lost by the combined fleets of France, Spain, Holland, Russia, Turkey and the USA. The first thing these figures suggest is that the Royal Navy faced two enemies. On the one hand there were the naval forces of France and her allies and on the other there were the forces of nature. Of these two, the latter was the primary cause of work in Portsmouth

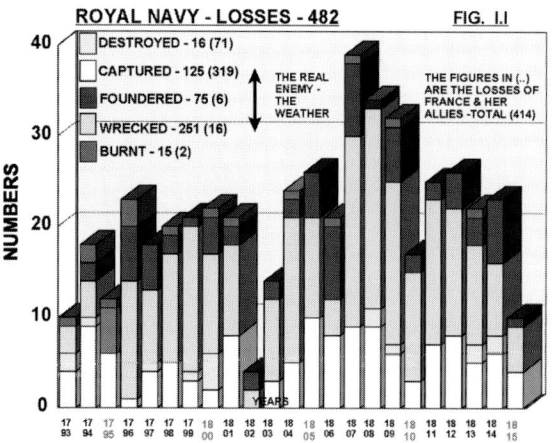

Dockyard.

At the start of the war the Government and Admiralty Board's focus was on the prevention of a French invasion of the United Kingdom or the seizure of its overseas possessions; the weight of the consequential operations fell on the line of battle ships and their supporting frigates. After the battle of Trafalgar, whilst this threat diminished; or at least became contained, the increase in the nation's overseas possessions, and the corresponding growth in trade with them, called for a steady expansion of the naval forces devoted to the protection of the trade routes. To this growing tasking was added the support of the Army whose presence in Portugal and Spain increased steadily from 1807 to the extent that at its peak over 80,000 military personnel were being directly supplied by sea from this country. This called for hundreds of small merchant ships regularly to make the perilous journey across the Bay of Biscay and France's Atlantic seaboard where, unless they were well protected by the Royal Navy, they were at real risk from French privateers.

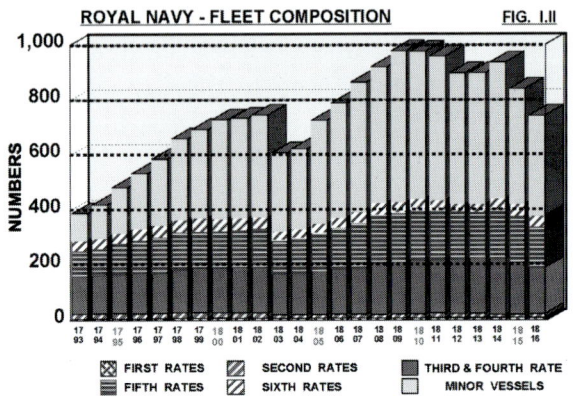

During the war the size of the fleet (Figure I.II) grew from 390 ships of all sizes in 1793 to a maximum of 979 in 1809. In terms of types the major growth in the fleet was in the area of the minor warships which made up the bulk of the convoy escorts. Their numbers stood at only 99 in 1793 but by 1809 had risen to no less than 549. The number of ships of the line increased from 136 in 1793 to a maximum of 202 in 1809. Those pure numbers are misleading, in terms of operational capability, since they take no account of the status of the ships. This is illustrated in Figure II.I under four headings: operational, that is, deployed on, or directly available for, service with the fleet at sea; in ordinary for sea service, that is, in reserve but available at relatively short notice to join the sea going fleet; harbour service, or ships employed as floating barracks, stores etc and not in a fit state for sea service; and in ordinary for harbour service, or ships in

reserve for harbour service – there is the strong suggestion that most vessels in this category were really only waiting to be taken to pieces or disposed of. Looked at this way it can be seen that the actual numbers of ships of the line which were operational, or in ordinary for operational service, remained remarkably constant throughout the war at around 110. In fact it was the increase in ships not fit for sea service that was the real cause

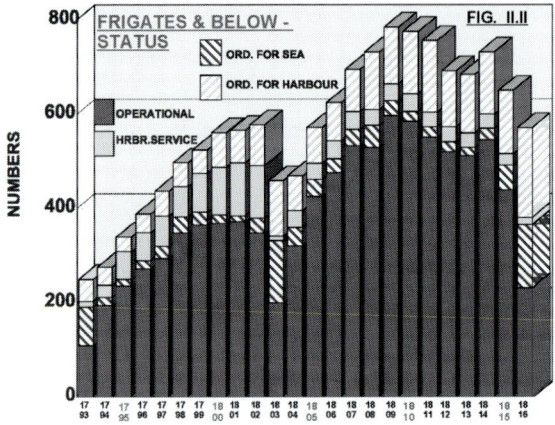

of the rise in total numbers to around 200.

The picture for frigates and below (Figure II.II) was significantly different. Here the numbers operational, or in ordinary for operational service, grew steadily from around 200 in 1793 to nearly 600 in 1809 even though, as with the ships of the line, the later years of the war saw a significant number of vessels in ordinary for harbour service, or awaiting disposal. The difference in the employment patterns of the two groups of ships is best shown by the percentages which were operational (Figure III.I). Prior to the Peace of Amiens both groups were maintaining an availability of between 60% and 70%, with the smaller vessels averaging close to 70% and those of the line something

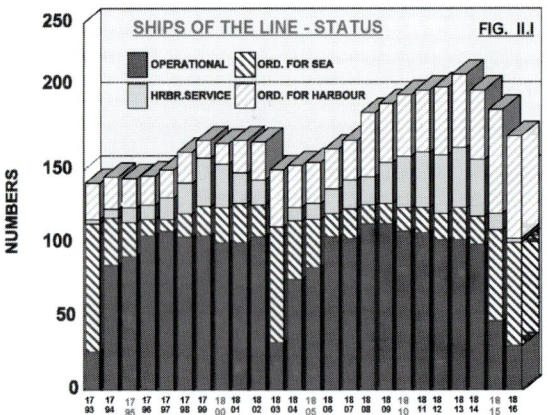

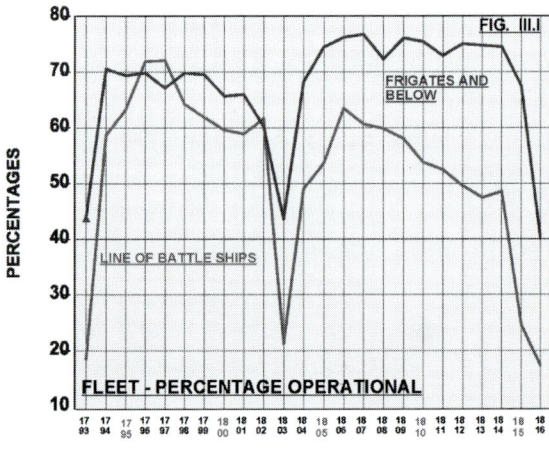

less than 65%, with the exception of one brief period when they actually exceeded 70%.

After the Peace of Amiens the situation changed markedly. The smaller vessels averaged something close to 75% until the actual invasion of France. However the

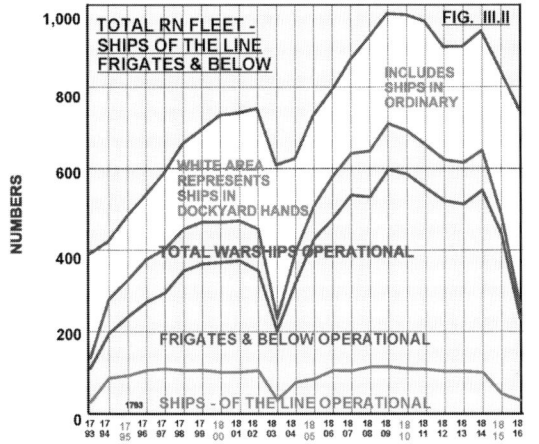

availability of ships of the line progressively declined to less than 50% by 1812.

It can be seen from Figure III.II that the number of ships in Dockyard hands, which included those in harbour service and in ordinary for harbour service, hovered around the two hundred mark (except during the Peace of Amiens) until about 1807, when it progressively rose towards the three hundred mark; this rise was primarily due to the increase in the numbers in ordinary for harbour service, or more likely awaiting disposal. When the fleet size peaked in 1809 at 979 there were 709 ships operational, 46 in ordinary/reserve for sea service, 64 in harbour service and 160 in ordinary for harbour service or awaiting disposal, which gave an overall operational availability figure of 77%. That this should be the situation after 17

years of war redounds greatly to the credit of the Royal Dockyards.

It is against this background that the work load at Portsmouth is examined. For that Yard the priority was refitting, with repairs (equating to major upgrades, re-builds or conversions) as a second priority, and new construction as the third. Figure IV.I[2] shows how the tasking was distributed between the three types of work. The extent to which the Yard was under pressure at a particular time is reflected by the degree to which refits dominated the loading; as was the case between 1797 and 1799 when the conversion of the dry docks was taking place. It may well be argued that whilst the Admiralty did not welcome the Peace of Amiens the Dockyard at least was grateful for the opportunity to consolidate.

From the point of view of the Navy's operational commanders the significant measure of Portsmouth's contribution to the forces at their disposal was the numbers of ships that sailed from the dockyard to join the fleet. Figure IV.II summarises these by type. It can be seen that in the second half of the war there was a progressive rise in the number of minor vessels sailing whilst the figures for the line of battle ships, and to a lesser extent even the frigates, remained relatively stable. What the graph tends to hide

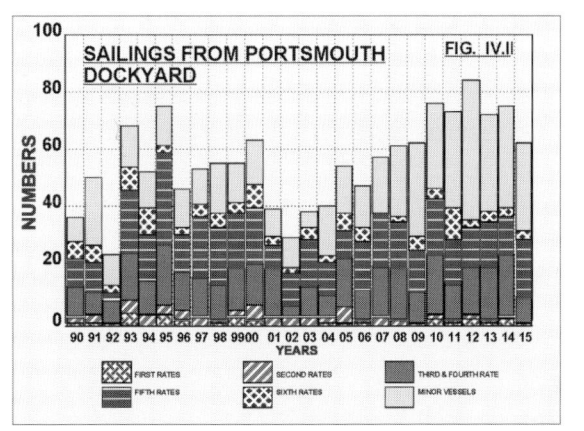

is the increasing workload involved in keeping the hard worked ships in a sea-going state.

Clearly, the number of sailings is not a reliable way to assess the Dockyard's workload since it in no way reflects how long any ship was in the Yard. However, a more accurate measure is available from the

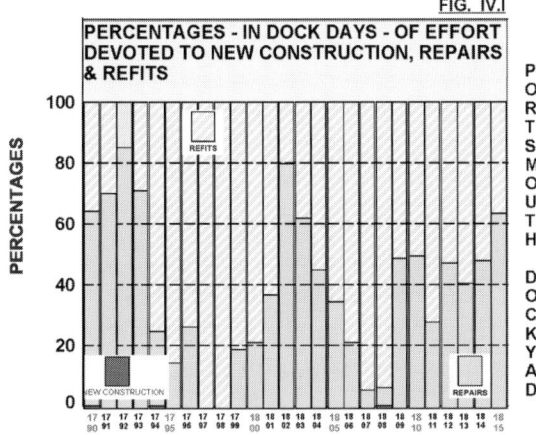

National Archives which still holds remarkably complete records of all ships entering dockyard hands (some 1,810 are shown in the *Progress Books*[3] for Portsmouth across the period). Secondly, those records showed that more than 80% of ships entering the Yard actually passed through the dry docks, and hence it appeared entirely reasonable to use the *Progress Book* records of the days individual ships spent in the dry docks as relative, and representational,

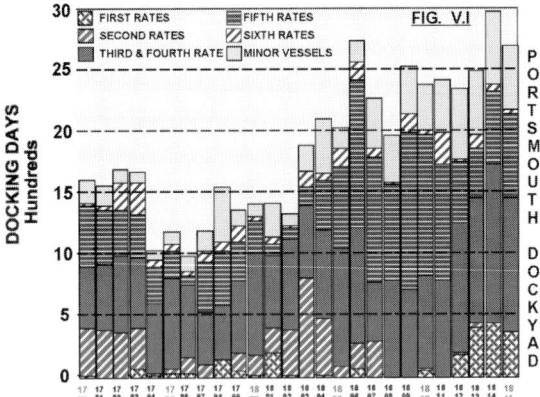

figures for the dockyard output. The results are shown graphically in Figure V.I. Nevertheless, the use of such a measure still does not allow for the difference in size of the various classes of ship and the corresponding difference in the amount of work involved in refitting them. This shortcoming can be overcome by multiplying each dock day for a particular ship by the tonnage of that vessel to give ton dock days. Figure V.II shows how the third and fourth rates dominated the scene. It should be emphasised that whilst the resultant year on year figures are shown in absolute numbers their significance and veracity, as a form of representative measurement of Dockyard loading or output, lies in the relationship

between the figures for one year and another.

The picture portrayed by Figures V.I and V.II is slightly distorted at the beginning and end of the war due to three major ships being in dry dock for excessive periods of time, when it is open to question whether they were being continuously worked on. On 7 August 1789 the second rate *Queen (90)*,[4] entered dry dock and did not undock until 1 October 1792 (1,151 days in dry dock). She was followed by *Barfleur (90)*[5] on 28 September 1792 and she did not undock until 18 November 1793 (323 days). At the other end of the period *Victory (100)*[6] entered dock on 26 March 1814 and did not undock until 15 January 1816 (658 days). It is thus suggested that a more accurate figure of ton dock days per year in Fig. V.II for the period 1790-1793 would have been 1.6 million, as opposed to 2.05 million ton dock days. Similarly the figures for 1814-1815 would be better represented by 3.3 million ton dock days rather than 4.01 million. These refined figures give a 107% increase in ton dock days across the war. Whether the presented or adjusted figures are used, two things stand out. Firstly, as the fleet progressively aged the work load involved in keeping it in a sea-going state steadily increased. This was especially true of ships of the line. Secondly, the output of the Yard as represented by the annual ton dock day totals effectively doubled across the period.

However, what makes the development of the Dockyard as a whole so interesting is the extent to which the developments in one area so often complemented those in another. Indeed, it seems totally appropriate to suggest that the Office of Naval Works, in working out its overall plan for the Yard, was certainly aware of the very real synergies that existed and was indeed markedly successful in realising their potential. That organisation was equally enterprising in the way it exploited the various approaches to introducing new technologies, both in terms of progressing in a series of sequential development steps, generally referred to today as "spiral developments", and also in not restricting itself to any one particular approach to the types of technological advances that it adopted. For instance, the types of the new technologies introduced

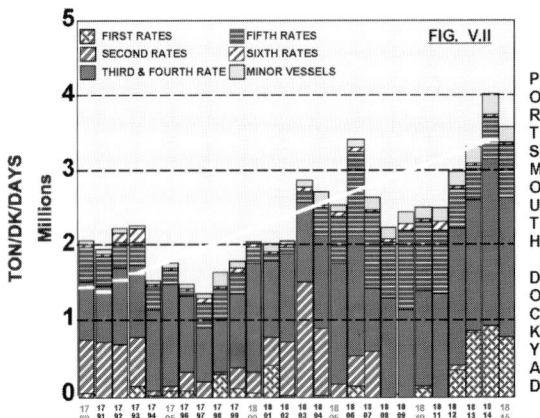

ranged from the low risk acquisition and direct implementation of commercially established and proven developments (today called COTS or commercial "off the shelf") – as was the case in the Metal Mills, through the bringing together of proven technologies but in a new environment as happened in the dry docks, or to the outright development and introduction of new leading edge technologies, with all their attendant difficulties and risks, as happened in the Wood Mills.

Much criticism down the years has been levelled against the Navy over its management of its procurement and maintenance programmes, but when the development of Portsmouth Dockyard in the period of the Napoleonic Wars is considered against the fundamental principles of today's much talked of Defence "SMART Procurement", it can be seen that those principles were actually in place, and exploited some two hundred years ago. There was the Office of Naval Works, which conceptually was very much akin to today's Integrated Project Management Teams (IPTs), with Bentham as the IPT Manager. There was "spiral or evolutionary" development in the areas of the docks and Metal Mills. Also there was undoubtedly real "risk management" in the Wood Mills and certainly there were strong partnerships with the private sector in the form of Marc Brunel and Henry Maudslay.

In essence Portsmouth's development during the Napoleonic Wars undoubtedly conformed to the best practices of today's "SMART" Procurement. It is true there may well have been some time overruns; but nothing like in the many developments the Parliamentary Defence Accounts Committee is seeing today. There were also relatively minor (in percentage terms) cost overruns although these were principally due to changed requirements. However, far from there being the all too common performance shortfalls, there were in fact notable performance increases, well above what was originally called for and which, over time, generated major through life cost savings for the Navy, specifically in terms of copper and block procurements.

It would be unfair also to the Navy Board and Bentham, with his IPT-like team, to leave this relating of the management of technological developments in the early 1800's with those of today without mentioning the really impressive achievements that were secured in the re-cycling of metal products. More than two thirds of the Navy's requirements for copper were coming from re-cycled material and the copper products being taken out of service were being fed back into the re-cycling process, and what is more, at an outright financial profit. It therefore seems entirely reasonable to suggest that today's top Defence Procurement Agency's Management would be most likely to firmly applaud Portsmouth's development record in this period.

Dry Docks

Turning from an overall view to the broad details of the individual areas of development in the Dockyard, the starting point has to be the dry docks through which nearly all ships entering the Yard passed and in which much of the dockyard work done on them was undertaken. Figure VI.I[7] portrays the dry docks in a simplistic "before" and "after" improvements form. Undoubtedly the greatest innovations in this area were the replacement of the double dock by numbers 2 and 3 docks together with re-development of the reservoir and the introduction of steam powered pumps. The architectural aspects of the rebuilt dry docks and the associated reservoir are relatively well documented and are therefore not discussed further. Sufficient to say that the primary new technologies which were introduced, such as steam pumps and stone construction, were already well

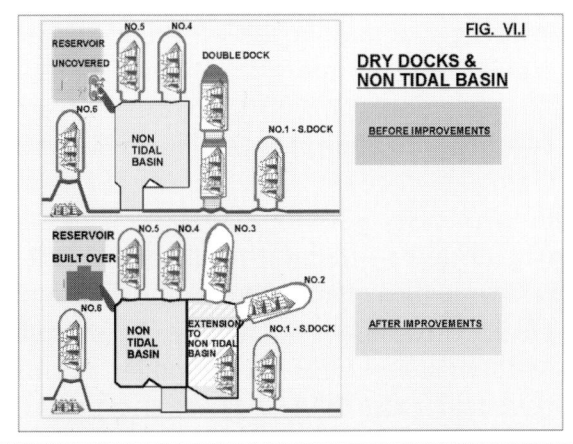

established outside the Dockyard. Instead the focus is on contributions of a number of developments in the complex which led to the near doubling of output or productivity.

Undoubtedly the replacement of the double dock by two separate ones increased the flexibility in the use of the two, but the enlarging of the size of the non-tidal basin was to have a wider effect in that it significantly increased the total number of vessels that the dock area as a whole could hold. This in turn increased the number of vessels that could be moved in and out of dry dock independently of the state or time of the tide. Other advances too which made a marked contribution such as the introduction of caissons, the concept of which had previously met with considerable opposition. However, they not only made the sealing of the docks more effective, and their subsequent draining quicker, but they also provided a series of invaluable "bridges" across the entrances of the dry docks for moving personnel and stores around the area, in line with the growth in output that traffic level would have doubled by the time the wars ended.

For the largest ships in the fleet to enter the docks area it was generally necessary to wait for high spring tides to provide the requisite depth of water in the immediate approaches to the tidal entrance. However that dependence on spring tides was effectively removed with the introduction into service in 1802 of one of the first steam dredgers in the world. This was built at Portsmouth and it was reported by Bentham in May 1803[8] as being in service and capable of raising one and a half tons of soil a minute.

However, in terms of increasing the ability of the docks complex as a whole to meet the growing demands made on them, it can be argued that the most rewarding innovation was the conversion of the North Boat Pond and boat channel into the North Basin and Camber Docks (Figure VI.II[9]). This theoretically provided for seven or eight frigates to be fitted out in the basin with the erstwhile boat channel becoming the Camber Docks capable of docking two large frigates or three sloops. This development seems to have taken less than a year to effect and cost

little more than £6,000,[10] or between £1 million and £2 million at today's prices. As such it may well rank as one of the most

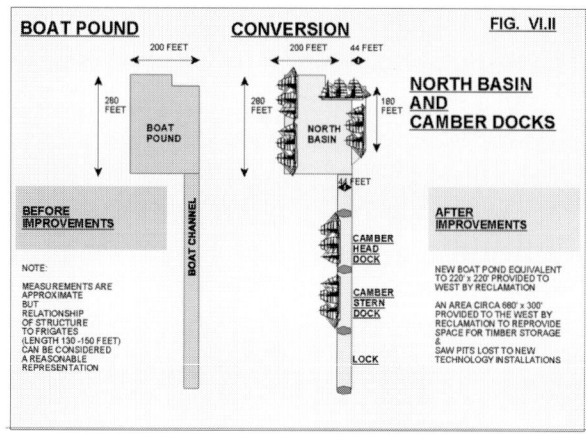

cost effective improvements in the history of the Royal Dockyards.

Metal Working

The second area in which there were major developments was the Metal Mills which are illustrated in Figures VII.I[11] and VII.II.[12] The idea originated in 1797 with a proposal for a small melting furnace,[13] as used commercially, to solve the problems of dealing with old copper sheathing removed

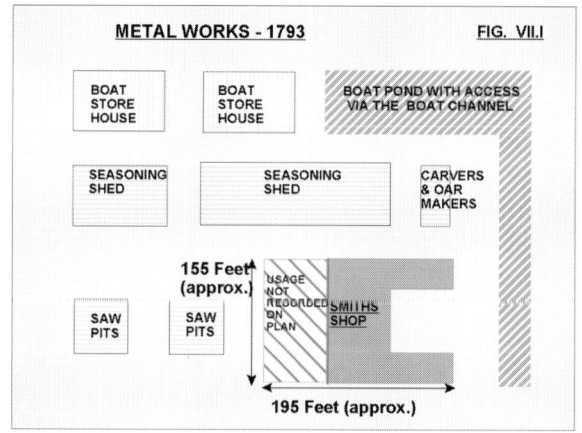

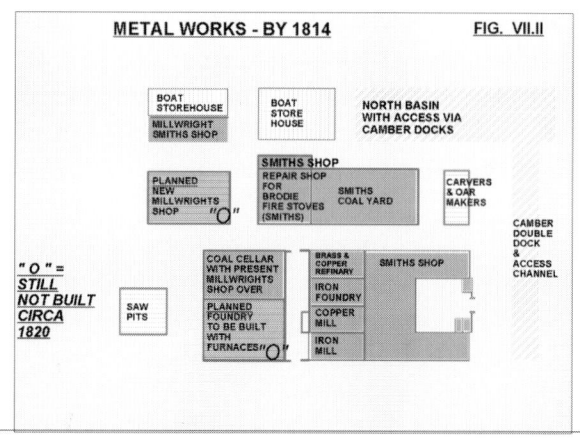

from ships. Until then the practice had been first to burn off the weeds on the sheathing and then remove the old material before returning it for re-cycling by the original commercial supplier. By 1802 the concept had grown into one which was to see Portsmouth re-cycling old copper and then re-processing it into new sheeting and bolts; again using commercially proven equipment. By 1807 Portsmouth was producing 800 tons of re-cycled copper annually which Goodrich stated was about two thirds of the Navy Board's annual requirement between 1804-1806 of 1,172 tons.[14] By 1808 capacity had risen to 1,000 tons[15] annually when it would seem that Portsmouth was handling all the material recovered from the fleet. Thus from the relatively modest local ambitions in 1797 Portsmouth Dockyard had developed into the major supplier of copper for the Royal Navy in just ten years.

It would be a mistake to believe that the development of the Metal Mills was confined to copper working. Across the period there was a steady increase in the use of metal in the Yard and in warships, for example wooden "knees" (deck supports) were being replaced by iron ones. This new work is reflected in the smiths whose numbers stood at 68 in 1793[16], but twenty years later there were 185.[17] Furthermore the progressive introduction of steam powered machinery in the Yard brought with it the arrival of a new trade, the millwright. The first appeared in the records in 1805 and by 1813 there were 77.[18]

Fibres

The fibre working area is the only one in which the Yard did not develop significantly. Like all the other Royal Dockyards, Portsmouth bought in all its canvas ready made but also like the other Yards it had a substantial rope-making capability of its own. For reasons that defied investigation it has not been possible to establish why Portsmouth in 1805 produced just 1,633 tons of rope – only 13% of the total amount of rope produced in all the Royal Dockyards – against the 7,696 tons obtained from contractors, the 2,120 tons made at Plymouth and the 1,938 tons produced at Chatham.[19] Given that Portsmouth undertook some 42% of the refits carried out for the fleet in that year the Yard would have been heavily dependent on external supplies and this would seem to run contrary to the management thrust of reducing dependence on contractually supplied material wherever possible.

It is possible to offer three hypothesis for this. It could have been that the Navy Board made a conscious decision to restrict developments in rope making to Chatham which subsequently was to become effectively the "lead" Yard in this area. Such a decision could have arisen as a consequence of deliberately spreading the Board's investment in new technologies across more than one Yard. An alternative hypothesis is that the management at Portsmouth formed the view that investing in steam power for rope-making represented an unacceptable fire risk. Indeed before even the start of the war the rope house at Portsmouth had burnt down no less than three times in the second half of the eighteenth century, in 1760, 1770 and again in 1776.[20] The last hypothesis is that the Master Ropemaker, possibly due to the earlier fires, or as a matter of personality, lacked the standing within the management structure to attract support for any requests for investment in his area and consequently he, and his area, became effectively side-lined.

Wood

Other research has addressed the structure and machinery of the Wood and Block Mills in considerable detail, so here attention is confined to consideration of the level of output or finished products and the manning levels within that complex. Since unquestionably Portsmouth's biggest "input" to the work it undertook was its workforce, this is considered first in its totality prior to looking at the activities and levels of the manpower in the Wood and Block Mills. Today's researchers are fortunate to have available to them in The National Archives the original Dockyard *Pay Books*. These show in fine detail, for each quarter of the year, not only the numbers of people being paid in the Yard but also how much, at what scale and for what duties. Thus it is possible to build up a comprehensive year on year measure of the changes in the size of the work force and relate them to the developments that were taking place in the Yard. Furthermore, using the relative changes in manpower levels to represent "inputs" as a whole – in the same way that ton dock days are taken to represent "outputs" – the two can be equated to give a measure of quantification of the change in efficiency of the Yard during the period..

Figure VIII.I presents the work force in terms of work groups and shows a curious plateau between 1795 to 1800 and an outright reduction between 1802 and 1805. This situation directly reflects the Royal Dockyards' inability to recruit the manpower they needed because the pay rates in equivalent commercial organisations were some two to three times higher than the rates being paid in the Yards which dated from the early eighteenth century. With the departure of the Earl of St Vincent, who was notoriously unsympathetic to the problems of the

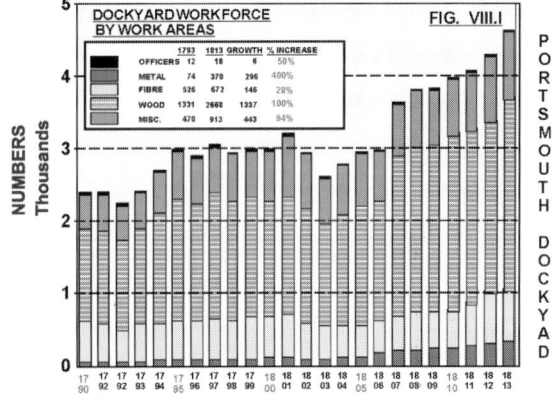

Dockyard workforce, from the position of First Sea Lord in 1804 the situation progressively improved and the undoubted manpower "crisis" of 1803 was overcome.

The biggest growth occurred in the metal group which has already been discussed. There the numbers rising from a total of 74 in 1793 to a total of 370 in 1813 (a 400% increase). That number included the surprisingly modest figure of just 69 involved in the mills on tasks like copper working which had previously been undertaken by commercial contractors. The least growth – only 28% – occurred in the fibres group whose 1793 numbers stood at 526. From that level it steadily decreased to a low of 432 in 1804

and it did not return to the 1793 level until 1811, rising thereafter to 672 by 1813, an increase of only 28%. Numerically by far the biggest group of workers were in the Yard worked in the wood area which, excluding consideration of the Wood and Block Mills, was least affected by the introduction of new technologies. This workforce stood at 1,331 in 1793 and that rose to 2,668 by 1813 (a 100% increase). Of these no less than 1,428 were shipwrights with the next biggest sub grouping being the 336 apprentices.

Figure VIII.II looks at the workforce in terms of skill levels and shows that by far the largest element were the skilled men who numbered 1,401 in 1793 with this number growing to 2,466 by 1813 – an increase of 76% – with the semi-skilled numbers increasing by 79% – from 541 to 969, and the less numerous unskilled, or labourers, numbers rose from 396 to 784, an increase of 98%. This figure is hardly surprising when it is considered the fleet itself grew from 390 in 1793 to 899 in 1813 – an increase of 130%; this would have greatly increased the sheer bulk of stores and material being supplied to it through the Yard. Nevertheless the biggest proportional increase was actually in the apprentices who numbered just 55 in 1793, but increased by no less than 609% to 390 in 1813, following the realisation of their

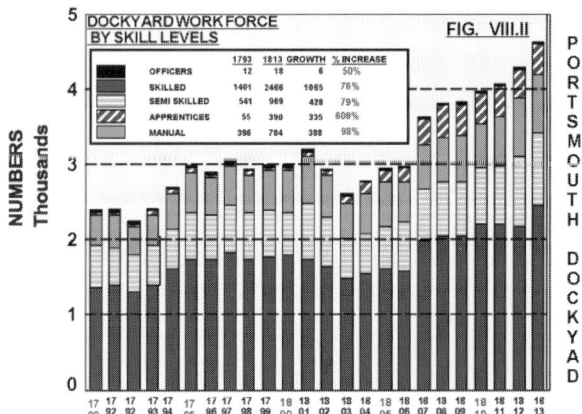

fundamental importance to the long term future of the Yard. Perhaps the most interesting change is the number of Yard officers – just 12 in 1790 and only 18 in 1813.

Overall, from 1793 up to 1813 the workforce increased by 92% against a ton dock day increase of 107%, which suggests that the efficiency of the Yard, as deduced from these two prime relative "input" and "output" measurements, rose by around 15%. But that takes no account of the fact that by the end of the period the Yard was providing all the Navy's re-cycled copper requirements

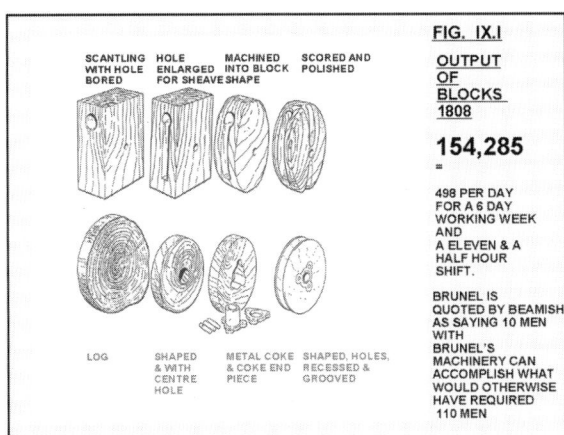

and all the Navy's block requirements. Factoring out the workforce engaged in working the copper and making the blocks – tasks previously undertaken by civilian contractors – we arrive at a figure of fractionally under 80% in the growth of Portsmouth Dockyard's baseline workforce. This therefore suggests that a truer indication of the increase in the efficiency of the Yard was around 27%.

in the Block Mills where Brunel is quoted as saying "Ten men by the aid of this machinery can accomplish with uniformity, celerity and ease, what formerly required the uncertain labour of one hundred and ten men".[21] The Block Mills have long been, very rightly, a subject of real historical importance and other papers address their architecture and the then "leading edge" nature of the technology involved with the introduction of Brunel's machinery. This article therefore directs its focus towards the productivity, or out put, of the Mills and the efficiency of the workforce.

A block may appear a simple and uncomplicated object – as indeed it is – but that hides the fact that firstly it has to be strong. Typically the test weight for a 10 to 18 inch block would be measured in tons rather than just pounds. Secondly its manufacturer had to be precise since any inadvertent misalignment between the moving and the standing parts stood to result in a rope jamming and the consequences of that at sea could be very serious indeed. Lastly, as Figure IX.I shows, there were at least eight separate stages in the manufacture

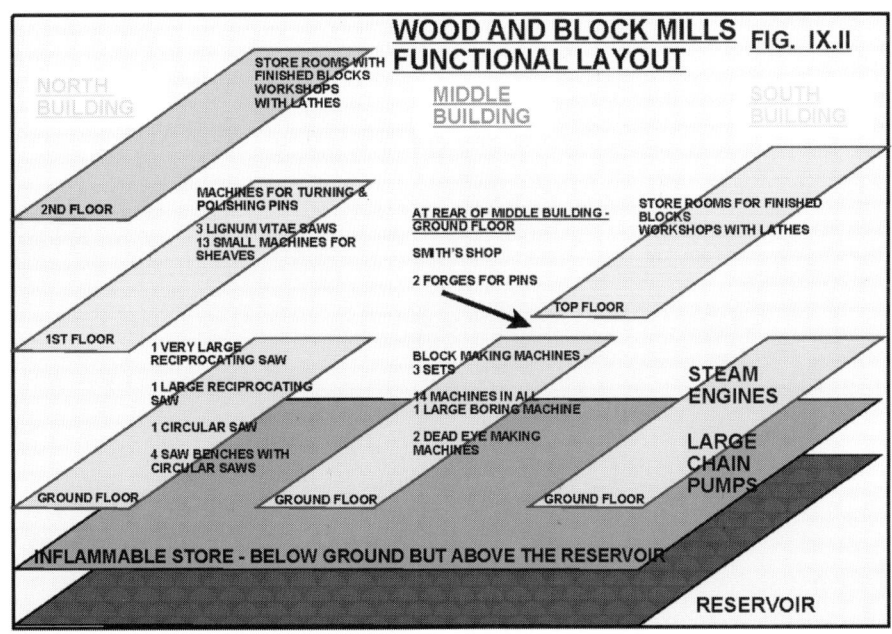

Undoubtedly, if Brunel's claim, as reported by his biographer Beamish in 1862 is correct, by far the biggest increase in efficiency was

of even a single purchase block and that number doubled with a three fold purchase. Precise records of the annual output of the

FIG. X.I

WOOD MILLS - MACHINES & THEIR MANNING -1808

PART OF THE MILLS	SUB AREA	MACHINE TYPE/ ACTIVITY	TOTAL No. OF MACHINES	Nos. OF MACHINES PER SET/PROD. LINE (BLOCKS ONLY)	MANNING - Nos. OF PERSONNEL		
					OPERATOR	SUPPORT TO OPERATOR	NON MACHINE SUPPORT ACTIVITIES
WOOD MILLS	WOOD TURNING	LATHES - NOT BRUNEL MACHINES	8		8		
		WOOD SAWING	10		10	12	
			SUB TOTAL 18		SUB TOTAL 18	SUB TOTAL 12	
BLOCK MILLS	SHELLS		SUB TOTAL 14		SUB TOTAL 15	SUB TOTAL	
	SHEAVES		SUB TOTAL 14		SUB TOTAL 16	SUB TOTAL	
	PINS		SUB TOTAL 5		SUB TOTAL 3	SUB TOTAL	
		HAND ASSEMBLY OF BLOCKS					6
TOTALS			45+8		44+8	12	6

WOOD MILLS - TOTAL MANNING - 1808   FIG. X.II

PART OF THE MILLS	SUB AREA	MACHINE TYPE/ ACTIVITY	TOTAL No. OF MACHINES	Nos. OF MACHINES PER SET/PROD. LINE (BLOCKS ONLY)	MANNING - Nos. OF PERSONNEL		
					OPERATOR	SUPPORT TO OPERATOR	NON MACHINE SUPPORT ACTIVITIES
WOOD MILLS & BLOCK MILLS		LATHES - NOT BRUNEL MACHINES BRUNEL MACHINERY & OPERATORS	45+8		44+8	12	6
WOOD & BLOCK MILLS		MASTER OF WOOD MILLS					1
		FOREMAN & CABIN KEEPER					3
		ENGINE KEEPERS					2
		MACHINE REPAIRS					2
		TRAINEES/BOYS					10
		RAW MATERIAL - RECEIPT					2
		TRANSFER OF MATERIAL AROUND THE MILLS					5
		FINISHED PRODUCTS - OUT					2
		CLEANING					5
							SUB TOTAL 32
TOTALS			53		52	12	38
		MANPOWER TOTAL TOTAL ON PAYBOOKS - 1808					102 102

blocks from the Block Mill are not available. However Admiralty records[22] show that even in 1808 the fleet used no less than 154,285 new blocks of various sizes all of which would have been made in Portsmouth. If it is assumed that the working week was six days and the working day was eleven and a half hours that output would have equated to 498 blocks a day or 43 per hour. That figure can very crudely be multiplied by ten to give in excess of 430 machine stages.

Whilst the new machinery broke new grounds in terms of alignment, accuracy, automation, on-line power engagement/ disengagement and variable speeds it did not include, as in today's factories automated transfer of components, finished products or waste material around the Mill. Figure IX.II sets out to show the functional relationship between the various parts of the Wood and Block Mills. As can be seen there would be a considerable need for people to move things around. Raw materials would have been introduced on the ground floor at the north end with the lignum vitae sheaves being cut out on the first floor and the blocks made in the Middle Building. Subsequently finished products had to be moved to one of the

Making machines.[24] In Figure X.I those machines and their manning are identified separately, but they are shown because their operators do feature in the one definitive set of original records which are available, namely, the pay records. The sources from which Figure X.I were deduced were Rees's *Cyclopaedia*, the works of Carolyn Cooper, K.R Gilbert and Bentham's proposed manning and pay scales.[25] The end suggestion is that some 64

FIG. X.III

PORTSMOUTH DOCKYARD'S CONTRIBUTION TO THE FLEET'S SUCCESS

1,810 SHIPS PASSED THROUGH THE DOCK COMPLEX

FOR FITTING, REPAIR

OUTPUT TON/DOCK/DAYS +107%

BOAT POND CONVERTED TO NON TIDAL BASIN & CAMBER DOCKS

DRY DOCKS RESERVOIR & NON TIDAL BASIN ENLARGED & RE-BUILT

OR REFIT IN THE PERIOD 1793-1816

INPUT WORK FORCE Nos + (92) 80%

STEAM DREDGER

PORTSMOUTH ROYAL DOCKYARD INVESTMENT IN NEW TECHNOLOGIES

CASSOONS

BY 1808 150,000 BLOCKS PER YEAR WERE

BEING PRODUCED TO MEET THE ENTIRE

NAVY'S NEEDS

WOOD MILLS & BLOCK MILLS

METAL MILLS

COPPER MILLS

BY 1808 THE COPPER MILLS WERE PRODUCING 80% OF THE NAVY'S ANNUAL COPPER REQUIREMENT FROM RECOVERED FLEET MATERIAL

EFFICIENCY GAIN + (15) 27%

storerooms on the top floors of the two outer buildings. Furthermore, much of the machinery would have generated waste material in large quantities and this would have had to be removed. Whilst it is not known to what use, if any, the waste wood material was put to, it is known that the metal swarf from the pin turning machines was recovered and returned to the foundry to be re-melted and cast into coaks, that is, the metal bearings let into each side of the pulley.[23]

Relating the machines to people calls for compromise and deduction since agreed and definitive records are not available. For instance, the Wood Mills undoubtedly served other purposes than just to produce blocks and we have evidence of eight lathes that do not feature in most listings of the Block

people were directly involved with working the machines and a further six were employed on hand assembly of the completed blocks.

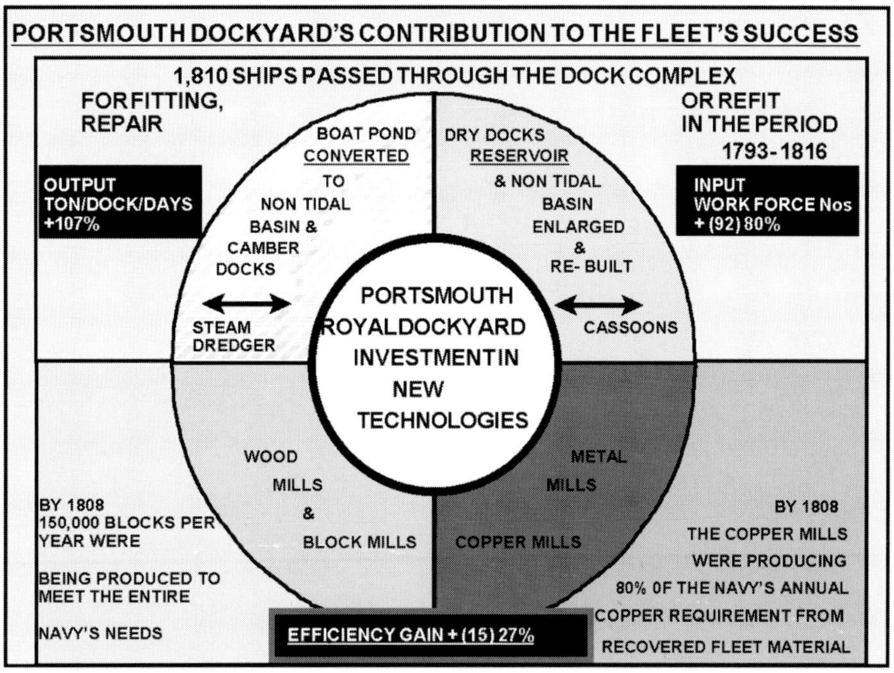

That left, as Figure X.II shows, a further 38, of whom Bentham only suggested individual tasking for eight, namely the Master of the Wood Mills, a foreman and two cabin or storekeepers, two engine keepers and two machinery repairers. For the remaining 24 the only proposal seems to be that 10 should be trainees or boys, leaving just 14 as the primary ancillary task force to carry the out the bulk of all the receipt of raw material, the movement of processed material, the removal of waste and the essential cleaning to keep the fire risk within bounds. The allocation of numbers to these various tasks has no more authority than a "best guess", but it does show how "lean manned" the Mill undoubtedly was, as well as being very efficient. Indeed, Gilbert states categorically "the capital cost was recovered in three years from the saving in the cost of production".[26]

Lastly, Figure XIII attempts to summarise in a single graphic the main developments and consequential output levels, and hence contributions to the success of the fleet, that the Royal Dockyard at Portsmouth achieved. Foremost of these is the 1,810 ships that emerged from the Yard. This achievement owed much to what would now be called the highly integrated nature of the development of the docks and directly associated facilities, not forgetting the north tidal basin with the Camber Docks, the introduction of caissons and steam-powered dredging.

On a broader front, Portsmouth became a prime supplier to the whole Navy in two vital areas. The Metal Mills, by the end of the period were producing some 80% of the Navy's requirement for new copper from re-cycled material. This was an achievement which far exceeds most of the re-cycling targets the present Government has put in place. Then there was the Block Mills where the Yard was, by 1808, producing the Navy's entire needs for blocks using Brunel's new generation machinery and just 102 men. Lastly, equating the representative output increase of 107% in ton dock days with the equally representative input increase of 92% in the Dockyard workforce suggests an efficiency increase of 15%. Indeed a truer figure would be 27% arrived at by factoring out the manpower for re-processing the copper and making blocks, both of which tasks were previously undertaken by suppliers outside the Yard.

Conclusion

This paper has attempted to show that the categorisation of the Dockyard during the Napoleonic Wars as "corrupt, inefficient and incompetent" would seem to be both totally unjust and not supported by the available facts. Indeed, if the psychological impact on the French fleet and the boost to the British morale are discounted it seems entirely reasonable to suggest that Portsmouth Dockyard's contribution to the success of the

Royal Navy in the Napoleonic Wars was probably greater than the victory Sir John Jervis achieved at Cape St.Vincent, which has a firm place in our history. It therefore appears that there is a good case for the Dockyard, and the principal architects of its success in the period – Bentham, Goodrich and Brunel – also to receive rather more recognition and acclaim from both naval and technological historians than it has been accorded in the past.

References

1. Sources for Figures I.I, I.II, II.I and II.II in W James, *The Naval History of Great Britain*, Captain Chamier Royal Navy ed, (6 volumes, R Bentley, London, 1847) Abstracts 1 – 25 for 1793-1817.

2. Sources for Figures IV.I and IV.II, ADM 180/ 4-13, *Admiralty Progress Books*, 1767 to 1866, The National Archive (TNA), Kew.

3. ADM 180/ 4-13, *Admiralty Progress Books*, TNA.

4. ADM 180/6, *Progress Book for 1st to 3rd Rates*, 1759-1820, TNA.

5. *Ibid.*

6. ADM 180/10, *Progress Book for 1st to 5th Rates*, 1792-1862, TNA.

7. Sources for Figure VI.I ADM 140/555/13-18, *Portsmouth Dockyard Maps*, TNA.

8. ADM/Q/3321, Letter of 4 July 1803, National Maritime Museum, Greenwich.

9. Source for Figure VI.II, ADM 140/555/13-18, *Portsmouth Dockyard Maps*, TNA.

10. ADM 1/3525, Letter of 8 April 1797, TNA.

11. Source of Figure VII.I, ADM 140/555/15, *Portsmouth Dockyard Map* dated 1 August 1793, TNA.

12. Source of Figure VII.II, ADM 140/555/18, *Portsmouth Dockyard Map* dated 10 September 1810 and 31 December 1814, TNA.

13. ADM 1/3525, Letter of 7 November 1797, TNA.

14. ADM 1/3527, Letter of 21 September 1807, TNA.

15. ADM 1/3527, Letter of 4 April 1808, TNA.

16. ADM 42/1310/2, *Portsmouth Dockyard Pay Book, Misdummer Quarter, 1793*, TNA.

17. ADM 42/1355, *Portsmouth Dockyard Pay Book, Midsummer Quarter 1813*, TNA.

18. *Ibid.*

19. R Morriss, *The Royal Dockyards during the Revolutionary and Napoleonic Wars*, Leicester University Press, 1983, 87, Table 19.

20. J G Coad, "Historic Architecture of HM Naval Base Portsmouth 1700-1850", *The Mariner's Mirror*, 67, 1981, 20.

21. R Beamish, *Memoir of the Life of Sir Marc Isambard Brunel*, Longmans, London, 1862, 98.

22. ADM 106/3519, *Papers Relating to Machinery, 9 February 1808*, TNA.

23. A Rees, ed, *Naval Architecture*, Longmans, London, 1819-20,174.

24. ADM/Q/3322, Letter of 27 May 1803, National Maritime Museum (NMM)

25. ADM/Q/3323, Letter of 21 February 1805, NMM. A. Rees, ed., *Cyclopaedia*, 29 volumes, 5 books of plates, Longmans, London, 1819; C. Cooper, "The Production Line at Portsmouth Block Mill", *Industrial Archaeology Review*, 6, 1981, 28-43; C. Cooper, "The Portsmouth System of Manufacture", *Technology and Culture*, 25, 1982, 182-225; K R Gilbert, *The Portsmouth Blockmaking Machinery*, HMSO, 1965.

26. Gilbert, *op.cit.*, 6.

Dr. Sue Wilkins *is an academic researcher with a special interest in eighteenth century technology.*

THE BLOCK MILLS: NEW LABOUR PRACTICES FOR NEW MACHINES?

Ann Coats

Abstract

This paper, based on the Simon Goodrich Papers, focuses on personnel and working practices. The Papers detail recruitment, rates of pay and the status of managers and skilled workers in the Wood and Metal Mills. They reveal working relationships between Marc Brunel, Goodrich and Samuel Bentham and political, commercial and patronage contexts. Although the machines were new and the workforce mostly recruited from outside the Dockyard, many working practices perpetuated traditional customs, despite Bentham's reforming aspirations.

Introduction

The Age of Nelson (defined as 1771-1815, from the year Nelson joined the navy until the end of the French and Napoleonic wars) was a period of tremendous change in dockyard administration and technology. Administrative changes were driven by the findings of successive and frequently conflicting parliamentary commissions of enquiry, beginning with the 1782 Commission on Public Accounts. St Vincent's 1802 Commission of Naval Enquiry and Lord Barham's rival 1803 Commission for Revising and Digesting the Civil Affairs of His Majesty's Navy had most impact during the period the Block Mills were established. Changes also resulted from ongoing friction over control of the dockyards between the politically appointed Admiralty Board and the permanent professional bureaucracy of the Navy Board. Political fortunes seesawed between ministerial whigs, opposition whigs and tories, and the ambitions of John Jervis/ Earl St Vincent, Charles Middleton/Lord Barham and Samuel Bentham.[1]

Implementation of task work by First Lords of the Admiralty Earl Sandwich, Earl Spencer and Admiral St Vincent; St Vincent's removal of dockyard apprentices from individual masters, introduction of Timber Measurers; commutation of chips[2] to a cash payment; and payment of weekly wages form the *minutiæ* of administrative changes.[3] These measures diminished the workforce's traditional working practices and privileges but weekly payments from 1805 of three-quarters of their pay due released artificers from a lifestyle of institutionalised debt caused by payment in arrears. The Navy Board and the workforce resisted the introduction of task work, and the workforce the abolition of chips, but the Admiralty was impelled by political and cultural initiatives to free the dockyards from waste, corruption and inefficiency and embrace new technology.[4]

The aim of the Admiralty and Samuel Bentham[5] was to switch naval administration from collective to individual responsibility, to enable best practice from public institutions and private enterprise to drive reform and innovation and save money. In April 1795 the Admiralty, noting the new French naval Inspector General, sent Bentham to inspect all the dockyards to suggest ways of improving them and introducing the 'application of mechanical powers'.[6] In June Bentham submitted his plan to reorganise Portsmouth Dockyard by enlarging the Basin and building two new dry docks.[7] Middleton promoted a major administrative reorganisation in 1796, deriving from the findings (1786-1787) of the Commissioners on Fees. This the Navy Board into three committees and initiated the Office of Naval Works as a Department of the Admiralty run by the two Secretaries of the Admiralty, with Samuel Bentham as Inspector General.[8]

Admiral Sir John Jervis, Earl St Vincent,[9] appointed whig First Lord of the Admiralty by Henry Addington in March 1801, believed 'the Civil Branch of the Navy is rotten to the very core' and dockyard workers were thieves. These beliefs were reinforced by reports from his allies at Plymouth Dockyard, brothers Clerk of the Cheque Benjamin Tucker and Master Shipwright Joseph Tucker. St Vincent believed the Navy Board defended abuses in dockyards and wanted to abolish it, using an Admiralty visitation in 1802 as the means of gathering damaging evidence. He wrote to Addington from Plymouth that the commissioners had 'found "abuses to such an extent as would require many months to go thoroughly into and the absolute necessity of a Commission of Enquiry... appears to the Admiralty Board here in a much stronger light than ever."' His Commission of Naval Enquiry was approved in December 1802, focusing on failures of collective responsibility and task work pricing.[10]

By January 1804 St Vincent had alienated Admiralty officials by the 'terrorist' methods used by the Commission for Naval Enquiry (Evan Nepean resigned as Secretary to the Admiralty). Reforms concerning timber contractors and cancelled private ship building orders were already affecting supplies of timber to dockyards and new ships. From March Pitt, seeking to regain office, accused him in Parliament of causing the navy to be unprepared for the renewed outbreak of war in May 1803. Even Nelson was worried about naval resources. As a result Addington resigned on 10 May and St Vincent left the Admiralty on 15 May, although a vote of censure brought by Jeffrey, Poole MP, was defeated in 1806. This ongoing struggle created the political background for the setting up of the Wood and Metal Mills.[11]

Samuel Bentham, the driving force for innovation, had trained as a shipwright at Chatham Dockyard in the 1770s under Master Shipwright William Gray. At Chatham fellow apprentices were Thomas Dunsterville (a Plymouth block making family) and John Peake, with Henry Peake as First Assistant Master Shipwright. In the 1790s, when Samuel Bentham became Admiralty Inspector General of Naval Works, Henry Peake was Master Shipwright at Portsmouth Dockyard and assisted with his expansionary plans there. Henry Peake was later Navy Surveyor and John Peake was later extra assistant Civil Engineer and Architect.[12]

One of Bentham's most revolutionary innovations was the utilisation of steam power to mass-produce blocks on Marc Isambard Brunel's block making machines

in the Wood Mills and to recycle copper from ships' hulls in the Metal Mills. Built in 1802 on vaults erected over Edmund Dummer's 1690s reservoir, the Wood Mills were powered by engines in the south-west corner, the Metal Mills utilising spare capacity from the steam engines pumping out the Docks.[13]

The 1802 Visitation minutes provide clear evidence of the Admiralty's partisan aims:

'The Lords taking into their consideration the extraordinary expences incurred in the several Dock & Rope Yards, beyond what were known in any former period of War, in proportion to the number of Ships employed, and having received Reports from various quarters of flagrant abuses and Mismanagement existing in the several Departments, which there is reason to believe are but too well founded, and being determined as far as in them lies to discover and remedy the same...'[14]

Not surprisingly, it is a catalogue of dockyard infringements which the commissioners, Earl St Vincent, Sir Philip Stephens,[15] William Elliot,[16] Sir Thomas Troubridge,[17] John Markham,[18] William Garthshore,[19] had set out to find.[20]

Blocks

The Royal Navy, which needed 1,000 blocks for a 74 gun ship, requiring around 100,000 blocks a year in 1800, depended on private contractors for blocks. The main contractors were the Taylors of Southampton and William Dunsterville of Plymouth, although, through connections with dockyard commisioner Samuel Hood, Portsmouth contractor Philip Varlo and then his widow Mary had supplied blocks in the 1770s. Walter Taylor II and III, supported by Southampton MP and Admiralty Commissioner Hans Stanley, had supplied the navy with blocks since 1759. After improving accuracy and reducing friction by sawing and boring the sheaves on machines, their blocks were tested at Deptford and they won the navy contract at Portsmouth in 1762.[21] First horses powered their machines, then water from a corn mill of Hans Sloane (a relative of Hans Stanley). Their experiments in the 1760s proved that smaller blocks were as effective as larger ones and reduced the weight borne by ships and cost

Fig. 1. The block mills photographed from the entrance to no. 6 dock in July 1996.

to the navy. Ordered to replace blocks destroyed by the dockyard fire of 27 July 1770, Taylor demonstrated the effectiveness of smaller blocks to the Navy Board, which directed him to draw up a new table of dimensions. Walter Taylor III probably used a circular saw from about 1781. In 1775 and 1784 Taylor applied for patents to insert metal bushes into the blocks and *lignum vitæ* (supplies of which were apparently controlled by him)[22] bushes into the sheaves to reduce wear. He was paid double the price Dunsterville received and supplied on average 100,000 blocks at £3,400 a year between 1797 and 1800.[23] In 1802 St Vincent found some of Mr Taylor's blockmakers in Portsmouth Dockyard: 'upon calling upon the Block Makers it appeared that several of them who had worked in the Yard for Mr. Taylor upon his Contract, had been ordered...to be borne on the Books of the Yard by the Commissioner for single days Pay'.[24]

The Taylors' contract ended in 1802 in expectation of Brunel's blocks appearing, but was renewed four times for limited periods from 1803-1805. It is clear from the following correspondence that they had been directly or indirectly supplying most, if not all, the navy's needs, creating a quasi-monopoly situation which they might have assumed would continue, until Admiralty investment in Brunel.[25] In December 1802 Woolwich Dockyard ran out of *lignum vitæ* and the Navy

Board asked the Admiralty if more could be obtained from the Taylors. The Admiralty asked what stocks the dockyards held. In January 1803 4cwt 1qr 14lb was sent from Minorca and 1cwt 2qr 14lb acquired from the Taylors. By September 1803 there was stock for one year to make the smallest blocks and the Jamaica Commissioner is asked to obtain more in December. By March 1804 London supplies, which were insufficient for the navy, cost £10-16 a ton compared with Providence prices of £8-12 a ton.[26]

On 11 March 1803 the Admiralty directed the Navy Board 'to advertise for tenders for supplying of Blocks and Blockmakers Wares' for twelve months, 'inserting therein a clause for giving Three Months notice of its Termination.' The Taylors replied representing 'the uncertainty of the continuance of their Contract and that the Stock of Materials they had, when their Contract was annulled in May 1802 is nearly exhausted'. As it was 'indispensably necessary for them to procure another Stock to secure to themselves a certainty of supplying the Demands made on them', they had asked General Bentham 'when he thought the Machinery which is erecting under his direction in Portsmouth Yard will be compleated so as to furnish all the Blocks and other Articles mentioned in the Blockmakers Contract.' Bentham had told them that 'the Machinery for making Blocks will be ready in Six Months to furnish all the Blocks wanted for the use of the Navy', together with all the other articles in the contract. The Navy Board, 'Not considering it prudent to rely wholly upon the supply of Block makers Goods which may be expected from this Machinery', asked Taylors for six months' supply, but they replied that 'they cannot continue the Contract unless they have an advantage of price.' On 14 November 1804 the Navy Board asked: 'as the whole of these transactions have been conducted under their Lordships directions…we request to receive their Lordships directions for our future guidance herein.' Marsden's turnover tersely directed the Navy Board to renew 'the contract with W Taylor or any other person for such description of blocks as the machinery will not yet furnish, and on the best and cheapest terms they can'. The Taylors responded that their 'Capstan bars, handspikes and other Ash goods, also Brass Shivers, Pumps & Dead Eyes' were in demand so they could not continue the contract unless they had an 'Advance of price'. They ended, not surprisingly, on a caustic note:

> '…we are compelled to say, that We cannot suffer ourselves to be so completely at the service of General Bentham and a Frenchman who we have no hesitation in asserting, will bring your Honble Board into great trouble and difficulty, for if our Manufactory is suffered to decay, which will be the case whenever the Contract ceases, the Fleet will never again be supplied, for double the money now Paid -'[27]

In June 1805 Samuel Taylor informed the Navy Board that his late father had delivered blocks to Plymouth Dockyard under Bartholemew Dunsterville's naval contract, 'in conformity to a general practice among the different contractors when one worked for the other, from the first introduction of the Brass Coaked Shivers, and Iron Pins much more than Thirty Years', because Dunsterville 'had not Lignum Vitæ for' the large blocks. Dunsterville had 'carried on his business mostly with Mr Taylor's money, and for several Years without any interest whatsoever'. Taylor was presumably hoping

to recoup the investment of 'many Thousands in his improvements' by calling in the 'very considerable arrears due' from Dunsterville 'to the Executors of Mr Taylor which was a part of the Moneys employed'.[28] Until Brunel's blocks materialised the Taylors still controlled Navy Board supplies.

Marc Isambard Brunel, who would oust the Taylors, arrived in England in 1799 from New York, where he had been Chief Engineer, with a letter of introduction from Major-General Hamilton, British aide-de-camp and secretary at Washington, to Earl Spencer, First Lord of the Admiralty. Spencer was 'a personal friend of Bentham', who was a half brother to Charles Abbot, Chairman in 1798 of the influential parliamentary Select Committee on Finance.[29] In 1799 Brunel married Sophia Kingdom, the daughter of Plymouth Dockyard contractor William Kingdom. Her brother John was chief clerk in the secretary's office at the Navy Office.[30] He met Maudslay who helped him perfect his machines. In 1801 Marc Brunel offered his own patented machine drawings and models to the Taylors through his brother-in-law, John Kingdom,[31] but they were satisfied with their machines. In 1802 Brunel showed his drawings to Bentham, who having patented his own machines in 1793 with the aim of manufacturing blocks in the dockyards, adopted them.[32] This network created the Block Mills project.

Construction was authorised in April 1802 and proposals for Brunel's machines agreed with Bentham in summer 1802, with the officers ordered to infill the space between the two ranges for the blockmaking machines in August.[33] On 8 September 1802 the Admiralty Visitation of the Dockyards[34] praised the progress of Bentham's improvements and 'Observed with Satisfaction the application of machinery particularly the Steam Engines, to Various purposes of Labour, by which the Expense must be considerably diminished.' Commissioners

> 'Proceeded to the Dockyard to examine the several plans proposed by the Navy Board, and the Inspector General for the improvement of the Basons, Docks, Mast and Boat Pounds, and other Naval Works, and by local inspection

to determine upon their respective merits.

Approved of the reduced Plan proposed by the latter for the extension and improvement of the Mast Pound (with the exception of the oblique Mast Houses at the upper angles) as Uniting the advantages of Œconomy of space and labour, with convenience of situation.

Observed with Satisfaction the application of Machinery particularly the Steam Engines, to Various purposes of Labour, by which the Expence must be considerably diminished.

The Inspector General took the opportunity of shewing an improved method of driving Treenails, which are prevented from Splitting by the intervention of an Iron Punch which receives the stroke of the Hammer: also a method of scarfing Timber by circular Cokes which is done by precision by an Instrument adapted to the purpose'.

On 10 September

'they examined plans proposed by General Bentham for erecting Furnaces and Machines for Melting, Refining, and working up the old Copper sheets, and also for Casting, Rolling, and Re manufacturing the Old Iron, which appear likely to be productive of considerable advantage to the Public, as those Materials have hitherto been taken off by the Contractor or Sold at an inferior price, and afterwards when wrought up re supplied to the yard'.

The Admiralty Visitation was St Vincent's propaganda exercise to highlight the progress of the Wood and Metal Mills.

The Block Mills

The Block Mills were more than a new building manufacturing an improved product on new machines. They embodied collaboration and conflict between public and private interests, the impact of the free market, innovation, labour practices (hours, wages and perquisites), and attitudes. This paper covers on the Block Mills during its establishment from the late 1790s to 1813, encompassing the Wood Mills making blocks, the Metal Mills recycling copper sheathing and making metal parts for blocks, and the Millwrights' shop. These aspects have been researched mostly from the Simon Goodrich Papers in the Science Museum Library,[35] relating processes, buildings, machines, personnel and working practices; detailing recruitment, pay rates and status of the managers and workers. They help to define the respective relationships and contributions of Samuel Bentham, Marc Isambard Brunel, Henry Maudslay and Simon Goodrich in research and design innovation. The least well known of these is Simon Goodrich, although the Newcomen Society published three articles about him and his rôle is appreciated.[36]

The Block Mills were conceived first by Bentham, outside the normal hierarchy; the Navy Board surveyor would normally have been in charge of such innovations. The surveyor from 1784-1806 was John Henslow (succeeded by Henry Peake 1806-1822), joined by William Rule from 1793-1813. Instead Bentham initiated and the Admiralty directed a Navy Board locale, then the Navy Board directed under Admiralty orders, while these boards were barely speaking to each other. Perhaps because relations were so bad, correspondence is remarkably detailed (not to say heavily ironic on the part of the Navy Board and disdainfully terse on the part of the Admiralty), as if all sides realised they might at some future point have to justify every action to a commission. Commission reports are naturally a good source of information.

An example of Navy Board beleaguered circumlocution is a reply to the Admiralty Secretary in July 1802, defending itself against criticism by Bentham:

'We desire you will please to acquaint their Lordships, that a deference to their superior Judgment will induce us to offer some observations upon that Letter, which otherwise we should not have deemed it necessary to have done, being conscious that on all occasions our best endeavors have been, and are exerted in the public service, and though on account of the multiplicity and pressure of business, imperfection and oversight may occasionally happen, yet we trust they will not, on the fullest investigation, appear of material consequence, or in a greater proportion than in the transactions of any Public Board whatever.'[37]

Of the two initiators, Brunel was a French contractor, while Bentham, also a naval contractor, was a problematical member of naval administration and mostly abroad.

Fig. 2. The interior of the block mills, the wooden columns and line shafting much in evidence. Photographed in July 1995.

They relied heavily on outside engineers Maudslay, Boulton, Watt for expertise and machines, but equally on Simon Goodrich as an Admiralty/Navy Board employee. He coordinated and implemented the amalgamation, drawing upon private engineering managers and workmen to run and man the new machines because the dockyards had no steam mechanics, until he could train ('breed' in dockyard terminology) the next generation. The building itself was designed by Admiralty/Navy Board architects Samuel Bunce and Edward Holl, built by Navy Board/Portsmouth Dockyard craftsmen directed by Master Shipwrights Henry Peake (at Chatham Dockyard with Bentham) then Nicholas Diddams.[38] The communication chain is demonstrated by Portsmouth Officers sending the Navy Board in November 1804 a drawing from Bentham 'shewing a small addition to the East end of the Block Manufactory designed to contain a Forge for repairing Tools and a Shop for branding Blocks.' Deputy Controller Henry Duncan and Surveyors Sir John Henslow and Sir William Rule requested the direction of Admiralty Board 'for carrying the same into

effect, if they approve thereof.'[39]

Although the machines in the Block Mills were far more elaborate versions of anything known previously, and the new workforce of millwrights was recruited from outside the dockyard, working practices perpetuated traditional customs, despite Bentham's reforming aspirations.

Simon Goodrich (1773-1847)

Simon Goodrich was born 28 October 1773. His father was Isaac, probably from Suffolk, and he had a brother, William, also an engineer, and a daughter Mary.[40] He married Susanna Lloyd on 25 December 1797 at Saint Martin-in-the-Fields Westminster, the Admiralty 'parish church'. She was probably a sister or daughter of 'John Lloyd, millwright, of Little Chapel St., Westminster' who made 'chain pumps and gearing' for the 30HP Sadler steam engine, supplied machinery for the steam dredger in 1800, erected the machinery and initially ran the Metal Mills. Goodrich may have studied under him before joining Reke.[41] Rhys Jenkins states that Lloyd, Goodrich and Burr had all worked for Bentham before 1796 and presumed he was part of Lloyd & Ostell. In 1810 Goodrich attended Arbitration Court when they were owed £2000 by the British Copper Company.[42]

Goodrich's correspondence covers flour mills, steam engines, a ballast vessel, fireproofing, cast iron pillars, ropemaking, heating tar by steam, foundation piling for a ropery, cisterns and dredging apparatus.[43] He won a 50guinea prize from the Society of Arts in 1797 for clock and watch mechanisms and in 1799 a 65guinea prize. In 1802 he shared the 50 guinea prize for plans for a fireproof building following the burning down in 1791 of John Rennie Sr's steam-powered London Albion Flour Mills.[44] They featured cast iron pillars, wrought iron ties and brick arches.[45]

The correspondence reveals a customised research team which advanced research and development through a free exchange of ideas and technology between public and private engineers much more quickly than individuals such as Walter Taylor III could on their own.[46] This follows the pattern of investigation, collaboration and testing carried out by Matthew Boulton, James Watt, Josiah Wedgewood and John Wilkinson.[47]

One example of such collaboration was Richard Trevithick's idea for a cast iron Thames Tunnel, discussed decades before its completion by Marc and Isambard Brunel in 1843 using a tunnelling shield patented by Marc in 1818 and constructed by Henry Maudslay.[48] From first idea to finished product an invention may have been through several minds. This was an era of outstanding self-made men, but within the Admiralty Marine Department Goodrich was awed by the Lords of the Admiralty, junior to Samuel Bentham, snubbed by a dockyard commissioner and felt threatened professionally by John Rennie Sr. But in the bicentenary of the Block Mills producing a full range of blocks it is right for Goodrich to receive the recognition due to him for his contribution to dockyards evolution.

Goodrich was appointed Mechanist in 1799 on a salary of £400. On 28 October 1807 he was transferred to the Navy Board on the same salary. He first ran the Block Mills operations from the Inspector General's office at the Admiralty, then on site. In July 1805 Samuel Bentham was ordered to Russia to arrange for ships to be built there for the Royal Navy.[49] Understanding that 'the several Works at present in hand should during my absence be put under the management of such one person as I might propose for this purpose,' he took the 'Liberty of recommending M:r Simon Goodrich, Mechanist, in my Office, as a person in whose intelligence & probity I can have full reliance, as the person whom taking all the business together I look upon as the most competent.'[50] This gave Goodrich the authority to act during Bentham's absence in the critical period of developing the Block Mills between August 1805 and November 1807.

A Mechanist was a mechanic, handicraftsman, one who constructs machinery, the *Oxford English Dictionary* cites S T Coleridge, *c.*1809: 'One State possesses Chemists, Mechanists, Mechanics of all kinds, Men of science; and the arts of war and peace; and its Citizens naturally strong and of habitual courage.'[51] Coleridge also wrote: 'To be a Musician, an Orator, a Painter, a Poet, an Architect, or even to be a good Mechanist, presupposes *Genius*; to be an excellent Artizan or Mechanic, requires more than an average degree of *Talent*'.[52]

An Engineer, on the other hand, was one who contrived, designed or invented bridges, roads, canals, harbours, a maker and manager of steam engines. The distinction was one of scale and status. Goodrich, clearly a rational, methodical, reflective, highly skilled man, referred bitterly to the difference. Helpfully for us he was an expansive writer to many correspondents, trusting them with revealing observations, expressed with candour.

Thanks to the Commission of Revision, Goodrich's services are clearly listed in his eleven page statement drafted in 1806, paraphrased here.[53] From the inception of the Office of Naval Works in 1796 the first Mechanist, Samuel Reke,[54] had erected a 12HP steam engine in the Pump House, two horse powered mills to mix mortar and the first experimental chain pump; he made a model of a machine to test comparative strengths of different metals, woods and other substances and advised the Inspector General on mechanical matters such as proposals for

Fig. 3. Brunel's swing arm circular saw, still in the block mills, used for cutting lignum vitae for the sheaves or pulley wheels. The lignum vitae timber is located centre in the lower part of the photograph, taken in November 2002.

slips, pumps, a method of combining small timbers and 'methods for working in wood by sawing, Rabetting[55] and Planing' and 'contrivances for Gun carriages upon the Non recoil Principle'.

Goodrich, having 'previously acted as Draughtsman to the late Mechanist' and 'been employed under him since the establishment of the Office', was appointed to succeed Reke on 25 October 1799, aged 26.[56] He planned and arranged the erection of the 30HP steam engine, six chain pumps and the 'Drains and Penstocks for communicating all the Docks and Basons with the Well and Reservoir so that the whole of the draining thereof is performed by the steam engine working these Pumps', furnishing drawings and directions and estimates of this machinery for the millwrights and engine makers. He made the first ground plans for

'...the Building containing the 12 & 30 HP Steam Engines and Pumping Machinery at Portsmouth Yard called the Woodmills, with a view to their being filled afterwards with various Machinery for sawing and otherwise working on Wood, with the spare power of the Steam Engines when not wanted for Pumping'

He then made plans and estimates for the shafts and wheels which transmitted the motion from the steam engines to the machines in the Wood Mills for sawing and making of blocks. He liaised with 'the Inventor of the Machines for making Blocks' (Brunel) over their introduction and erection. He produced drawings and estimates for the first reciprocating saw mill, the first two circular sawing machines for converting wood for block making, a long circular sawing bench for edging, rabbeting and cutting plank in scantling,[57] and two circular sawing machines 'on Gen[l] Bentham's Great Plans'. He made ground plans for the Metal Mills and new coal yard, consulting 'Metal Masters'. He also made plans for the 50HP steam engine and machines for

'remanufacturing the Old Copper into Sheets and Bolts and the old Iron into Bolts Barrs and other Uses, furnishing detailed Drawing and instruction, for the Guidance of the Engine Maker and Millwright for the execution and fixing of all this various and extensive

Machinery', which, Goodrich wrote, 'is not yet completed'. He made drawings and estimates for the 'Engine Maker' for a second 30HP steam engine at the Wood Mills to be erected 'in lieu of the present 12 HP engine'.

Interspersed with this work Goodrich made detailed drawings, directions and estimates for a ballast-heaving engine; a 12HP engine on a vessel for underwater excavation in Portsmouth harbour; and for the pump and machinery to raise water from Portsmouth's new freshwater well. He suggested repairs and improvements to Haslar Hospital water works; made plans and estimates for a 6HP movable steam engine at Portsmouth to supply power for pumping and raising water anywhere in the yard. He made plans and estimates to carry fresh water raised by the Woodmill pump through cast iron pipes of 8, 6 and 4 inches diameter to dockyard buildings and ships and to pump salt water from a well through pipes to extinguish fires in the dockyard. He made ground plans for the new smith's shop for repairing Brodie's fire hearths and a new coal yard for the smithery at Portsmouth. He made drawings and estimates for a new wharf crane at Portsmouth.

In Devon he designed an additional 8inch cast iron pipe with cocks to move water from Brixham reservoir to the watering quay. He made drawings for two circular sawing machines on Bentham's plan for the Joiners and Carpenters' Shop at Plymouth Dockyard. He also made plans and drawings for a reservoir supplying fresh water to Plymouth yard by a water wheel worked by the fall of water to the lower dock and instructed the millwrights there.

At Deptford Dockyard he made plans and estimates for a second ballast-heaving engine and directed millwrights to prepare a horse wheel pump for Deptford Victualling Office. At Woolwich he advised and assisted Mr Grimshaw of Sunderland in erecting a Rope Mill and machines to manufacture cordage day and night. He made drawings and estimates for three horse mortar mills at Woolwich Dockyard.

As well as these projects Goodrich examined associated tradesman's bills and assisted the Inspector General 'with an opinion on the subject of various references of a Mechanical nature that have come before him from time to time'. He acted during his absence in the:

> *'General superintendence of the business of the Office and has in addition to the ordinary duties thereof the preparatory Regulation untill complete establishments can be formed & proposed, for the three new Establishments in Portsmouth Dock Yard of the Wood Mill, the Metal and Millwrights, all entries and discharges, the rate of wages and weekly payment of the men being made by his certificate-'.*

He concludes, not surprisingly: 'The whole time & attentions of the present Mechanist since his appointment has been fully taken up in the execution of the constant duties required of him'.[58]

This document, itemising his actions between October 1799 and April 1806, indicates conclusively that the Wood Mills project was managed by Simon Goodrich. Mr Forward notes that he complained several times that he was so busy 'he did not know which way to turn. He seems to have worked early and late, often including Sundays...discuss[ing] business over the breakfast table.' Although he asked for remuneration as Bentham's deputy 'he received nothing but thanks.' In 1808 he sent a memorial requesting more salary but recorded no improvement. In 1810 he again asked, being told 'it could not at present be complied with.'[59]

Even more revealing than the letters are Goodrich's journals, each covering about six months. His first few months after taking over from Bentham must have been a steep learning curve. Pathos emerges occasionally. His first entry on 1 August 1805: 'Go to the Office, No one there but myself.'[60] On 7 August he was introduced to the Navy Board by Controller Sir Andrew Snape Hamond and commented 'S.r A. H. takes a more civil leave of me than at a former interview by wishing me good morning.'[61] In Portsmouth in September he was snubbed by Commissioner Charles Saxton. Goodrich had requested him to order beer for the Metal Mills, but two weeks later the Commissioner 'signified to me that I should write to the Navy Bd on that

subject and that he should not take notice of my letter to him.'[62] This undoubtedly represented Navy Board resentment over an Admiralty initiative, the Wood Mills, within the dockyard, echoing previous incursions into Navy Board responsibilities.[63] Aware as Goodrich was of the tensions between the two Boards, he was either naïvely expecting Saxton's cooperation or following Bentham's example of pushing the boundaries.

On Monday 5 August 1805 Goodrich had the delicate task of negotiating with Edward Holl, Architect and Engineer, the boundaries of their respective responsibilities. 'I judged it now necessary to enter into some conciliatory explanation with M.r H. We agree, and shake hands in token of acting cordially together.' Although Holl held more professional sounding titles, they were paid the same salary and Goodrich was senior by appointment.

Goodrich communicated regularly with Bentham in Russia, sending him information about new processes and notes from Mr Lloyd on copper experiments in the Metal Mills and his own experiments.[64] He visited sites pioneering belts transmitting power to machines.[65] He visited Mr Roper in Houndsditch who had applied for a Navy Board contract for blocks. He commented that his machines, driven by ¼ inch diameter flaxen cords, cost only £200, but 'his offer seems now too late and his means not sufficiently extensive'.[66]

The Metal Mills were as important to Bentham's plans as the Wood Mills. Bentham wanted to improve the quality, remove reliance on the copper merchants and control production of metal sheathing, so a mill re-manufacturing old copper was established between August 1803 and September 1805, Bentham approving Goodrich's plans on 30 July 1805.[67] In August 1805 Mr Beach[68] reported progress on constructing two furnaces: trials on copper waste showed that two men working one pair of rolls with one furnaceman, one man pickling and shearing and three boys assisting could produce six to seven tons of recycled copper a week.[69]

Pay and conditions

Time-work discipline was a thorny issue,

with engineers imported from private foundries bringing their own traditions and the Admiralty determined to rid the dockyards of traditional work practices and perquisites.[70] Applying Bentham's classification of workers, wage setting and hiring suitable labour was Goodrich's responsibility but Bentham's focus and Brunel's concern; as Bentham's justification and Brunel's financial reward depended upon the detailed costings whereby the Admiralty calculated the money saved. In 1804 the Navy Board reported pay for Block Mills labourers as 2s 6d a day in winter, in summer (5am-6pm) 2s 8d a day, including dinner time and excluding chip money. Brunel suggested that labourers working on mortising and shaping engines and turning iron sheaves should be paid 1s extra; those attending boring engines, scoring engines, turning pins and attending in the Cabin to be paid 8d a day extra. The Admiralty confirmed payment of 3s a day excluding chip money.[71] Artificers in the Wood Mills in 1805 were paid rates of between 4s a day 1st class and 3s 9d 3rd class; the wood millers 3s a day 2nd class, 2s 9d a day 3rd class; with boys between 1s 6d a day and 9d a day.[72] Although this was a new working site with jobs that could be broken down into repetitive tasks, they were still paid day rates. As woodworkers they were also allowed the traditional perquisite of graded rates of chip money, even though the Wood Mills had started work after chips were commuted to a cash payment, evidence of continuing traditions.

Chips were wood waste 'such as fall from the axe', the perquisite of dockyard woodworkers, but viewed by management as a pernicious cause of waste and theft. Dockyards had tried to abolish them since the 1620s, but while wages were paid in arrears the workforce needed this source of ready cash. London magistrate Patrick Colquhoun highlighted their abuses in a 'Treatise on the Police of the Metropolis' in 1796 which was praised by the Select Committee of Finance (chairman Charles Abbot) and Home Secretary the Duke of Portland. He estimated dockyards lost £140,000 through time, materials and concealed theft:

'The artificers in the dock-yards, availing *themselves of their perquisite of chips, not only commit great frauds through this medium, by often cutting up useful timber, and wasting time in doing so; but also in frequently concealing within their bundles of chips, copper bolts, and other valuable articles, which are removed by their wives and children, and often sold to itinerant Jews, or to the dealers in old iron and stores; who are always to be found in abundance wherever the dock-yards are situated'.*

From May 1801 chips had been commuted to a cash payment, and from September 1805 three-quarters of wages due were paid weekly, so chips could no longer be pleaded as a necessity.[73]

From 16 August 1805 Goodrich's journal relates his deliberations. From Friday 30 August he was in Portsmouth. On 6 September he took lodgings in St George's Square, Portsea, close to the Dockyard and Brunel's home in Britain Street. One problem arose when Mr Burr[74] raised 'a boys wages without application – it seems advisable to make a new rate between 1s/9d and 1s/6d per day for lads'. Goodrich told Burr not to make any new appointments or advances of pay without permission. Another difficulty arose from showing piecework on certificates from the Portsmouth Clerk of the Cheque. All the dockyards were having problems setting piece rates, designed to reward higher productivity with higher wages.[75] His notes reveal a system of Byzantine complexity, showing why the Navy Board had been reluctant to implement it for so long.[76]

Goodrich collected information 'of the wages given to labourers and Scavelmen[77] in order to fix upon proper wages to be given to the men to be attached to the Engines at the Wood Mills under the Master Mill wright for the Pumping &ca'. He took advice 'about making out the wages for each man in the certificates when several of them work together by the Piece'. He discovered that

'*...according to the Dock Yard management of the pay the whole earnings of a Scavelman at Present coming in at 5 and going out at 7 is 3s/7d per day being for a double day 3s/- one tide 4d Chips 3d – and of a Labourer 2s/9d per day being for a double day 2s/2d one tide 4d Chips 3d – To this must be added per Week upon the average 2/4 for working every 3rd night, and* *three single days when they work on a Sunday from 6 to 6 – in the one case 4ˢ/6ᵈ and in the other 3/3 –'.*

There followed notes of wages earned in the past five weeks 'for doing the same work and for staying every other week in Yard during Nights' amounting to £1 9s 9d. a week. Goodrich calculated this as the weekly pay for 'Scavellmen now proposed as 2ⁿᵈ Engine Keepers', broken down as follows:[78]

	£	s	d
Bare time per week from 6-5	0	18	0
Extra made at present in the woodmills 2 hours per day	0	3	6
Extra for Pumping and staying in the Yd every other Week during the night this is fixed	0	5	3
Sunday when necessary from 6-1, to pack Piston &ᶜᵃ· but not for Pumping	0	3	0
	1	9	9

Following Goodrich's format, the first Engine Keepers would be paid per week:

	£	s	d
Bare time per week from 6-5	1	4	0
Extra made at present in the woodmills 2 hours per day	0	5	0
Extra for Pumping and staying in the Yd every otherWeek during the night this is fixed	0	7	0
Sunday when necessary from 6-1, to pack Piston &ᶜᵃ· but not for Pumping	0	4	0
	2	0	0

And Labourers would be paid per week:

	£	s	d
Bare time per week from 6-5	0	15	0
Extra made at present in the woodmills 2 hours per day	0	3	0
Extra for Pumping and staying in the Yd every other Week during the night this is fixed	0	3	6
Sunday when necessary from 6-1, to pack Piston &ᶜᵃ· but not for Pumping	0	2	6
	1	4	0

After consulting with Lee, Linacre and Beach he proposed for the Cabin Keeper at the Metal Mills: '1..1..0 bare day and 4ᵈ per hour extra equal at present to 1..5..0 per week'.[79]

So that wages would be equivalent to rates paid for similar jobs in the dockyard he consulted the officers responsible: 'These wages were considered fair by the Builder and Clerk of the Cheque whose opinion I asked upon them'.[80] He needed information as to whether Mr Burr considered

'…the exertions of the Smiths… swedging[81] Block Pins so far extraordinary as to entitle them to the Great earnings they make per week, one man earned 2£..8ˢ..0ᵈ – The price given for Sweding Pins of all sizes is 1½ per lb, or whether the rate ought not to be reduced'.

Burr replied that these wages were earned from working from 4 in the morning and he does not think they will earn so much normally. He agreed with the blockmakers on piece work when they had to work by the day: '4ˢ/6ᵈ bare day 6ᵈ Chips = 5ˢ/0 and 6ᵈ per hour extra'.[82]

By 5 September Goodrich had completed his pay 'scheem' for the wood and metal mill engines and was focusing on entering workmen, some of whom came from the dockyard, when he had to consider the matter of 'beer to be allowed the men at the Metal Mills.' His understanding of their need, and recognition that this was one custom he could not alter, overcame his principles. On 10 September:

'The Men at the Metal Mills are very pressing about the allowance of beer. I had wished to have done it away if it had been possible and allowed money to those to whom it had been promised – But as for this work their [sic] is a real necessity for some kind of drink it may upon the whole be best to allow the beer instead of money'.

However, Commissioner Saxton was not prepared to help him obtain the 'allowance

Earnings of a Portsmouth shipwright 1805-1808

	Day pay	a week	a month	a year	Task pay a day	a week	a month	a year
1805	5s 5d	£1.63	£7.52	£90.19	6s 9d	£2.03	£9.36	£112.39
1806	4s 9d	£1.43	£6.59	£79.09	6s 10d	£2.05	£9.48	£106.84
1807	4s 9d	£1.43	£6.59	£79.09	6s 5d	£1.93	£8.90	£117.11
1808	4s 9d	£1.43	£6.59	£79.09	6s 8d	£2.00	£9.25	£111.00

of one Gal.ⁿ to each man employed about the Furnaces and hot Metal' and said he had to obtain it from the Navy Board.[83]

On 21 October 1805 Goodrich reported that '40 of the Wood Mill people had gone out of the Yard after dinner in consequence of being checked for not coming in time for call,[84] they having been ordered to shorten their dinner time by a quarter of an hour in consequence of the short daylight.' The next day he was determined 'not to give way to them. Call them together and speak to them on the subject. They are brought to reason and do not object to comply.' Dinner hours had traditionally been a thorny issue.[85] Forward noted that they did stop work earlier in the winter evenings with no loss of pay.[86]

The Metal Mills workforce came with expectations from private industry. On 21 July 1805 the furnacemen millwrights under Mr Lloyd, in response to Goodrich's terms, insisted on

'...the privileges that we at present enjoy That is that we shall be paid at the rate of 6s 3d pᵣ day which shall include 10 working Hours and all overtime to Be Paid as it has Hithertoo been in proportion to the advance Wages: With Respect to going to Cal[l] will by no means Complyed with as it is Contrary to all other [word erased] Millwrights ruls. To come to the Point we shall expect the advance wages for the incoming week and the privileges of London Millwrights which if Granted we have have [sic] no objections to Come to work but upon no other terms whatsoever'.[87]

In October 1805 Mr Lloyd had to deal with millwrights unsettled about the uncertainty of their employment after four had been discharged at short notice.[88] He protested to Goodrich:

'...without the least idea of giving offence what is intended to be done whether I may expect any of the Men will be continued in my employ or not, or whether you have any objections to inform me whether I may write to the Navy Board or the Lords of the Admiralty on the subject, and to which it would be proper for me to wright, if at all'.

He complained that 'what little money I gained for about 7 years industry I have laid out in shops & tools...with the expectation of finding some continuance of favors from the Quarter, which now seems to be in a tottering state.'[89] On 2 November Goodrich informed Mr Lloyd that 'no men can be continued in this Dockyard under your pay and directions, after Saturday the 16.ᵗʰ instant'. He added that some might soon 'be entered upon the establishment'.[90] In November 1805 Goodrich even had to negotiate time-work issues with Maudslay's workforce, who were definitely not his responsibility.[91]

Fig. 4. An assortment of pulley blocks on the floor of the block mills. July 1995.

Superintendent Mr Beach was paid £4 a week, the copper melter for one charge of two tons a day received £2 a week and 6s house rent, his assistant 27s a week. They worked 12 hours a day, starting at 5am in summer, 8am in winter. Smiths swaging block pins earned 48s a week, starting at 4am. Smiths were paid 6s 6d a day plus 8d allowance, with other classes paid 5s 3d a day with 6d allowance and 4s 3d a day with 5d allowance. Labourers earned 25s a week.[92] Dockyard smiths earned 2s 6d a day on day work at the time with no chips allowance.[93]

In the Metal Mills in 1805 were three workers called Ollis: John Sen[r], John Jun[r] and Sam[l].[94] In 1808 there were also a James and a Matthew Ollis.[95] This replicated the pattern of dockyard employment, where the same family names occurred within trades and shared the name of the leading craftsman. While artisans had no great wealth to pass on, they could confer a job on their sons and nephews through family hierarchies in dockyards. It is also typical that Beach passed on a message from Mr Linacre, Master Millwright,[96] 'respecting Tho[s.] Davis' being alow'd 4 Pounds to remove his Wife and Family here which I hope you will consider of as the Man appears rather uncomfortable'.[97] This signified what I have called the 'caring Navy Board' approach, much in evidence in dockyards through the seventeenth and eighteenth centuries.[98] But the Navy Board did not run the Block Mills. It is therefore confirmation of continued paternalistic behaviour in workplaces generally, evidence of E P Thompson's 'moral economy',[99] proof that even as mechanised processes took over from hand tools in the early nineteenth century, paternalism was still active. Individual skill was still valued. Beach: 'I think it would be better to have [copper sheets] from the plain Casting as Ollis with some directions will turn them better then you are likely to get them done any were else.'[100]

Goodrich selected a new Master of the Metal Mills 'after a number of applications to the advertisement'. On 18 December 1806 he visited the iron works at Fontley near Portsmouth once owned by naval contractor Henry Cort, but following his bankruptcy, by Adam Jellico. While noting the process of rolling old iron, he also spoke to Mr Vernon.

'He appears to understand the iron business practically, not chemically, for he seems unacquainted with the terms of the Science, but that part would be easy to acquire. He seems also to understand furnace work, brick and sand, has mechanical invention without science or a sufficient knowledge of first principles'.

Despite Vernon's lack of drawing skill Goodrich valued his practical experience 'in Copper Mill business'. He was appointed Master of the Metal Mills from 19 January 1807 on a salary of £4 a week (£17.33/month, £208/year) but could not leave Jellico until the end of the quarter. On 22 January Vernon observed to Mr Rogers that he would inform himself, 'not only for the purpose of being enabled to discharge his duty here in a satisfactory manner, but also for his own pleasure and information, which he would endeavor to do both by reading and practical experiments'. On 8 March Rogers reported that Vernon had moved his family to Half Way Houses the previous day, 'so that now he will have nothing to interrupt his attendance at the Metal Mills.'[101]

On 6 September 1806 thirteen millwrights and five smiths struck over refusing to appear at call in the morning. Goodrich paid them off the next day and 'intended to do away with all remains of their London rules'. He would only deal with them individually if they agreed to 6s a day without the half-hour watering time. Most returned on these terms.[102] By 1808 in the Metal Mills had a workforce of 42 day workers and 15 piece workers with a weekly wage bill of £89. 13s 9¾d. The skilled day workers earned between £3 7s 1d (£3.35p) a week (foreman John Ollis sr) and £1 10s (£1.50p) a week for a furnaceman and also got a beer allowance, with some receiving house rent and firing of 6s (30p) a week. This was for a day rate of 7s 8d (£2.30 a week) for the foreman and 6s 4d (£1.90 a week) for a furnaceman, 1d a day more than they had asked for initially. The pay of the piece workers casting iron and brass varied from £3 14s 11¼d (£3.75p) a week for producing 27cwt of iron to £1 17s 9¼d (£1.89p) a week for casting 4cwt of brass. They did not get a beer allowance.[103] This is compared with Morriss's table of earnings of a Portsmouth shipwright on day pay and task pay after pay rises 1805-1808, estimated for a

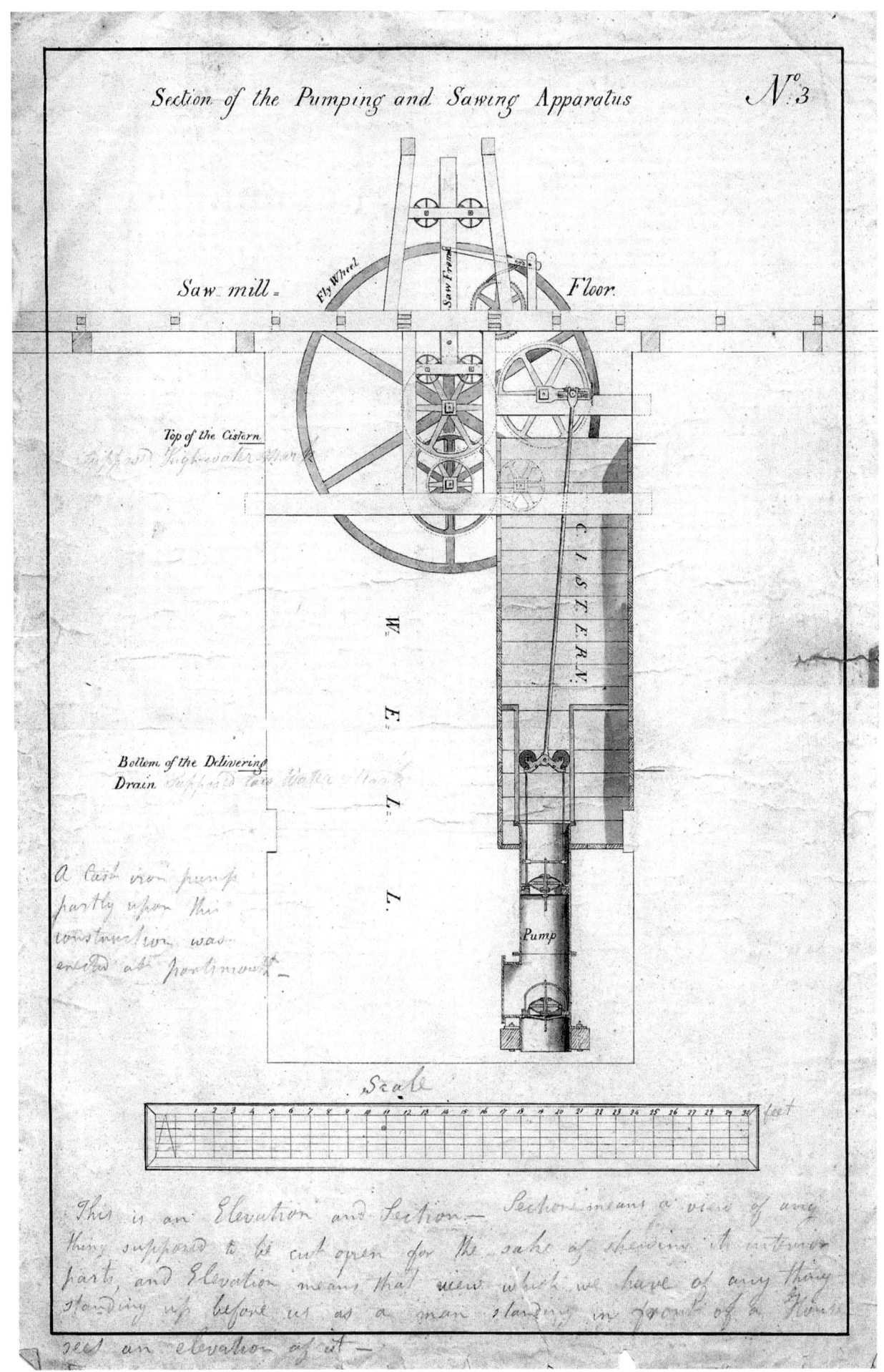

Section of the Pumping and Sawing Apparatus

Saw mill =   Fly Wheel   Saw Frame   Floor.

Top of the Cistern

CISTERN:

W=

E=

L=

L.

Bottom of the Delivering Drain

Pump

A cast iron pump partly upon this construction was erected at portsmouth =

Scale

This is an Elevation and Section — Section means a view of any thing supposed to be cut open for the sake of shewing its interior parts, and Elevation means that view which we have of any thing standing up before us as a man standing in front of a House sees an elevation of it —

Fig. 5. Drawing of the pump and saw operated from the same engine, probably 1797 by Bentham. *Courtesy the National Archives.*

week, month and year in decimal currency.[104]

The most skilled day workers and piece workers in the Metal Mills were therefore earning more than dockyard shipwrights, even those on higher task rates. Furnacemen were also earning more than dockyard labourers, who earned 2s 5d by the day (73p a week, £3.35 month, £40.24 pa) from 1805-1808 or up to 3s 9d (£1.13p a week, £5.20 month, £62.44 pa) by task by 1808. Goodrich was adamant in contradicting 'Workmen who state that they are over worked when in fact they are not stinted to any quantity of work, but work by the piece and do only as much as they please and [it is] the Masters and Foremens business to see that it is well done.'[105]

In 1810 Goodrich noted smiths' wages in private foundries, reporting that they are paid by day rates because 'the men cannot nor could not take proper pains with their work if the price is so straitened that the[y] cannot get their wages.' This experience was shared by others:

> 'Boulton & Watt's men are now all by the day and keep a looker-on for the different sets of men, the same as Mr. Murray. Messrs Murray, and Boulton & Watt, say that engine work is not got up with that accuracy as it would be if done by the piece, which was the reason they both established over-lookers to the different classes'.[106]

Success?

A landmark in the history of the Block Mills was reached on 3 October 1805 when Brunel responded to Goodrich's request of 2 August[107] on 'The Present State of the Wood Mills'. Forty machines were complete, four were at Maudslay's and more were planned: 'Apparatus for converting Timber', to 'cross cut Logs of the largest dimensions and if necessary to fletch and square the pieces'; also 'An Engine for Rivetting the Brass Coaks' and one for turning 'pins or cylindrical pieces of metal 38" in length by 5" diameter' and less. These produced blocks of 4-7 inches, 7-10 inches and 10-18 inches long, the sizes required by the navy, though not yet in sufficient quantity.[108]

In 1806, however, the future of Portsmouth Block Mills was still precarious. In 1802

William Marsden, Second Secretary to the Admiralty,[109] hoped that 'the Commission [of Naval Enquiry] will in fact be a sort of protection to the inferior boards...to crush them was the object of the bill and the frauds in the dockyards (which we are daily detecting and punishing) are only a pretext'.[110] But St Vincent, although no longer First Lord of the Admiralty, used his Commission of Naval Enquiry to further his aims.

Goodrich reported on the activities of the Commissioners of Revision in May 1806: 'it is not thought by M.r Darch, that what they might propose would be readily listened to by the present Administration'.[111] Mr Darch, First Clerk at the Admiralty Naval Works Department, was referring to the political upheavals following Prime Minister William Pitt's death on 23 January 1806 and a coalition of the parties of Grenville, Fox and Addington. On 10 February Lord Barham, James Gambier, Philip Patton, W Dickenson, Sir Evan Nepean and Lord Garlies were replaced by First Lord Charles Grey (soon to be Viscount Howick), John Markham, Sir Charles Morice Pole, Sir Harry Burrard Neale, Lord William Russell and William Lord Kensington, leaving Sir Philip Stephens as the only continuous element at the Admiralty Board. Grey was replaced by Thomas Grenville in September 1806. The warring commissions continued to exacerbate relations between the Admiralty and Navy Boards.[112]

In June 1806 Marsden wrote sympathetically to Goodrich directing him to analyse *Hibernia*'s recycled copper, following St Vincent 'complaining of its adulterated quality' and despite their own analyst, Mr Davy, finding only 5 and 3 parts of iron per 1,000. Marsden believed a trial coppering a sloop with the softest copper possible would establish the truth, but 'I am well aware that merely an Order to the Navy Board, however well inclined the Members may be to have it duly executed, will not answer the purpose unless some executive person takes it zealously in hand.'[113] Goodrich replied to Marsden the next day:

> 'The only sloop sheathed with the copper Which has been on a Cruize is the Amazon frigate[114]

which when lately in this port was reported to me by the officers here to have had the cleanest and brightest bottom of any ship lately observed- 'The only other ships coppered with this Copper are two of the Line just turned out of Dock and now lying here the Colossus and another whose name I have forgotten. The people at the Storehouse who receive and Mark the Copper gave ours the best Character of any they have had to handle. The Cabin Keeper told the Builder some time ago and myself today unasked that he was sure the copper made in the Yard was the best as it was the softest and did not wear out upon the sheets half so fast as the Contractors copper did in general-'[115]

Alluding to 'confusion' arising from 'our circumstance of the bad start of the Copper on the Hibernia' which has been complained of by L^d St Vincent, Goodrich urged Marsden to correct misunderstandings:

'If the mistake about our Copper has spread at all, I will thank you to do all in your power to contradict it and point out to your Brother[116] that he may point out to others, how it has arisen, for it may have a bad effect that any prejudice should arise altho' by a mistake- But I do not wish prematurely to give our copper a good Character as any little circumstance against it may then have a worse effect; till further experience is had of it, and till we have completed our machinery and modes of working, let the Judgement be suspended'.[117]

This was a mark of Goodrich's reflective sense.

In a letter to Mr Grimshaw, Ropemaker from Sunderland in October 1806,[118] he elegantly and succinctly unravelled the politics affecting the future of the Block Mills:

'The Board of Commissioners for revising the Civil Affairs of the Navy was an appointment made by the King at the suggestion I suppose of Mr. Pitt soon after his coming into administration the last time. It was said that this Board was intended to counteract the measures of the famous Board of the Comm[ission] of Naval Enquiry appointed by Parliament at the suggestion of Lord St. Vincent and his party. At the head of the Board of Revision was Sir Charles Middleton...noted as a man versed in the business of the Civil Department of the Navy and as a manufacturer of Rules and Regulations. After Lord Melville

was brought with a scrape by the Board of Enquiry Mr. Pitt's Party could find nobody for the first Lord of the Admiralty but Sir Charles Middleton and he acted under the new name of Lord Barham preserving at the same time his seat at the head of such Board of Revision. Things were then beginning to go on swimmingly with the Board of Revision for the regulations would be no sooner proposed by that Board, before they were approved of and acted upon by the Admiralty Board, when Mr. Pitt's death caused such a loss of weight in that scale that Mr. Fox's and Lord St Vincent's again preponderated – Lord Barham gave place at the Admiralty to Lord Howick[119] and Lord St. Vincent's Party, he however kept to his post as head of the Board of Revision and this Board proceeded and finished their first Report containing instructions for the Commissioners and the six Principal Officers of each Dock Yard...'[120]

Goodrich continued:

'However during Lord Howick's time it was not thought by many who were likely to be judges that anything from the Commissioners of Revision would be readily attended to or carried into effect. I found however from many quarters that the enquiries of the Comm[issioners] of Revision by the reports they called for from the Master Smiths of the Dock Yards and other noted private manufacturers such as Mr. Bramah, that they were descending into the minutiae of the manufacturing Branches of the Dock Yards with a view I suppose to propose improvements, tho' I very much suspect that there is no Body at that Board who are judges in such matters of improvement, but a certain rage now seems creeping into that Department for new schemes and inventions so probably what has been brought forward at this Dock Yard may have given birth to it, and they seem determined to come in for their share of the Glory tho' I believe they are not willing to allow the General any credit. I who am behind the scenes cannot help smiling to observe men see only with their eyes and not with their judgement'.[121]

Politics continued to intrude on manufacture: in March 1807 Mr Rogers[122] wrote from the Wood Mills to Goodrich, describing almost a French farce of visitors with different agendas:

'We were a good deal thronged yesterday at the

Metal Mills with Visitors. Lord Melville[123] *and a great number of great folks with him paid us a visit about 4 oClock. Their attention was a good deal taken up with the process of manufacturing Copper, and one of them (I rather think Adm.ʲ Young)*[124] *questioned me very closely and particularly respecting the expense and waste of metal in re:manufacturing the Old Copper. From his enquiries he seemed to be aware of the Storm that appears to be gathering over these Works. However terrible and tremendous, I think the Copper Mill will resist sufficiently so as to stand its ground in spite of the endeavors of the whole body of Copper Gentlemen to undervalue it. I think Grenfell & Williams' observations ought to be immediately replied to, in order to remove any prejudices or unfavorable impressions which they, as well as perhaps the malicious Reports of others, may have made upon the minds of the Admiralty Board....The Copper folks may well begin to squeak.– The price of Copper sheath*ᵍ *& Bolts, and of every other article of Copper brass or mixed Metal supplied to the Dock Yards fell a penny per lb the day before yesterday'.*

Amongst other visitors yesterday was M.ʳ Marsden.[125] He was at the Metal Mills about half an hour before Lord Melville and Party, and was accompanied by Sr. Isaac Coffin.'[126]

Why were William Marsden, Sir Isaac Coffin,[127] and two ex-members of the Admiralty Board enquiring about the cost of re-manufacturing copper?

The reason was copper's price, availability and government relations with the merchants. On 4 July 1807 William Whitmore,[128] who had supplied Goodrich with machinery for the Metal Mills, wrote advising him to obtain the report of the House of Commons Committee on the Copper Trade.[129] His letter explains the reasons for unstable copper prices and production which had prompted Bentham to re-manufacture copper sheets for the navy.[130] Until 1792 the copper trade had been almost totally controlled by Thomas Williams,[131] owner of the Parys Mine Company with rolling mills in Flintshire, North Wales which produced copper and copper nails for naval sheathing by a cold-rolling method. In 1790 the price for Cornish ore was set at £74 a ton and

Williams had obtained a five year monopoly of selling Cornish copper. In 1791 the price was raised to £86 a ton but Williams refused to sell to Birmingham due to a shortage of copper to satisfy all markets (Birmingham manufactures, East India Company, Royal Navy and coinage). Whitmore outlined the control over prices and output: Williams

'...and his partners of whom he may be said to be Manager (being bred up a Lawyer), raised about 3500 Tons of Copper from the Anglesea Mines and I think he had by contract with the Miners in Cornwall, which he had so compleatly under his command from the Circumstance of his being able to Under Cooke Copper in the Market at 38 Pʳ Ton, confined them to 40,000 Tons of Ore, the produce abᵗ· 4000 Tons of fine Copper. They had till then raised much more and the price was about 76 to 84 and Cake Copper then was abᵗ· £10 over the Standard of Cornwall. He lower'd it from time to time to 65, being anxious to have the sole Management. He proposed a Second Contract which they refused and I recollect he said 'Well Gentlemen if we cannot agree upon this point can we agree on another which was shall Copper be at £70 or £60 Pʳ Ton the next Quarter?' This was like the Fable of the Frog to the Cornish Men for they cou'd not work to profit at less than abᵗ· 76 and this would have brought it to abᵗ· 50. While they were under this alarm he proposed to purchase all the Ores at a standard of £74 Pʳ Ton and as he was in no Want, as he pretended, they shou'd be equally divided amongst the whole of the Smelting Companys, these were 11 at that time. This had on first view such an appearance of fairness that a meeting was called of All the Copper Smelters to be held at the George & Vulture Corn Hill'.[132]

At this meeting Williams controlled 'ten or Eleven sixteenths of the Cornish as well as all his own Ores' and Whitmore called for an adjournment to consult manufacturers in Birmingham. He was told by a Mr Simeon 'that if we did not come in Cake Copper should be 17ˢ Pʳ lb and the poor of the Town of Birmingham should want bread.' But Whitmore knew this was a gamble on Williams's part as his Anglesey ores were depleted and extraction costs were rising. His monopoly ended in 1792 and by the time of

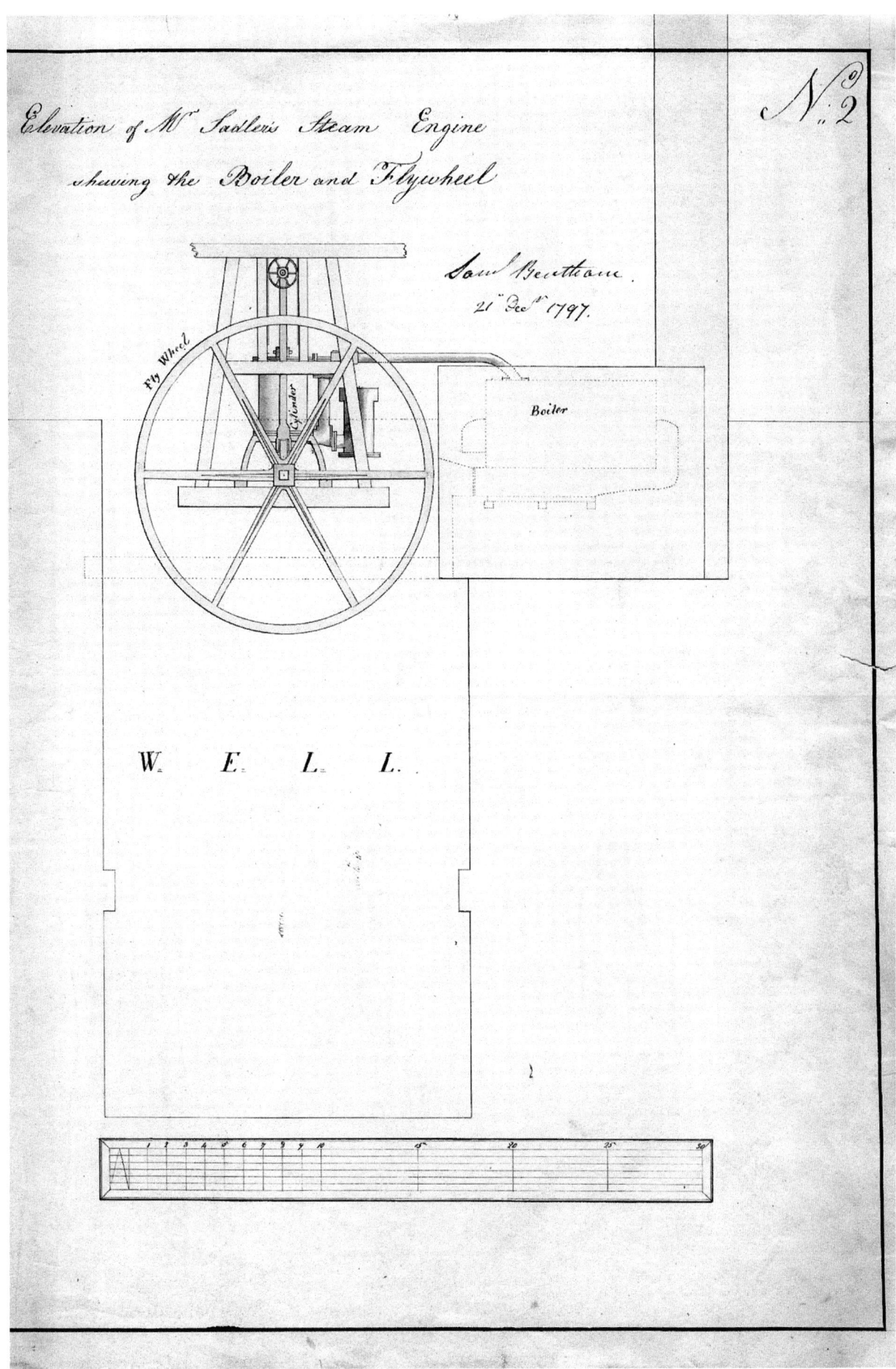

Elevation of Mr Sadler's Steam Engine
shewing the Boiler and Flywheel

Saml Bentham.
21st Decr 1797.

Fly Wheel

Cylinder

Boiler

W. E. L. L.

Fig. 6. Drawing of the small Sadler steam engine used for pumping the well beneath the block mills and for driving saws, signed by Samuel Bentham, 21 December 1797. *Courtesy The National Archives.*

the parliamentary enquiry in 1799 Williams was also losing control of Cornish production.

The Admiralty desperately needed the Metal Mills to start producing copper supplies for the navy. From 1803 Navy Board reported prices and demands from Grenfell and Spedding of Mines Royal Co for old copper, offering 1s a lb. The dockyards had stored old copper since August 1802 rather than sell to the contractors, the copper melting furnace was ready by October 1803, but the Metal Mills were not ready.[133] In January 1805 the Navy Board reported that the two contractors had again requested old copper for remanufacture, 'alledging that…the State of the Wind and Weather might impede their Supply of copper from the Smelting Works in Wales by Sea and by Canal, and that they now learn the Frost has suspended it entirely by the latter', so they could not deliver supplies for two months. The Navy Board was awaiting 500 tons of supplies from them and asked the Admiralty if they could release another 100 tons of old copper to each contractor, who had already had 150 tons each

'…since their Lordships order of the 20th Septr 1803 directing Us to keep the whole in Store until the Machinery for remanufacturing the same will be ready, but which is not yet nearly finished as £10,000 is demanded by the Officers for completing it this Year'. [134]

In February 1805 the Navy Board reported price rises for copper sheeting from 1s per lb in 1795, to 1s 4d in 1802-1803, and 1s 6d in 1805. As the market price was 1s 9d/1s 10d a lb they anticipated the contract price rising further unless the government 'put a stop to the Exportation of that Article'.[135] Whitmore ended his letter in 1807 'I am happy to hear the Works go on so well and hope you will find no difficulty in refuting every misrepresentation'. Goodrich noted underneath that, working night and day, he was producing 16 tons of copper sheathing a week, not sufficient to replace the contractors.[136]

In 1808 Goodrich still had to counter Surveyor Henry Peake reporting, 'as the Hints appear of importance to me', the insinuation of St Vincent's ally Joseph Tucker, Plymouth Master Shipwright. When Tucker visited the Metal Mills he claimed to Portsmouth Master Shipwright Diddams that 'copper sheets served into Plymouth Yard from the Metal Mills were not so good in appearance as those served by contractors.' Goodrich noted 'NB M:r Tuckers brother married one of Mr William's (the great Copper Contractor's) Daughters – or one Grenfell's'.[137] By 1812 the Metal Mills were saving £41,000 a year by recycling copper.

Results

The crucial landmark came on 3 September 1807 when Brunel reported to Goodrich:

'After an enquiry into the state of the several articles requisite for making blocks of all sizes and other articles of the blockmakers contract; I beg to…inform you, that the Wood Mill will be able within the 15th of next month, to make and furnish all the Blocks necessary for supplying the whole of His Majesty's Navy, provided the Wood Mill is furnished with all the articles necessary to make the same'. [138]

His caveat illustrated supply bottlenecks which hindered full production and delayed Brunel's payment from the Admiralty. Continuity of supply was now vital, as the navy's requirement for blocks was greater than in 1797-1801 and the Taylors were demanding higher prices. Brunel 'observes' that there has been for some time a 'want of brass Coaks', preventing completion of blocks, the reason given by Mr Vernon, Master of the Rolling Mill, as lack of men at the foundry, but 'another foundry is nearly complete to afford assistance when he is furnished with some more hands.'

Finally, by mid-October 1807, the Block Mills produced all the navy's requirements, saving £17,000 a year. In 1808 ten men, replacing 100 blockmakers, produced 130,000 blocks, securing the navy's annual requirements.[139] The Taylors would still be supplying private firms, including possibly the East India Company. Dickinson suggested they also made ships' pumps.[140] They did not cease their criticism. In 1808 Peake asked Goodrich to 'ascertain if M.r Taylorys [sic] assertion Respecting the Price of Blocks are double at Portsmouth to what he supplies. It has made an impression on some of the Members of this [Navy] Board and of those of the most Weight.'[141]

Goodrich did not now anticipate a favourable future for him or Bentham. In February 1807 he had written to John Grimshaw that the Board had

'...lately sent down to Portsmouth Dock a Corps of Civil Engineers, consisting of Mr Rennie, Mr Watt, junr, Mr Southern, Watt's partner and Mr Whidby Master Attendant of Woolwich Yard &c accompanied by their Secretary–; to inspect the Works of the Dock – What their immediate object is I cannot say, but I begin to feel, that many unfavorable observations have been made by this Committee of Engineers, respecting the Chain Pumps, Steam Engines, Copper Mills &c &c. Rennie disapproved of every steam Engine excepting Bolton and Watts-'.

He continued:

'Between ourselves the Admiralty have just sent a letter to the General, ordering him positively to return home by the 24th next June, or they shall consider his situation vacant.' Bentham's mission to build ships in Russia had failed, although he was still hopeful in 1806 of obtaining timber.[142]

The General has many enemies who take advantage of his absence and perhaps fear his return....I apprehend that if the General does not come back, the Office will be done away and some of the Members of it put under the Navy Board to assist them, if an opinion good enough of us is entertained for that; but I do not expect at any advanced salary – How can I who am only called a Mechanist pretend to contradict any general assertion of those who are called Engineers?'[143]

Goodrich, having completed the task assigned to him, was transferred with the Naval Works Department to the Navy Board in October 1807. He seems to have established a good relationship with them. He advised Bentham to take the Navy Board offer, reminding him that 'you are Engineer Comm:r and that all Works must go thro' your hands – You will now have an opportunity to show some of the Na. B that you are not that strange creature they may suppose you to be.'[144] Bentham returned to England in November 1807. In August 1808 he agreed to move to the Navy Board because the

alternative was retirement on an inadequate pension.[145]

In 1812 when Goodrich heard that Bentham's office was being abolished he knew his own post would again be at risk. He prepared a memorial for compensation in the loss of office, discovering from Brunel that the Admiralty suspected him of being concerned in Bentham's private business. Despite the Navy Board Comptroller, Sir Thomas Boulden Thompson,[146] telling him that he might be taken on at an increased salary of £600 (actually recommended by the Navy Board in 1811), his position was abolished on 25 December. A proviso that he would be given preference over others when his services were required seems to have ensured that he continued working until April 1814.[147] He was then re-appointed engineer and mechanist to the Navy Board on £600 a year, moving to Portsmouth where he rented Mile End Cottage and later Friends Cottage although he also had an official residence in the dockyard.[148]

Goodrich translated Bentham's *Desiderata* into actuality: those things which Bentham perceived were wanting and required were now in place. From 1805 Portsmouth Dockyard employed around 4,000 of 10,000 artificers in naval dockyards, serving a fleet of 700 ships and 120,000 men. Goodrich ensured its lead in technological innovation, arising through a synergy of politics, geography and technology, exchange of ideas and combined public and private enterprise. Bentham planned the

'...introduction, against great opposition, of steam engines into the dockyards, and the setting up of the wood mills, metal mills, and millwrights' shop, in Portsmouth Dockyard, for the more economical manufacture of naval requirements. The success of these establishments is indicated by the facts that the savings on the blocks made during 1808 was nearly £17,000, while that on the work done in the metal mills during 1812 was nearly £41,000'.

But Goodrich 'carried into effect the various engineering schemes prepared by Bentham'.[149]

Starting as a government draughtsman, he spent his whole career as a government engineer and project manager. The

Newcomen Society noted: 'Goodrich was a good example of the Government official, for he never went anywhere without picking up information.'[150] It is virtually impossible to distinguish where Bentham's initiatives were translated into working machines by Goodrich's endeavours, illustrated in his letters, journals and drawings; they both contributed engineering ideas and skills and collaborated with private engineers Brunel and Maudslay. It was an ongoing process; they tested and modified Boulton and Watt's and Maudslay's engines, making site visits and poaching engineers from private companies as Boulton and Watt had done before.[151]

Postscript

After Bentham left in 1812 Goodrich became the 'prime mover in the industrialisation of the Dockyards.'[152] At Portsmouth he built up a group of skilled engineers, training sons of dockyard workers as steam ship apprentices. In 1822 37 men worked in the Wood Mills, 56 in the Metal Mills, 20 in the Millwright's Shop, 17 in the Engine Shop, 7 in the Smiths' Shop and 8 in the Engine Shed.[153] He continued to visit private manufacturers to assess the most effective machines and parts. From Portsmouth he introduced more steam power at Chatham, Woolwich, Sheerness and Plymouth Dockyards for draining dry docks and for driving mills, forges, tilt hammers, lead and paint shop, cable testing and finally, ships. George Smith, Navy Board Secretary, promoted steam development enthusiastically, and suggested a new steam department headed by Goodrich, the Navy Board investing in an innovative boiler house at Portsmouth in 1830. At the Science Museum website you can see six images, including his model of a tilt hammer, 1802, a plan of Plymouth Dockyard, 1802, a section of a well in Portsmouth Dockyard, 1825 and a diagram of the Deane brothers' diving demonstration to remove the wreck of the *Royal George* from Spithead.[154]

Ironically, Benthamism which had led to his first appointment, and politics which had dogged his career, drove Goodrich into early retirement. With the fall of the Tory government in 1830, whig First Lord of the Admiralty Sir James Graham wielded a retrenching axe. The Navy Board offered Goodrich a job at Somerset House. But in January 1831 he and the Masters of Metal Trades at Portsmouth were discharged with pensions (his was £400, two-thirds of his salary). In March the total dockyard workforce was reduced to 6,000 and nearly all the Masters of Trades were abolished. Goodrich left Portsmouth Dockyard at the end of March, to work briefly as a consultant for the Navy Board until that was abolished the following year, then moved to Portugal in 1834.[155]

When Prime Minister Lord Grey abolished the Navy Board on 1 June 1832 another circle was completed, as he had briefly, as Lord Howick, been first Lord of the Admiralty in 1806. The Admiralty, which had since 1628 tried to dominate the Navy Board through reform, subvention and procedural control, subjugated it finally in 1832 by abolition.[156]

Conclusions

From the seventeenth century the sourcing of naval *matériel* went in cycles: in-house to control quantity and quality; out to private contractors to reduce manpower, costs and risks. Bentham wanted to control the quality and quantity of blocks and copper sheathing within the dockyard *and* save money, whereas the Navy Board wanted the risk to be borne by contractors. For £17,000 paid to Brunel, £12,000 to Maudslay, the initial Admiralty investment of £54,000 and annual running costs,[157] the Block Mills brought quality and production under navy control and produced blocks until 1965. Ironically, through steam-powered processes for making wooden blocks for sailing ships, the Block Mills were arguably the birthplace of the steam-driven navy, by introducing fundamental steam technology and skills to the dockyards.[158]

Family networks and political patronage were embedded within the new structures. Samuel Bentham's pivotal place within dockyard and parliamentary networks enabled his ideals of individual responsibility, classification of labour and central financial control to become enshrined within nineteenth century naval administration.

This was not wholly accomplished while he was in office, but his disciples rose to power in the 1820s, eventually effecting the abolition of the Navy Board in 1832. George Smith, Assistant Secretary to the Navy Board 1807-1813, drove Benthamite changes when Secretary 1820-1832, providing Sir James Graham with the actuarial means to restructure naval administration. Smith retired 11 June 1832.[159] St Vincent, who raged against fraud, made extensive use of his own patronage networks to influence events, especially through the Tucker family.[160]

Task work with its associated classification of personnel could only have been introduced to the largest contemporary industrial workforce once their work had been reduced to measurable, repetitive and de-skilled tasks, with a large clerical staff to classify time-motion studies and record data. The principles of Taylorism[161] (applied to offices, shops and steel mills in the early twentieth century) or Fordism (applied to assembly line production in factories) were employed embryonically in the factories of Boulton and Wedgewood from the 1770s and in the Wood Mills in the early 1800s. The principles involved standardised work, selected workers, successive processes and division of labour, using piecework rates and classification as an incentive to increase output. Wedgewood wrote in 1769 'I have been...preparing to make such *Machines* of the *Men* as cannot err.' James Watt's view was that workers were 'mere acting mechanical powers...it is scarcely necessary that they should use their reason'.[162]

The Block Mills were an early physical embodiment of the number-crunching exercises which led to massive dockyard reductions in the 1820s. As in the Taylor system, they required expert managers to monitor and set norms for performance, quality and output, as men became less craftsmen and more machine operators. The willingness of the men to submit to the new discipline was negotiated through penalties and the prospect of higher earnings. George Smith used figures 'to justify a very large reduction in the number of Shipwrights and others in the Dock Yards at this time', the selection of discharged men made in 1824 as a 'consequence of those mechanics having

petitioned' the Admiralty for more work.[163] Within the dockyards the once recalcitrant but often deferential workforce had to accept nineteenth century discipline because deference could now be enforced where it had once been courted.[164]

So, new labour practices for new machines? Task work was not new, as it had been used before 1694,[165] but by 1805 was being implemented on a wide scale. Goodrich had to blend workers from private industry with dockyard workers, each with their own expectations, until he could 'breed' up his own apprentices. He lost some workers at the beginning. He systematically reviewed current pay rates so that his should be 'fair' to both his workers and the other dockyard workers. Some of the Wood Mills workers were working day work and some piecework; on the whole they were earning more than craftsmen or labourers in the rest of the yard. Problems arose over conditions such as beer, to which Goodrich acceded, and shorter winter dinner breaks so they could finish earlier (because of the fire risks of candles in a wood mill), on which he insisted, but the men did not lose pay. Later he bought lanterns from Grimshaw to get over this problem. Blockmakers as woodworkers received chip money, as chips had been commuted to a payment in 1801, but Metal Mills smiths were also paid allowances (dockyard blacksmiths were paid chip money, but not smiths). Goodrich assessed a situation, set out his reasons and reached a compromise with his workforce, a blend of old and new.

Were the machines new? They were certainly new in being assembled in a dockyard to mass produce blocks by steam power, but in their complexity and aggregation, they were the logical conclusion of at least half a century of increasingly sophisticated power-driven, ordered flow of mechanical processes. Engineers in Europe and America were problem-solving in similar ways and the more they communicated the faster they thought of new solutions.

Like Boulton's or Wedgewood's factories, the Wood Mills attracted the great and the good, who marvelled.[166] As this conference focused on Portsmouth Dockyard in the Age of Nelson, it is only fitting that Nelson himself should have visited the Block Mills, accompanied almost certainly by the ubiquitous Sir Isaac Coffin.[167] On Saturday 14 September 1805, his last day ashore before the Battle of Trafalgar, Goodrich records briefly: 'Lord Nelson in the Dock Yard visits the Wood & Metal Mills.'[168] It is to be hoped that 2005's legacy will bequeath to the future the survival of the unique Block Mills building.

References

1   See J Ehrman, *The younger Pitt*, 3 vols, Constable, London, 1969, 1983, 1996; N A M Rodger, *The insatiable earl*, Norton, London, 1994; G R Barnes, J H Owen, eds, *The private papers of John, Earl Sandwich 1771-1782*, Navy Records Society, 69, 71, 75, 78, London, 1932-1938; N A M Rodger, *The command of the ocean*, Allen Lane/National Maritime Museum, London, 2004, 475-488; J E Talbott, *The pen & ink sailor. Charles Middleton and the king's navy, 1778-1813*, Cass, London, 1998; J K Laughton, ed., *Letters and papers of Charles Lord Barham*, vols I, II, III, Navy Records Society, London, 1906, 1909, 1910.

2   Traditional woodworkers' perquisite of 'Lawfull Chips such as fall from the axe'. N(ational) M(aritime) M(useum), POR/A/101, fos 165-169, 17 October 1698.

3   J M Haas, 'The introduction of task work into the royal dockyards, 1775', *Journal of British Studies*, VIII, 2, 1969, 44-68; J M Haas, 'The royal dockyards; the earliest visitations and reform 1749-1778', *Historical Journal*, XIII, 1970, 191-215; J M Haas, 'The pursuit of political success in eighteenth century England: Sandwich, 1740-1', *Bulletin Institute of Historical Research*, XLIII, 1970, 56-77; J M Haas, 'Methods of wage payment in the royal dockyards 1775-1865', *Maritime History*, 5, 1977, 99-115; J M Haas, 'Work and authority in the royal dockyards from the seventeenth century to 1870', *Proceedings of the American Philosophical Society*, 124, 6, December 1980, 419-428; J M Haas, *A management odyssey: The royal dockyards, 1714-1914*, University Press of America, Maryland, 1994; R J B Knight, 'Sandwich, Middleton and dockyard appointments', *Mariner's Mirror*, 57,, 1971, 179-183; R J B Knight, 'From impressment to task work: strikes and disruption in the royal dockyard, 1688-1788', in A Day, K Lunn, eds, *History of work and labour relations in the royal dockyards*, Mansell, London, 1999, 1-20; R Morriss, *The royal dockyards during the revolutionary and Napoleonic wars*, Leicester University Press, 1983; Talbott, *The pen & ink sailor*, 1998. R J B Knight, *Portsmouth Dockyard Papers 1774-1783: The American War*, Portsmouth Records Series, 6, City of Portsmouth, 1987.

4   R Morriss, *Naval power and British culture*, Ashgate, Aldershot, 2004, 4n.

5   J Coad, *The Portsmouth Block Mills*, English Heritage, Swindon, 2005, 23. Admiralty Inspector General of Naval Works 25 March 1796-28 October 1807, Navy Board Civil Architect and Engineer 3 December 1808-25 December 1812, J C Sainty, *Admiralty officials 1660-1870*, University of London, 1975, 110; J M Collinge, *Navy Board officials 1660-1832*, University of London, 1978, 86.

6   Morriss, *Naval power*, 2004, 4; Coad, *Block Mills*, 2005, 21, 29-31, 63.

7   Coad, *Block Mills*, 2005, 24-27.

8   These findings were submitted to the Privy Council in 1788 and referred to the Admiralty in 1792. Sainty, 1975, 10, 91, 110; Collinge, 1978, 8-12, 19; P K Crimmin, 'The financial and clerical establishment of the Admiralty Office, 1783-1806, *Mariner's Mirror*, LV, 1969, 299-309. See *17th Report on Finance*, 331-332; Rodger, *Command of the ocean*, 2004, 475.

9   1st Lord of the Admiralty 19 Feb 1801-15 May 1804. Sainty, 1975, 149.

10   Morriss, *Naval power*, 2004, 28, 52, 160-162, quoting D Bonner Smith, ed., *The Letters of St Vincent 1801-1804*, II, Navy Records Society, London, 1926, 141, 193-194.

11   P K Crimmin, 'John Jervis, Earl of St Vincent, 1735-1823', in P Le Fevre, R Harding, eds, *Precursors of Nelson. British admirals of the eighteenth century*, Conway, London, 2000, 345-347.

12   T(he) N(ational) A(rchive): P(ublic) R(ecord) O(ffice), ADM42/220, 1774; ADM42/221, 1775; ADM42/222, 1776; Coad, *Block Mills*, 2005, 62-63; Collinge, 1978, 128. At Portsmouth a Henry Peake was Master Boatbuilder 1762-1765 and one was Assistant Master Shipwright 1793-1799 then Master Shipwright 1799-1803. NMM, Dockyard Officers Lists.

13   Coad, *Block Mills*, 2005, 20, 29; SML, GA, Copy S Bentham to Admiralty, 12 April 1800.

14   NA: PRO, ADM7/663, fos 5-5v.

15   First Admiralty secretary from 1783-1795, having started as a Navy Board clerk in 1739, became an Admiralty clerk in 1751. He was appointed Admiralty Commissioner by First Lord Spencer in 1795 aged 70 and created baronet the same year, presumably as a reward for faithful service and over 50 years' experience. Morriss, *Naval power*, 2004, 24; Collinge, 1978, 141; Sainty, 1975, 152.

16   Hon. William Eliot, Admiralty Commissioner 10 July 1800-17 January 1804. Sainty, 1975, 123. A whig friend of Edmund Burke, a Treasury Commissioner March 1807-January 1812.

17   Created Baronet in 1799, Admiralty Commissioner 19 February 1801-15 May 1804, appointed Rear Admiral of the Blue in 1804. Sainty, 1975, 154; D Syrett & R L DiNardo, eds, *The commissioned sea officers of the royal navy 1660-1815*, Navy Records Society, Aldershot, 1994, 445.

18   Captain John Markham, Commissioner 19 February 1801-15 May 1804 and 10 February 1806-6 April 1807. Sainty, 1975, 138. Elder brother of Osborn Markham appointed to the Navy Board by St Vincent in August 1803. He was regarded by them as a spy and refused to support this board's collective letter to the Admiralty in 1804 because he supported the 1803 Admiralty direction that Navy Board commissioners should take on individual responsibilities. Morriss, *Naval power*, 2004, 163, 177-180. A Navy Board Commissioner from 27 August 1803-15 July 1805, when his patent was revoked. Collinge, 1978, 141.

19   A whig, secretary to Henry Dundas in the 1790s, MP for Weymouth and Melcombe Regis 1796 to 1806, Admiralty Commissioner, 19 February 1801-17 January 1804. Sainty, 1975, 126.

20   NA: PRO, ADM7/663, fos 5-43v. Only Markham and Garthshore came to Portsmouth with St Vincent.

21   H W Dickinson, 'The Taylors of Southampton: their ships' blocks, circular saw, and ships' pumps', *Transactions of the Newcomen Society*, 29, 1953, 170-172; K R Gilbert, *Portsmouth Blockmaking Machinery*, HMSO, London, 1965, 2-5. Knight, *Portsmouth Dockyard Papers*, lx, 114, 149.

22   J E Horsley, *Tools of the maritime trades*, David & Charles, Newton Abbot, 1978, 220.

23   Dickinson, 'The Taylors of Southampton', 174; Goodrich visited Dunsterville's Plymouth factory in 1802. E A Forward, 'Simon Goodrich and his work as an engineer - compiled from his journals and memoranda Part I, 1796-1805', *Transactions of the Newcomen Society*, 3, 1922, 7. Dunstervilles were shipwrights at Chatham and Plymouth in the 1770s, when Bentham was a Chatham shipwright apprentice.

24   NA: PRO, ADM7/663, folio 30; Portsmouth Dockyard 1774, British Library, Maps K.Top.XIV.45/2.

25   Coad, *Block Mills*, 2005, 75.

26   NMM, ADMB/206, 22 Dec 1802; 207, 10 Jan 103; 211, 24 Sept 1803; 212, 7 Dec 1803; 214, 21 Mar 1804, 22 Mar 1804. My thanks to B Vale, Naval Dockyards Society Navy Board Project, for researching these letters.

27   NMM, ADMB/217, Navy Board to William Marsden 14 November 1804, enclosure of Taylors to Navy Board, 8 November 1804. (Brian Vale)

28   NMM, ADMB/217, S Taylor to Navy Board, 6 June 1805.

29   Coad, *Block Mills*, 2005, 24, 31.

30   C Drunel Noble, *The Brunels father and son*, Cobden-Sanderson, London, 1938, 10; R Beamish, *Memoir of the life of Sir Marc Isambard Brunel*, Longman, Green, London, 1862, 16.

31   Collinge, 1978, 43, 117; Coad, *Block Mills*, 2005, 51.

32   Dickinson, 'The Taylors of Southampton', 172-175; Forward, 'Goodrich I', 7. Patent 1838. K R Gilbert, *Portsmouth Blockmaking Machinery*, HMSO, London, 1965, 2-4; Coad, *Block Mills*, 2005, 50-53.

33   Coad, *Block Mills*, 2005, 49, 52, 53.

34   NA: PRO, ADM7/663, folios 35v-36, 43v.

35   S(cience) M(useum) L(ibrary), G(oodrich) A(rchive). I cannot praise too highly the help of the Science Museum Librarians, despite 2005 staffing cutbacks.

36   E A Forward, 'Goodrich I', 1-15; E A Forward, 'Simon Goodrich and his work as an engineer - compiled from his journal and memoranda. Part II 1805-1812', *Transactions of the Newcomen Society*, 18, 1937, 1-27; A S Crosley, 'Simon Goodrich and his work as an Engineer (compiled from his journals and memoranda) - Part III, 1813-23', *Transactions of the Newcomen Society*, 32, 1959, 79-92; F S Wilkin, 'The application of emerging new technologies by Portsmouth Dockyard 1790-1815' (PhD, Open University, 1999), *passim*; D Evans, *Building the steam navy*, Conway/English Heritage, London, 2004; Rodger, *Command of the ocean*, 2004, 475; Coad, *Block Mills*, 2005, *passim*.

37   NMM, ADMB/22b, 26 July 1802.
38   NA: PRO, ADM42/220, 1774; ADM42/221, 1775; ADM42/222, 1776.
39   NMM, ADMB/217, Portsmouth Yard to Navy Board, 8 November

1804. Sainty, 1975, 113, 132; Collinge, 1978, 98, 110, 112, 136.

40   Or Goodrick. Coad, *Block Mills*, 2005, 40, 42, 56, 58, 63, 70; Sainty, 1975, 113, 132; Collinge, 1978, 98, 110, 112, 136; Forward, 'Goodrich I', 1. SML, GA, A60, 1802; A206, 18 Feb 1807.

41   My thanks to J Greenwood for family information. SML, GA, A162, 1 Oct 1805. Was Thomas Lloyd, Superintendent of the Block Mills in 1831, his son? Coad, *Block Mills*, 2005, 62, 105-106.

42   Forward, 'Goodrich II', 22, 16.

43   Précis created by the Science Museum Archivist, Robert Sharp.

44   SML, GA, A11, 1797; A65, January 1802; A73, 11 March 1802.

45   Forward, 'Goodrich I', 6; SML, GA, A59; A62, 1802

46   Coad, *Block Mills*, 2005, 23.

47   J Uglow, *The Lunar Men*, Faber, London, 2003, 210-212, 252-257.

48   Forward, 'Goodrich II', 11-12; SML, GA, A251, Goodrich, 5 Sept 1808.

49   Forward, 'Goodrich I', 13. By April 1806 Russia had forbidden this. Even obtaining permission to purchase timber was not certain. SML, GA, A183, W Heard to S Goodrich, 26 April 1806.

50   SML, GA, A153, S Bentham to Admiralty, 30 July 1805.

51   *OED*, quoting S T Coleridge, *c.*1809. Barbara E Rooke, ed., Essay IX, *The Friend* I, 2 volumes, Routledge & Kegan Paul, 1969, 251. 1st eds 1809-1810, 1812, republished 1818-1819.

52   B E Rooke, ed., *The Friend*, 10, 19 October 1809, II, Routledge & Kegan Paul, 1969, 139.

53   SML, GA, A182, Goodrich, 16 April 1806.

54   Or Rehe. Sainty, 92, 147; Coad, *Block Mills*, 2005, 61.

55   Also rebating, the process of grooving boards or fitting rabbeted boards together or preparing boards to receive the edge or end of another piece or pieces or making a tongue to fit the groove.

56   Samuel Reke became ill in 1799, died 16 October. Sainty, 1975, 92, 147; Coad, *Block Mills*, 2005, 61.

57   Measured or prescribed dimensions, thickness and breadth, of a piece of timber.

58   SML, GA A182, S Goodrich, 16 April 1806, folio 11.

59   Forward, 'Goodrich I', 13, 15; Forward, 'Goodrich II', 12, 16.

60   SML, GA B10, Journal 1805, 1 Aug. 1805, folio 1.

61   SML, GA B10, Journal 1805, 7 Aug. 1805, folio 10. The Controller was normally the senior naval officer on the Board, was the only MP allowed on the Board and coordinated all Navy Board business. Hammond was Controller 1794-1806. Collinge, 1978, 5, 14, 21, 107; Rodger, *Command of the ocean*, 2004, 479.

62   SML, GA B10, Journal 1805, 11, 23 Sept. 1805, folios 65, 70.

63   See Admiralty attempts to direct Portsmouth Dockyard officers in 1746. D A Baugh, *British naval administration in the age of Walpole*, Princeton University Press, New Jersey, 1965, 90-91; D A Baugh, ed., *Naval administration 1715-1750*, Navy Records Society, 1977, 21-24, 28-32, 92. In 1804 St Vincent gave port admirals, rather than the Navy Board, the power to decide the order in which ships should be repaired. Morriss, *Royal dockyards*, 1983, 179.

64   SML, GA A187, S Goodrich to S Bentham, 17 May 1806.

65   Forward, 'Goodrich II', 26.

66   Forward, 'Goodrich II', 5-6.

67   Forward, 'Goodrich I', 10-12; SML, GA, A14, Bentham to Admiralty 12 April 1800; A155, Goodrich to Admiralty 30 July 1805.

68   Samuel. Named as suitable for the Metal Mills. SML, GA, A134, Goodrich, 13 Feb 1805.

69   SML, GA A159, Samuel Beach to S Goodrich, 8 Aug 1805.

70   E P Thompson, 'Time, work-discipline and industrial capitalism', *Past and Present*, 38, 1967, 56-97.

71   NMM, ADMB/214, 29 Mar 1804, 12 April 1804. (B Vale)

72   Coad, *Block Mills*, 2005, 70-72; SML, GA A147, Mrs & S Bentham to Goodrich, 30 June 1805.

73   A Coats, 'The œconomy of the navy and Portsmouth. A discourse between the civilian naval administration of Portsmouth Dockyard and the surrounding communities, 1650-1800', DPhil thesis, unpublished, University of Sussex, 2000, 113-114; Morriss, *Royal dockyards*, 1983, 93, 102, 104; Mr. Colquohoun's [*sic*] 'Observations on Naval Embezzlement', *Naval Chronicle*, II, 1799, 390.

74   Before working in Portsmouth James Burr had been in the Royal Navy, then a draftsman, Naval Works Department, 13 May 1796-28

April 1805, when he left office. Sainty, 1975, 93, 114. He had also made machinery for Bentham. Coad, *Block Mills*, 2005, 62.

75   Morriss, *Royal dockyards*, 1983, 24, 102, 115-9, 140, 207; Morriss, *Naval power*, 2004, 31, 45-7, 156-50, 162, 167, 230-232, 243n.

76   A Coats, 'Efficiency in dockyard administration 1660-1800: a reassessment', *Age of Sail*, 1, Conway, London, 2002, 121, *passim*.

77   Labourer who assisted shipwrights by cleaning and pumping the docks.

78   SML, GA B10, Journal, 4 Sept 1805, folio 53-54.

79   SML, GA B10, Journal, 4 Sept 1805, folio 55.

80   SML, GA B10, Journal, 4 Sept 1805, folio 55. Nicholas Diddams, Master Shipwright 1803-1823. The Master Shipwright was also called the Builder.

81   Swage, to shape or bend. *OED*.

82   SML, GA B10, Journal, 4 Sept 1805, folio 55.

83   SML, GA, B10, Journal, folios 57, 64, 65, 70, 5-23 Sept 1805.

84   A roll call, muster of workmen by name at the beginning of the day and when they returned from dinner to check their presence. If late or absent, pay was deducted.

85   A Coats, 'Breakfast and chips – symbols of power relations in Deptford and Woolwich dockyards in the seventeenth and eighteenth centuries', in J R Owen, ed., *Shipbuilding on the Thames and Thames-built ships*, Owen, West Wickham, 2004, 105-122.

86   Forward, 'Goodrich II', 3, 26.

87   SML, GA, A151, Memo Millwrights, 19 July 1805; A152, Millwrights to Mr Linacre, 21 July 1805.

88   Forward, 'Goodrich I', 4, 5.

89   SML, GA, A162, Mr Lloyd, 1 Oct 1805.

90   SML, GA, A164, S Goodrich to Mr Lloyd, 2 Nov 1805.

91   Coad, *Block Mills*, 2005, 70.

92   Forward, 'Goodrich I', 12; 'Goodrich II', 3; SML, GA, A147, Bentham to Goodrich, 30 June 1805.

93   Morriss, *Royal dockyards*, 1983, 101 gives the traditional day rates of all dockyard trades.

94   SML, GA A159, Samuel Beach to S Goodrich, 8 Aug 1805.

95   SML, GA A261, Weekly pay list, 14 Nov 1808.

96   Linacre was dead in 1816. Forward, 'Goodrich II', 11, 24. Coad, *Block Mills*, 2005, 66.

97   SML, GA A159, Samuel Beach to S Goodrich, 8 Aug 1805.

98   Ann Coats, 'The moral economy in action: the Navy Board as a caring seventeenth century employer', Naval Dockyards Society Sixth Annual Conference: *Naval dockyards as employer-employee communities*, 2002.

99   A Coats, 'The œconomy of the navy and Portsmouth', 2000, 13-15.

100   SML, GA, A159, Samuel Beach to S Goodrich, 8 Aug 1805.

101   Forward, 'Goodrich II', 7; SML, GA, A201, 13 Jan 1807; A202, 19 Jan 1807; A204, 22 Jan 1807; A209, 8 March 1807. NMM, Dockyard Officers Lists: Hamlet Vernon Master of the Metal Mills 1814-1830.

102   Forward, 'Goodrich II', 6.

103   SML, GA, A261, Weekly wages, 14 Nov 1808.

104   Morriss, *Royal dockyards*, 1983, 103. Multiplying d x 6 days/week; d x 333 days/year (excl. Sundays).

105   Morriss, *Royal dockyards*, 1983, 103; SML, GA A235, Goodrich to Henry Peake, Surveyor of the Navy, 12 Feb 1808; A261, Weekly certificate of wages, 14 Nov 1808. Stint, a restriction on the work allowed.

106   Forward, 'Goodrich II', 15.

107   SML, GA B10, Journal, 2 Aug 1805.

108   SML, GA A163, Present State of the Wood Mills by Mr Brunel, 3 Oct 1805; Forward, 'Goodrich I', 8.

109   2nd Admiralty Secretary 3 Mar 1795-21 Jan 1804, 1st Secretary 21 Jan 1804-24 June 1807 when he retired. Sainty, 1975, 36, 139. Marsden served two whig ministries and one tory ministry and was a distinguished orientalist scholar, so may be characterised as a public rather than political servant. In 1831 he gave up his Admiralty pension of £1,500 a year, an indication of his views on whig cuts to naval expenditure? See footnote 116.

110   *Memoir of the Life of William Marsden*, 1838, 103-104, quoted Morriss, *Naval power*, 2004, 162-163.

111 SML, GA A187, Goodrich to Bentham, 17 May 1806. Thomas Darch, First Clerk at the Admiralty Naval Works Department, 1796-1800, Extra Clark 19 Dec 1800-3 May 1804, Junior Clerk 3 May 1804-1816. Sainty, 1975, 93, 120; NA: PRO, ADM7/820, p. 06.

112 Rodger, *Command of the ocean*, 2004, 475-481; Sainty, 1975, 26.

113 SML, GA A189, Marsden to Goodrich, 18 June 1806.

114 'Annason', query *Amazon*. I am grateful to P Ashley for identifying *Amazon* prize, *Subtile*, taken 1746, re-named *Amazon*, 38 guns, 1,038tons (bm), 150 x 39.5 ft, the 5th of 10 ships to date named *Amazon*. T D Manning, C F Walker, *British Warships' Names*, Putnam, London, 1959.

115 SML, GA, A190, S Goodrich to W Marsden, 19 June 1806.

116 Marsden's brother John was his partner in the East India agency they established in Gower Street in 1785 after returning from working for the East India Company in Sumatra since 1770.

117 SML, GA, A190, S Goodrich to W Marsden, 19 June 1806.

118 An engineer as well. Forward, 'Goodrich II', 2; Coad, *Block Mills*, 2005, 73.

119 Charles Grey, Viscount Howick, later Earl Grey and leader of the whig administration in 1830. Sainty, 1975, 26, 128; N A M Rodger *Admiralty*, Dalton, Lavenham, 1979, 69, 97-98.

120 SML, GA A197, Goodrich to Mr Grimshaw, 20 Oct 1806; Rodger *Admiralty*, 1979, 85-86.

121 SML, GA A197, Goodrich to Mr Grimshaw, 20 Oct 1806.

122 Heigham Rogers, 1st Clerk Naval Works Department, 5 July 1804-28 October 1807, when he transferred to the Navy Board as Clerk Secretary's Department, employed at the Navy Board until 1829. Sainty, 1975, 93, 148; Collinge, 1978, 135.

123 Henry Dundas, 1st Viscount Melville, First Lord of the Admiralty 15 May 1804-2 May 1805. He had resigned prior to being impeached in April 1806 for financial irregularities while Treasurer of the Navy, 1782-1800, discovered by St Vincent's Commission of Naval Enquiry's 10th Report, Jan 1805; acquitted June 1806.

124 Admiral William Young, under Spencer and in Pitt's ministry a junior naval Admiralty Commissioner 20 Nov 1795-19 Feb 1801. Sainty, 1975, 26, 159.

125 1st Admiralty Secretary, 21 Jan 1804-24 June 1807, when he retired.

126 SML, GA A209, Mr Rogers to Goodrich, 8 March 1807. Grenfell and Williams were copper contractors.

127 Rear Admiral Sir Isaac Coffin (1759-1839), (Bart 1804), commissioner of Halifax Dockyard 1799-1800, Sheerness Dockyard 1801-1804, appointed Rear Admiral of the White April 1804, created baronet May 1804, Rear Admiral of the Red November 1805. A whig, patronised by St Vincent since 1798, he shared and collaborated in St Vincent's reforming aspirations for dockyards. Syrett & DiNardo, *Commissioned sea officers*, 1994, 89; Morriss, *Royal dockyards*, 1983, 92, 93, 142, 144, 149, 153, 177-179.

128 Engineer and partner in Messrs Whitmore & Norton of Birmingham who built weighing machines; worked as an engineer on the Stratford-upon-Avon Canal (opened 1816); Forward, 'Goodrich I, 10-11.

129 Coad, *Block Mills*, 2005, 66. House of Commons Committee into the State of the Copper Mines and Copper Trade of this Kingdom 'Copper mines and copper trade of this Kingdom', Session 1798-1799, vol. 54, House of Commons, 7 May 1799, 520; 'The Copper Mines and Copper Industry of the United Kingdom', House of Commons Reports X, *British Parliamentary Papers*, 5 April 1799, 651-728.

130 The situation was not helped by inflation rates at the end of the eighteenth century of around 40%.

131 (1730-1802) MP for Marlow in Berkshire where he owned Temple Mills copper works. Cornish production rose from 1798 as Anglesey sales declined. After his death his mines were bought cheaply by John Vivian, his Cornish rival, and production prolonged by deep mining expertise facilitated by steam driven pumps. See J R Harris, *'The Copper King', A Biography of Thomas Williams of Llanidan*, Liverpool University/University of Toronto Press, 1964.

132 SML, GA A217, W Whitmore to Goodrich, 4 July 1807.

133 NMM, ADMBP/24a, 1803-1804; ADMB/214, 20 Mar 1804. (B Vale)

134 NMM, ADMB/217, 5 Jan 1805; NMM, ADMBP, 24a, 5 May 1804.

135 NMM, ADMB/217, 16 Feb 1805.

136 SML, GA A217, W Whitmore to Goodrich, 4 July 1807.

137 SML, GA A234, Henry Peake to Goodrich, 10 Feb 1808.

138 SML, GA A219, Brunel to Goodrich, 3 Sept 1807.

139 Forward, 'Goodrich I', 8; Coad, *Block Mills*, 2005, 63; Gilbert, *Block Making Machinery*, 1965, 6.

140 Dickinson, 'The Taylors of Southampton', 175-177; Gregory Clark, 'The Royal Navy's blockmaking boffins', *Proceedings of US Naval Institute Press*, Annapolis, Maryland, nd, *c*1980. My thanks to Cdr J Bingeman for giving me a typescript copy.

141 SML, GA A234, Henry Peake to Goodrich, 19 Feb 1808.

142 Forward, 'Goodrich II', 4; SML, GA, A183, Wm Heard in Russia to Goodrich, 26 April 1806. He was Goodrich's draughtsman 1814-1830, NMM Dockyard Officers Lists.

143 SML, GA, A208 23 Feb 1807.

144 SML, GA A223, Goodrich to Bentham 30 Nov 1807.

145 Forward, 'Goodrich II', 10, 11.

146 Controller 20 June 1806-24 Feb 1816. Collinge, 1978, 21, 143.

147 Sainty, 1975, 10, 92, 103, 127; Collinge, 1978, 32, 104; NA: PRO, PC2/194, pp. 67–70, Order-in-Council 28 November 1812.

148 Correspondence indicates that he was very close to Quakers. SML, GA, B70, 1830, inside front cover 'Friend Wm Allen Paradise Row Stoke Newington'. (J Greenwood) NA: PRO, ADM 7/819 lists of officers 1816; ADM7/861, lists of officers 1828; Forward, 'Goodrich I', 1; A P Woolrich, *Simon Goodrich (1773-1847)*, *Biographical Dictionary of Civil Engineers*, I, 2002; *Oxford Dictionary of National Biography*, 2004; Wikipedia www.en.wikipedia.org.

149 Forward, 'Goodrich I', 2, 7.

150 Forward, 'Goodrich I', 14.

151 Forward, 'Goodrich I', 8, 14; Uglow, *Lunar men*, 2003, 210-215, 290-291; SML, GA, A134, 13 Feb 1805; NMM, ADMB/219, 15, 17 July 1805.

152 Evans, *Building the steam navy*, 2004, 15.

153 Crossley, 'Goodrich III', 90.

154 www.scienceandsociety.co.uk I am indebted to J Greenwood for this information.

155 Evans, *Building the steam navy*, 2004, 15-27.

156 Forward, 'Goodrich II', 24.

157 Forward, 'Goodrich I', 8; Coad, *Block Mills*, 2005, 6, 99, 110.

158 Evans, *Building the steam navy*, 2004, 15.

159 2 & 3 Will IV.c.40, June 1832, The *Act to Amend the Laws relating to the business of the Civil Department of the Navy*, abolishing the Navy Board, was passed in June 1832. Morriss, *Naval Power*, 2004, viii, 150, 194-8, 201-2; O A R Murray, 'The Admiralty', VI, *Mariner's Mirror*, 24, 1938, 329-352; Sainty, 1975, 110; Collinge, 1978, 86, 139; NA: PRO, ADM7/821, fo 64.

160 R(oyal) N(aval) M(useum) A(dmiralty) L(ibrary) M(anuscript) C(ollection), MSS 259, Papers of Admiral Sir John Jervis.

161 Frederick Taylor, *The principles of scientific management*, Harper Bros, New York, 1911.

162 Wedgewood Archives, Special Collections, University of Keele, J Wedgewood to T Bentley, 9 September 1769, W. E25-18265; J Watt, Minutes of the Evidence, Committee of House of Lords (1785), 252, 253; quoted Uglow *Lunar Men*, 2003, 213-217, 466.

163 NA: PRO, ADM106/3371, July 1822, No1 Mcmd:m on the orders for reducing the Establishments at the Dock Yards; No2 Memdm in continuation of No1 in the late orders for reducing the Establishments at the Dock Yards, orders of 22d Aug 1822; RNMALMC, MSS 302/14, np, Admiralty Orders 18 & 21 December 1824, 'Mechanics in the Dock Yards'. My thanks to Chris Donnithorne for the last reference.

164 Morriss, *Naval power*, 2004, 233-235; Evans, *Building the steam navy*, 2004, 23.

165 A Coats, 'Efficiency in dockyard administration', 2002, 123-125.

166 Uglow *Lunar Men*, 2003, 20, 210-212, 376, 399; Coad, *Block Mills*, 2005, 12-13, 96-99, 101-102.

167 R J B Knight, *The Pursuit of Victory. The life and achievement of Horatio Nelson* (Penguin, London, 2005), 500.

168 SML, GA, B10, Journal, 14 Sept 1805, fo. 66. Researched by A P Woolrich, announced by Jonathan Coad, English Heritage Buchanan Seminar, Swindon 19 Nov 2004. Coad, *Block Mills*, 2005, 12, 101.

Dr Ann Coats, *is at the School of Environmental Design and Management, University of Portsmouth.*

MARC BRUNEL'S PULLEY BLOCK-MAKING MACHINERY: OPERATION AND ASSESSMENT

Ray Riley

Abstract

The importance of Marc Brunel's pulley block-making machinery for naval vessels is widely known and therefore needs no rehearsing. Less understood is the significance of the machines themselves in the history of technology. This paper describes the operation of those machines held in the Science Museum, London, and at Portsmouth Dockyard, and endeavours to assess their innovatory characteristics. It is argued that while many, but not all, of the principles were already in the public domain, it was Brunel's genius, with some possible assistance, that caused them to be refined and collectively employed in what must be regarded as a major technological leap forward.

Introduction

For most historians Marc Brunel's pulley block-making machinery is seen variously within the framework of the industrialisation process, or more specifically, the beginnings of mass production and deskilling, or the emergence of the machine tool industry, or the cost effective measures brought to bear on naval shipbuilding. Seldom do the machines themselves – there were 45 constructed between 1801 and 1808 – receive attention, and then largely from disciplines other than history. The definitive work is the monograph by Gilbert[1] who was a mechanical engineer. The aim of this brief paper is to examine the 14 Brunel machines held by the Science Museum, London, and in Portsmouth Dockyard, with a view to explaining in simple terms how they worked. Emphasis will be placed on their main features and comments made on their innovatory characteristics. It is not intended to introduce biographical and other background details since they are widely known. The contribution made by Henry Maudslay, arguably the finest machine tool-maker of his day, is merely noted since the extent of his advice is unclear, although it is generally thought that it was Maudslay's ability to interpret Brunel's drawings which

rendered the whole project viable. There is also a strong possibility that Samuel Bentham and Simon Goodrich, who was mechanist to the Navy Board, made a contribution to the machines.[2] Indeed, since all four worked closely together during the years when the machines were being manufactured, it is justifiable to suggest that the outcome was the product of four minds, with Brunel the leading light. Some preliminary remarks may be helpful. It is sometimes thought that Brunel's machines were automatic, requiring operatives only to start and stop them. This was hardly the case, rather the machines represented a transition phase between hand and automatic production. They were therefore semi-automatic; in every case, save one, which was fully automatic, and a second which was operated manually without the aid of a lever, operatives controlled the machines by activating levers. It is worth noting that Walter Taylors' (father and son) block mill at Southampton, whose contract was terminated as a result of Brunel's machines, contained some semi-automatic machines, although they were relatively unsophisticated. However, it would be incorrect to suggest that Brunel was responsible for the introduction of machine tools, rather it was a gradual process. Hence the assertion that his machines represented the first example of metal, as opposed to wooden, machine tools.

In essence, the machines reflect the stages in the manufacture of pulley blocks. They may be grouped into three separate processes. Firstly, the production of the shell, that is, the wooden frame containing the pulley wheels. The shells were fabricated in six stages: sawing the log, boring a hole for the pulley wheel axle, making an aperture to take the pulley wheel, smoothing of the shell in two stages, and gouging a recess to take the rope from which the shell was suspended. Secondly, the making of the pulley wheel or sheave in three stages: sawing the log, giving it a rounded form and at the same time utting a hole in the centre, and finally making a setting to take the metal bearing or coak for the axle. The third process concerned the manufacture of the axles or pins on which the pulley wheel rotated; since no pin-making machines appear to have survived the process is not described in this paper. Different sized pulley blocks could be made and some of the machines were sized accordingly, although their mode of operation remained unchanged. No attempt is therefore made to distinguish between the variously sized machines.

The Manufacture of Shells

1. Sawing Logs

The cutting of logs was traditionally carried out by sawyers in a saw pit, an arduous and slow process. The Taylors at Southampton c.1765 used a horse-driven wheel to which was attached a crank linked to a traditional saw,[3] and Bentham patented a circular fixed saw in 1793.[4] Brunel, however, employed a circular pendulum saw which could be adjusted through levers to saw the sides and top of logs, thereby making it possible to saw logs of greater diameter than previous arrangements. Power was delivered through belting tensioned by jockey rollers, enabling the saw assembly to be moved while sawing was in progress. The literature on belting is sparse; it is possible that its use in this manner was novel. The principle of a mobile circular saw certainly was.

2. Boring

The boring machine drilled the hole for the pivot pin on which the sheave rotated. Taylor had taken out a patent in 1762, but as Pannell remarks, this was primitive,[5] even if it did embody some of the principles later used by Brunel. In his machine the drill was mounted on a slide; the drill was pushed home via a long lever worked by the operator. To accommodate shells of different sizes the slide could be moved at right angles to the line of the drill by worm gear turned by the operator (Figure 1). The use of metal in the slide, worm gear and framework made for great precision, although it is likely that the accuracy of the worm gear owed much to Maudslay and Joseph Bramah from their 1794 slide rest for holding metal being cut by a lathe.[6]

Fig. 1. The boring machine held in the Science Museum, showing the mechanism for drilling a hole for the sheave pin.

A further novel feature of the boring machine was that the same frame was employed for a second drilling operation, this time to make the starter holes for the chisels of the mortising engine, which cut the space for the sheave. Taylor's practice had been to make use of a circular saw as a start, and then to cut out the waste by hand chisel.[7] To overcome the problem posed by different sized blocks, the drill was moved vertically into position though gearing worked by the operator (Figure 2). Brunel used this stage to make locating marks on the shell while it was clamped to facilitate positioning in the later mortising and shaping machines.[8]

Fig. 2. The boring machine held in the Science Museum. On the left is the drill for making a hole for the chisel of the mortising engine; the mechanism for setting the vertical position of the drill is clearly visible.

A comparison of the boring machines in the Science Museum and in Portsmouth dockyard reveals that while both bear the same characteristics, they are not identical. For instance, the drive wheels for the drills are different, and in the Portsmouth example the levers moving the drills into the shells are pivoted at a common point enabling the table to be shaped as the segment of a

Fig. 3. The Portsmouth boring machine showing push levers and drive wheels which are different from those in the Science Museum machine.

further difference between the two machines concerned the drive belts. The Science Museum example has conventional flat belting driving flanged wheels, whereas in the Portsmouth case the machine has circular, leather belting. The latter is unusual and may have represented an attempt to prevent the belt from slipping off the wheels as the drill moved into the shell.

3. Mortising

The space, or mortice, in the shell for the sheave was begun as has been noted above in the second stage of the boring machine. By means of chisels the mortising machine simply completed the process; a vertically set chisel, or twin chisels in the Science Museum example, cut into the shell and on its withdrawal the shell moved forward to receive the next downward stroke (Figure 4). To use the word 'simply' is in one sense highly inappropriate since not only was the mortising machine the largest machine tool to have been built, but also in all probability it was the world's first fully automatic machine. In the other Brunel machines, with exception of one which was worked manually, the operator contributed to the actual process

circle(Figure 3); the levers in the Science Museum example are pivoted separately and the table is rectangular. Furthermore, the detailing on the Science Museum machine appears more sophisticated. One possible reason for the differences is that the Portsmouth example was manufactured first, improvements in the design of the second being made in the light of experience. It is hardly surprising that experimentation should take place given the innovatory nature of the machinery. The smaller size of the Portsmouth machine probably indicates that it was employed to bore smaller shells. A

Fig. 4. The Portsmouth mortising machine illustrating the flywheel, cone clutch and lever, the cam on the drive shaft activating the carriage holding the shell, the crosshead and the single chisel.

by working levers; in this case all he did was to start and stop the machine and remove and replace the shell. A powerful indication of the technological leap made by the machine was its speed of operation. It was capable of up to 400 strokes a minute, far outstripping the ability of a craftsman.[9] Curiously enough, all the mechanical principles were already in the public domain, but it required someone of Brunel's vision to combine them in a single machine. Four aspects are worth considering.

Firstly, because of the need to ensure even running in a machine where the downward application of the chisels was intermittent, a substantial flywheel was fitted. It was the intermittent pumping action of beam engines that had led James Watt to introduce a flywheel in his experimental rotative beam engine of 1779,[10] although the principle

Fig. 5. The mortising machine at the Science Museum showing provision for twin chisels, the crank and on the right the lever operating the cone clutch.

appears in a sketch by that towering genius, Leonardo da Vinci, drawn c.1480-2.[11] Secondly, in order to overcome the inertia of the working parts, and to allow the drive to be disconnected from the flywheel when

changing shells, a cone clutch mechanism operated by a lever was inserted between the flywheel and the main drive shaft. The principle of the clutch, or friction drive, had long been known to millwrights, for example, who had incorporated it into windmills in order to allow the drive to be taken up without stopping the sails and windshaft. Much later Taylor used the notion, causing his machines to be independent of the horse gin which powered them.[12] However, Brunel's modification is thought to be the first instance of a cone clutch.[13] Thirdly, the problem of converting the rotary movement of the drive shaft to the vertical movement needed for operation of the chisel was solved by fitting a crank to the end of the drive shaft. The crank was linked to the chisel by a connecting rod enabling the chisel to move vertically through slide bars (Figure 5). The principle of the crank appeared in a sketch made in 1480-2 by Leonardo da Vinci;[14] it had been applied to wood turning lathes in the 17th century,[15] and was certainly used by the Taylors to drive their horizontal saw in the 1760s.[16] The patent was taken out by James Pickard in 1780.[17] The use of slide bars and crosshead to ensure linear motion was also not new. Watkins believes that it was invented by William Murdoch, an employee of Boulton and Watt, probably in the 1790s.[18] Maudslay used the principle in his table engines which were contemporary with Brunel's design, and of course possibly influenced by them. Fourthly, the movement of the carriage holding the shell was synchronised with the stroke of the chisel by employing a ratchet wheel which was turned by one tooth for each revolution of a cam on the drive shaft; the

Fig. 6. The corner saw at Portsmouth. The two wooden blocks are a later modification.

wheel was linked to a screw causing the carriage to move forward. The cam was a medieval, or earlier, device used for instance in fulling mills to drive fulling stocks, tilt hammers in metal working, and ore crushing stamps illustrated in Agricola's *De Re Metallica,* 1556, while the ratchet principle had been used by clock makers for some time. The mortising machine is thus an excellent example of Brunel's skill in harnessing known technological principles and adapting them for his own purposes.

As in the case of the boring machines, the Science Museum and the Portsmouth mortising machines exhibit a number of differences, quite apart from the smaller scale and single chisel of the Portsmouth example. In the Portsmouth machine the jockey roller is mounted on a strip of looped flexible metal, the roller being forced to follow the cam by a piece of cord suspended from a spring. This inelegant solution is avoided in the Science Museum machine by means of a counterbalance. The shell is clamped on the carriage by three worm rods in the Portsmouth machine, but by only one in the Science Museum case. The latter difference may not be of great import, but the rather primitive use of a cord to tension the jockey roller would suggest that the Portsmouth machine was the prototype.

4. Corner Sawing

The smallest range of shells was shaped by a corner saw. Shells mounted on an inclined rest were presented to a circular saw set vertically and moved against it by the operator without the aid of levers. This was the simplest of Brunel's machines, but even

Fig. 8. The scoring machine at the Science Museum. The rotating gouges, former and two levers may be seen.

here there was an indication of his thoughtful approach, for the base of the rest incorporated bars which ensured that it was always parallel to the saw should the distance be altered (Figure 6).

5. Shaping

Fig. 7. The shaping machine at the Science Museum. The shells are rotated by rods with worm gear at one end and by bevel gear at the main axle end. The gouge mechanism is on the left.

Thus far, with the exception of the small shells shaped by the corner saw, the shell is still angular; its distinctive smooth contours are imparted by the shaping machine. In this ingenious device, 10 shells are clamped between two wheels (Figure 7). As they rotate the shells themselves are caused to rotate so that at each revolution of the wheels a different part of the shell is presented to the gouge or cutter. The gouge can be moved in two planes by levers worked by the operator: proximity to the shells and lateral positioning by moving the gouge on a frame whose curvature is that of the shell. The principle of adjusting the position of the gouge has been seen in the boring machine, but what makes the shaping machine novel is the use of bevel and worm gears to rotate the shells while the two wheels between which they are clamped are themselves rotating. This is achieved by a bevel gear wheel mounted on the main drive shaft, driving 10 spindles at the end of each there is worm gearing which causes the clamps and hence the shells to rotate.

Cast iron gear wheels incorporating a bevel shape, replacing the Greco-Roman wooden lantern gearing, in which the teeth meshed with each other at right angles, were probably first made by John Smeaton c.1750.[19] A drawing by Leonardo da Vinci dated about 1500 depicts worm gearing;[20] wooden worm gears were almost certainly used to rotate windmill caps in the 18th century, and has been pointed out above, metal worm gearing had been pioneered by Maudslay and Bramah. However the use of bevel and worm gearing in combination is likely to have been a Brunel innovation. The motion could be stopped by means of a friction brake comprising a simple metal band depressed by the operator, although in the absence of a clutch the belting itself must have been disconnected from the layshaft to allow the machine to cease turning. This friction brake also pre-dated Brunel, being used in windmills to slow or stop the rotation of the windshaft.

6. Scoring

Fig. 9. The scoring machine at Portsmouth, in situ in the Block Mills in 1968. The wheel-driven worm rods are in contrast with the machine in the Science Museum.

The final shell-making process scores a groove in the shell to take the rope by which it is suspended. By comparison with mortising and shaping, scoring is a relatively unsophisticated process, but one which may nevertheless have incorporated a novel principle, that is, the use of a wooden guide or former whose edge was shaped to the required profile, and which is followed by the rotating gouges. In the Science Museum example twin gouges are mounted on a common shaft, the centre of which follows the former as the operator works a lever causing the shells to move against the gouges. The wooden former may easily be changed to allow different sized shells to be scored. A second lever enabled the gouge assembly to be disengaged (Figure 8). In the Portsmouth

example there is a single gouge, but more interestingly, in place of the lever causing the gouge to follow the former is a wheel and worm rod altering the position of the former. A second worm rod is employed to press the shell into position. The use of wheel driven worm rods suggests that the Portsmouth machine was made after that at the Science Museum (Figure 9).

The Manufacture of Sheaves
1. Sawing Logs

As in the case of sawing logs for the shells, Brunel's solution for the manufacture of sheaves or pulley wheels was a mobile or swing arm circular saw, but in this case set in a horizontal plane, the lignum vitae log from which the sheave is made being vertical. With his left hand the operator works a lever which, through geared wheels, causes the log to rotate, while with his right hand he moves the saw into the log. The height of the log can be adjusted by manually turning a spoked

Fig. 10. The swing arm circular saw used for cutting lignum vitae logs for sheaves in Portsmouth Block Mills. The frame for adjusting the height of the log can be seen between the two main upright columns.

wheel which is pivoted on a worm rod, itself attached to a frame between the two main upright columns of the machine. Uniquely of all the block-making machinery one of these saws is still in its original position in the Portsmouth block mills since it is secured into both ceiling and floor. The same remarks regarding earlier circular saws apply: previous saws were fixed and so did not require a flexible belt drive system. Figure 10 shows the Portsmouth saw in situ in the Block Mills.

2. Rounding

Fig. 11. The rounding saw at the Science Museum. The lever controls the horizontal movement of the cutter and drill. The larger drive wheel works the cutter against which may be seen the rough wood towards the right end of the main shaft.

The rounding saw cut the lignum vitae section to give it circular form and ingeniously at the same time bored a hole through it to take the axle, or pin, for the sheave. This was achieved by having the drill operating within the shaft driving the circular saw-toothed cutter. Both the drill and the circular cutter advanced at the same speed by virtue of a long lever depressed by the operator. Both drill and cutter rotated at different speeds, this being achieved through independent drive wheels of different sizes, the larger driving the cutter, which thus rotated more slowly than the drill (Figure 11). As has been observed, the Taylor patent on boring dated from 1762, but the notion of a circular cutter was almost certainly new, as indeed was the combination of drill and cutter, enabling the machine to do the work of two. There was consequently a saving of both capital and labour costs. Since the operations were carried out simultaneously, in this sense the rounding machine was an

advance on the boring machine where the two processes were carried out sequentially.

3. Coaking

Fig. 12. The coaking machine at the Science Museum. The sheave with its three 'necked' coak in place is visible in the centre.

The coaking machine drilled three recesses in the sheave to take the metal coak or bearing for the pivot or pin. The sheave was rotated beneath the drill through 120 degrees exactly to match the three 'necks' of the coak. This apparently simple step was an important stage in the development of mass production for it meant that each coak would match any sheave, something which was not easily achieved in craft manufacture. The speed of advance of the drill was determined by downwards pressure exerted on a lever by the operator, while the positioning of the sheave under the drill was also worked by a lever mechanism. The rotation of the drills in the boring and rounding machines caused no difficulties since the drills were in the horizontal plane rendering it a simple matter to power them by belting from an overhead layshaft; in this instance the drill was vertical, requiring the belting to be taken through a right angle. This was achieved by two guide pulleys, a solution which may have been novel, a literature search having failed to locate an earlier example of the arrangement (Figure 12). However, the use of a metal coak as a bearing, thus substantially prolonging the life of the sheave, had been previously developed by Taylor.[21] For no apparent reason the coaking machine was accorded a measure of ostentation, its belt guides being made of brass, and the frame being surmounted by brass finials.

Conclusion

While recognising that the finished machines were the work of Maudslay, and that it is reasonable to suppose that he, and almost certainly Bentham and Goodrich, had a role in the interpretation of Brunel's original designs and conceivably also in the modification thereof, it seems clear that the various principles incorporated in the block-making machinery were either Brunel's extensions of existing techniques, or his own creations. It is reasonable to suppose that Brunel was familiar with the work of Da Vinci, and doubtless of other contemporary engineering developments, but in any event it was his genius to bring the old and the innovatory together in what must be regarded as a major technological leap forward in the process of mass production. Had Brunel's other machines been available for inspection, arguably further insights into his inventiveness would have been possible.

References

1. Gilbert, K.R., *The Portsmouth Blockmaking Machinery*, HMSO, 1965.

2. Wool rich, A.P., 'Portsmouth Block Mills', English Heritage Seminar, Swindon, 2004.

3. Pannell, J.P.M., 'The Taylors of Southampton: Pioneers in Mechanical Engineering', *Proceedings of the Institution of Mechanical Engineering*, 169, 1955, fig.4.

4. Rowland, K.T., *Eighteenth Century Inventions*, David & Charles, 1974, 84.

5. Pannell, *op.,cit.*, 927.

6. Rowland, *op.cit.*, *86*.

7. Pannell, *op.,cit.*, 928.

8. Gilbert, *op.cit.*,12.

9. Strandh, Sigvard, *Machines: An Illustrated History*, Nordbok, 1979, 57.

10. Rowland, *op.cit.*, *29*.

11. Rolt, L.T.C., *Tools for the Job. A History of Machine Tools to 1950*, HMSO, 1986, 34.

12. Pannell, *op.cit.*, *926*.

13. Gilbert, *op.,cit.*,12

14. Rolt, *op.,cit.*, 34.

15. Rowland, *op.cit.*, *29*.

16. Pannell, *op.,cit.*, plate 2.

17. Rowland, *op.cit,*. 29.

18. Watkins, George, *The Stationary Steam Engine*, David & Charles, 1968, 12.

19. Rolt, *op.cit.*, *130*.

20. *Ibid.*, 33.

21. Pannell, *op.cit.*, *926*.

Acknowledgements

The author is most grateful for the assistance of Ben Russell, Curator of Mechanical Engineering and Manufacture at the Science Museum, London, in establishing the modus operandi of the machines in his care, and for the comments of an anonymous referee.

Dr. Ray Riley *is Associate Director of the Institute of Maritime and Heritage Studies at the University of Portsmouth.*

PORTSMOUTH YARD AND TOWN IN THE AGE OF NELSON (1758-1805) – A RELATIONSHIP EXAMINED

James H. Thomas

Abstract

During Nelson's lifetime a tortuous relationship developed between Portsmouth, Portsea and the dockyard. Admiralty and military interests, urban authoprity, religion and institutional landowners influenced late Georgian Portsmout. A symbiotic thouf the relationship was bewteen yard and town, an international trading ventures made the situation even more delocate. War's demands and the desire for yard reforms were not always compatible. Dockyard workers, changing over time, their lifestyles, and complex relationships are delineated against a backdrop of tensions.

Late in April 1805 Hampshire's county newspaper carried the following item:

The Directors of the Hants, Sussex, and Dorset Fire Insurance Company have presented Mr. Collins, of the Victualling-office, Portsmouth, with a silver cup, value five guineas, with a suitable inscription, as an acknowledgement of his active exertions at a fire which lately broke out in the dwelling-house of Thomas Sharpe, Esq. in the High-street, Portsmouth.[1]

At first sight, such an entry would appear to be slight. On further consideration, however, it reveals something of the links between yard and town, of the threat of fire to both and of an insurance venture's role in Nelsonian Portsmouth. Employing, at its height, more than 500 men, the Victualling Office was an important institution in eighteenth-century Portsmouth, but only one of many. While the yard existed to build, repair and fit out ships, vessels such as the Indiamen *Hartwell* and *Belvidere*, fitted out following their launch at Itchenor in April and May 1787,[2] and the 14-gun brig launched at Hythe in late May 1805,[3] it had acquired a momentum and grandeur of its own. By 1774 the yard had six docks – North Dock, North and South Basin Dock, the Double Dock and South Dock, beautifully modelled by shipwrights for George III that year.

Increased numbers were drawn to working in the yard which soon became the largest local employer on Portsea Island and a fine national example of early large scale employment. Its significance was summed up pithily in a 1774 survey of royal dockyards:

The Dock Yard is situated on an Island and inclosed with so strong a Fortification as to render it securer and more defensible against an Enemy than any other in the Kingdom .... It has a more spacious and safer Roadstead before the Harbour than any other in England or indeed than any other known in the World, so that the greatest Fleets and Convoys may Rendezvous and lay there in perfect safety.[4]

The yard had also become a tourist 'must' for those who flocked to Portsmouth in increasing numbers, being drawn by the Fleet Reviews of 1773 and 1778 and to witness the return of Black Dick Howe's victorious forces in June 1794.[5] Visiting diplomats included the outgoing ambassadors from Morocco and Tripoli in July 1774 and from the latter in late April 1787, weighed down with £15,000 worth of gifts, mostly destined for his master the Bey, and the Russian Ambassador and his wife in mid-November 1790. Late in December 1803 the imposing Elfi Bey, the 'Mameluke Chief', toured the site and was suitably impressed. So, too, was Mirza Abul Hassan Khan, the Persian Shah's representative, who was taken to see the yard's new blockmills in mid-July 1810. 'The yard contains', he observed, 'some 100 steam-powered machines, which only two years ago had to be operated by hand'.[6] Royalty visited too. The Prince of Monaco was shown round the yard complex in May 1768; in September 1786, it was the turn of the Duke of Palma, the Holy Roman Emperor's brother, while in October 1800 the Prince and Princess of Orange paid a visit. The Prince and Princess of Wales, visiting in 1803 and 1805 respectively, were followed by the Margravine of Anspach and the Duc de Berri[7]. During July 1794 Franz Joseph Haydn (1732-1809), needing a holiday, journeyed to Portsmouth, and endeavoured to tour the dockyard, only to be told that he "could not go there, because I am a foreigner".[8] Moreover, much of this activity had taken place at the height of the prolonged struggle against Revolutionary and Napoleonic France.

Opinions as to the people who worked in the dockyard and lived either in the town or its burgeoning satellite of Portsea varied considerably. The Southampton-born itinerant cleric Dr. Richard Pococke (1704-1765) waxed lyrical in 1754 at seeing the yard workforce, between 1,000 and 1,500 strong, 'go out at the toll of a bell at noon and night'. James Wolfe, by contrast, referred to 'the diabolical citizens of Portsmouth' adding, almost as an afterthought, 'It is a doubt to me if there is such another collection of demons upon the whole earth'.[9] The population of late eighteenth-century Portsmouth was highly cosmopolitan. Russian sailors, particularly after 1769, rubbed shoulders with Hessian and Scottish soldiery, lascar seamen, timid Malay and Indian servants, with dejected Chinese, Polish lancers, negroes, mulattos, Jews, French refugees and many others. While all had needs, fears and aspirations, the yard workforce needed discipline, payment and food.

To make sense of the relationship between yard and town in the age of Nelson, six key questions need answering. What were their comparative sizes over time? To what extent was the relationship affected by war? Did the key institutions in the life and work of Portsmouth during the half century after 1758 generate tensions? What part did seaborne commerce play in the relationship? What were yard workers' lifestyles like? Did the urban community's face change as a result of the relationship? Once answers have been provided, the lie might be given to the idea that Portsmouth's growth was explained wholly and solely by a naval presence.

The Yard Workforce: change over time.

Portsmouth's dockyard workforce experienced change and growth over time, the former being dictated, as with so many other aspects of the long eighteenth century, by war.

When war broke out, which it did with near monotonous regularity after 1739, and almost invariably against France, employment opportunities in Portsmouth increased substantially. Yard employment figures for the second half of the eighteenth century are tabulated below:

Table 1
**Portsmouth Dockyard Employment
1754-1805**

1754	1,000-1,500	1780	2,431
1762	2,033	1782	2,445
1774	2,883	1790	2,219
1776	1,999	1805	3,000
1778	2,234		

Sources: Vice-Admiral Sir H. Kitson, 'The Early History of Portsmouth Dockyard, 1496-1800', *MM*, 34(1948),94; P. McDougall, *Royal Dockyards* (David and Charles 1982), 90; B.L. King's MS. 44, f.5v; R.J.B. Knight (comp.), *Portsmouth Dockyard Papers 1774-1783 The American War*, (Portsmouth Record Series, 6, 1987), 157; *N.C.*, XIII, Jan-Jun 1805, 83; J. Fleming, 'The Greethams of Portsmouth: the Rise of a Professional Family' (unpublished dissertation for M.A. History, University of Portsmouth,1999), 20.

While the statistics reveal both change and fluctuation, they mask Portsmouth yard's stature nationally, for it was the largest of the royal dockyards, as figures for 1774 demonstrate quite clearly:

Table 2.
Royal Dockyard Employment in 1774.

	Yard	*Ordinary*	*Total*
Chatham	1,629	502	2,131
Deptford	1,066	199	1,265
Plymouth	1,995	527	2,522
Portsmouth	2,198	685	2,883
Sheerness	469	250	719
Woolwich	974	137	1,111
Total	8,331	2,300	10,631

Source: BL King's MS. 44, ff.5v, 12v, 16v, 20v, 27v, 32v.

Of the total workforce engaged in royal dockyards in 1774 Portsmouth had 27.1%. Quite clearly, this was a force with which to be reckoned, while also constituting considerable purchasing power in the local community.

Over time, the demographic size of that community was also to change, though the fact that there was no national census until 1801 needs to be borne in mind. The changes are tabulated below:

Table 3
**Population of Portsmouth and Portsea
1725-1811**

Year	Portsmouth Town	Portsea Town
1725	8,000	1,500
1788	7,500	20,000
1801	7,839	8,348
1811	7,103	11,004

Sources: HRO. B/3, Episcopal Visitation Returns of 1725; W.R. Ward (ed) *Parson and Parish in Eighteenth-Century Hampshire: Replies to Bishops' Visitations* (Hampshire Record Series, XIII, Winchester 1995), 314-316; *Victoria County History of Hampshire and the Isle of Wight*, V, (5 vols. 1900-12), 450.

Housing conditions within the town left something to be desired as Robert Wilkins explained in 1748:

'The Town, consisting of about Six Hundred Houses, is enclosed within a Stone-Wall several Feet thick and deep; and upon that, a very thick Mud-Wall, as high, or rather higher, than the Tops of the Houses; so that the Inhabitants are constantly buried in Smoak; But as the greatest Part of them are Natives of the Place, and upon that Account inured to it, they seldom mention it as an Inconvenience. They are badly supplied with Water,…'[10]

Dockyard growth, however, would change that situation.

The relationship between yard and town was certainly influenced by war for this meant full order books and prosperity for Portsmouth. There was money to be made from billeting troops, from supplying food and drink to soldiers, yard workers, sailors and marines, and from contracting. The fact that the armed forces contracted for everything, from buckets to food, from bricks to soap and the feeding of prisoners of war, 50% of whom were in the Portsmouth area in late 1799,[11] fostered a situation where influence and patronage could be used extensively. The result was one where rivalries arose between those who secured contracts and those who were 'left out in the cold'. Close family connections between members of the Corporation turned some contracts into virtual family possessions. Thomas Fitzherbert (1746-1822) typified the contractor. A onetime coalmeter in Portsmouth yard, he described himself as a merchant in 1774 and supplied horses on contract to the yard for machinery work and to assist with drainage. With Lord Sandwich's backing and the judicious distribution of £3,000, he became Arundel's Member of Parliament in 1780. In that same year he leased Stubbington Manor on Portsea Island, becoming 'a progressive and successful tenant'. In the Commons he was active on many issues, drawing in some of them upon his Portsmouth experiences.[12] A 'local lad made good', Fitzherbert was just one of many successful contractors.

While much has been written about Portsmouth dockyard, insufficient is yet known about the workforce's dynamics, attitudes and spending power. Their response to war comes through quite clearly, particularly at the time of the struggle against Revolutionary and Napoleonic France. Wartime exigencies required extra effort, as was made apparent in December 1792:

*'The artificers of this dockyard worked the whole of Christmas-day, a circumstance which has not happened before since the peace of 1763….
So great is the emergency for getting the ships ordered ready, that the shipwrights and caulkers afloat, and in the yard, were obliged to work during the dinner hour, and they are to be put immediately on double time'.*

While war drew ever closer, the yard workforce held their own public meeting on 16 December to discuss protecting the Constitution, an operation that was followed by similar sessions in Bridport, Poole, Wincanton, Basingstoke, Wootton Bassett in Wiltshire and in Crewkerne, Somerset, on 1

January 1793.[13] Before the end of that month it was no longer a matter of 'if' but one of 'when?' :

War is now considered here as certain – an event ever acceptable at the dock-yard, where the exertions of the artificers are truly astonishing; and the orders of Government, in every department, are executed with an alacrity heretofore unexampled.[14]

The effect of war, in naval and dockyard terms, had always been to bring increased labour opportunities for bakers, caulkers, labourers, shipwrights and others and, in a mood reminiscent of the War of the Austrian Succession, the Seven Years War and that against the revolting American colonists between 1775 and 1783, the great two-decade struggle against Revolutionary France called for more hands. In July 1796 advertisements called for skilled painters familiar with large-scale work:

Wanted, several PAINTERS, that have been used either to SHIP or HOUSE-PAINTING. Good encouragement will be given to sober industrious men (none else need apply), constant employment, with extra hours all the winter as well as summer.

Enquire by letter, or otherwise, of Mr. PHIL. AVERY, Contractor for Painters-work, at his Majesty's Dock-yard, Portsmouth. If at any considerable distance, their travelling expenses will be paid at the rate of 2s. 6d. per day.[15]

Nor was it simply ship-orientated work for which employees were sought. Early in April 1790 William Bayly, Headmaster of the Naval Academy wanted, 'a sober, steady, single Man, to do the work of the house, and manage the Kitchen garden.'

Seven years later the post was again vacant, though this time the applicant was expected to be 'middle-aged' and able to 'bear confinement'.[16]

Yard employment was not, however, always safe, steady and assured. In mid-November 1780 yard Master Sailmaker Thomas Hills complained to local magistrates regarding errant indentured apprentice Edward Hall who 'hath several times lately absented himself from his Duty in the ... Dock Yard.'[17] In September 1802 caulkers were discharged 'for refusing to go to Woolwich to work'. Besides job losses, inadequate safety procedures resulted in danger to both life and limb. On 19 June 1802 it was reported that:

Part of the under-ground storehouses, now building at the Dock-yard upon the plan of General Bentham, have given way, and the bricks and material fell in; luckily, as it had the appearance of sinking some days before, no person was below, so that no one was hurt.

That yardworkers' efforts were not unappreciated was evident early in 1805 when an anonymous donor provided 'a pot of strong beer' to each of their 3,000-strong number.[18]

What was increasingly evident to the yard workforce was their collective power and how this could be used effectively in time of war. On two occasions, in June and July 1775, the yard's shipwrights went on strike and in April 1805 they again made their muscle felt:

The whole of the mechanics in his Majesty's Dock-yard, who partially struck on Tuesday last, in consequence of not being allowed to come out at meal times, have received the Board's order to have the grievance redressed by being allowed the usual time.[19]

Contrast this with the situation in 1806 when all but 100 or so of the yard's 3,000-strong workforce simply decamped to attend Portsdown Fair.[20] They had became increasingly aware of their power and this was to be an element of increasing significance in the relationship between yard and town.

The return of peace inevitably placed Portsmouth's inhabitants in a rather different situation. Many previously small-scale businessmen, puffed up by war's insatiable demands, encountered difficulty in adjusting to new circumstances. Fewer demands meant shrinking orders and the local incidence and level of bankruptcies rose. The heaviest failures by decade, coinciding with the restoration of peace, are tabulated below:

Table 4
Portsmouth and Portsea Bankruptcies by Decade, 1746-1785

1746 – 55	14
1766 – 75	14
1776 – 85	35
Total	63

Sources: *LG* 1746-1795, passim; *GM* 1746-95, passim.

Many businesses could have been the creations of war itself; with peace, they found it harder to cope with their larger competitors. Thus there was a heavy preponderance of slop sellers, bakers, butchers and vintners amongst those who failed. Savings, if any, the resources of local charities and the old Poor Law would be their only recourse and it would be insightful to see if there was a concomitant increase in the outgoings of those bodies over time.

Rivalries, Tensions and the Yard Workforce.

Did the key institutions in late Georgian Portsmouth generate rivalries, tensions and 'crossfire' in which yardworkers, perforce, found themselves caught? The relationship between the unreformed Corporation, the dockyard and the armed forces was certainly complex. The awarding of contracts to some businessmen at the expense of others, the use of contracts as a political lure and the return of naval officers as MPs, such as Naval Controller Maurice Suckling, created the impression that Portsmouth lay firmly in the grip of their Lordships at the Admiralty. The relationship between the Corporation and the armed forces could perhaps best be described as 'fraught', while 'love-hate' was another equally apt term. Concurrent jurisdictional issues, harsh treatment by civic authorities of forces' employees and the open flouting of privileges made for strained relations, intensified by the fact that all branches of the armed forces were present in Portsmouth.

There were other institutions to take into account as well. The great contemporary trading ventures used town and yard facilities. The Levant and Royal African Companies used Portsmouth, as did the greatest of the contemporary commercial ventures, the East India Company. The town was its most important provincial depot and the Company was not averse, particularly before 1760, to using yard facilities, generating a recipe for both tension and, eventually, a certain amount of friction. The vessels of the Danish, Dutch and Swedish East India Companies drew on the resources of Portsmouth yard and town too. While such an arrangement caused problems during wartime, other institutions also had a role to play in the convoluted relationship.

The institution of religion certainly needs to be taken into account if sense is to be made of the links between the town and the ever-burgeoning dockyard. The demographic expansion upon Portsea Island between 1750 and 1805 was not without effect. The main churches of St Thomas and St Mary were joined by the newly constructed St George's, built by yard workers in 1753 under the leadership of Master House-carpenter Nicholas Vass, by St John's in 1787 and by St Ann's, the yard's own church, opened in February 1786. Missionary ventures such as the Society for the Promotion of Christian Knowledge and the Society for the Propagation of the Gospel used Portsmouth's facilities. The S.P.C.K.'s links with the town went back to at least 1710 and some yardworkers were among its regular supporters. Similarly, S.P.G. missionaries had used Portsmouth as a departure point from the early eighteenth century onwards.[21]

While religion represented authority in its various forms so, too, did Portsmouth's phalanx of customs officers. Their propensity to interfere and to be as difficult as possible, did little for their image. As symbols and agents of the ever-interfering state, they were viewed with disfavour by townsfolk and yardworkers alike. And to complete the richness of the urban tapestry there were a small number of absentee institutional owners, always concerned about their Portsmouth interests. Prime among these were the Warden and Fellows of Winchester College who held the advowson for St. Thomas's and owned property at the northern end of Portsea Island,[22] the Dean and Chapter of Windsor who owned at least one building in the High Street and the authorities of Christ Church, Oxford, who had links with a school in Penny Street in 1771, if not before.[23]

The most important walled town in eighteenth-century England, Portsmouth was marked by contrasts. It had a teeming population, whose eighteenth-century growth would lead to the development of Portsea beyond the restrictive confines imposed by the defences. While civic life was governed by the 1627 ruling Charter, effective control of town life lay in the hands of the garrison Governor, the Mayor and the resident Dockyard Commissioner, replaced in 1763 by a Port Admiral. Military control was evident to residents, their very comings and goings being controlled by the opening and shutting of the town gates at prescribed hours, by the chain of military posts stretching to Hilsea barracks at the northern end of Portsea Island, which so irked visiting thespian Tate Wilkinson in June 1758, and by the regular, eventually monotonous firing of a curfew gun which could be heard many miles from Portsmouth.[24] The constant drama, colour and activity of Portsmouth life after 1750, exemplified in the dispatch of a squadron to retake the Falklands in 1770 and the First Fleet's departure in May 1787, was in some ways, a rather superficial part only of Portsmouth life. Beneath the surface lay a bewildering mass of seething tensions, which frequently erupted into open conflict. A garrison town, an expanding dockyard, an all-powerful Corporation, the presence of countless soldiers, sailors, royal marines, Ordnance Board employees and dockyard workers, an abundance of liquor, of money and of ladies of easy virtue were sufficient to ensure a basic recipe for social disorder.

Hostility between the various organs of authority, antipathy towards them and tensions among the citizens themselves meant Portsmouth was marked by both resentment and opportunities. The latent rivalry between successful contractors and those Aldermen hoping for preferment was further coloured and compounded by political differences within the Corporation. Public service and connections converted men such as merchant Andrew Lindegren, Town Clerk George Huish and Mayor Edward Linzee into giants who bestrode the Portsmouth stage with fingers, seemingly, in every pie imaginable. Linzee, highly successful local apothecary, eight times Mayor and father of the Corporation, assembled a substantial property portfolio, in Portsmouth, Catherington and the Isle of Wight. His immediate family included his namesake son, a naval Captain; his son-in-law, Samuel, later Baron and then Viscount,

Hood, resident yard Commissioner, and his brother-in-law John Walton, Headmaster of the Naval Academy. Declining a knighthood at the 1778 Fleet Review, Linzee died in mid-May 1782 aged 84.[25]

Frictions also existed between the various branches of the armed forces in Portsmouth. The military presence was clearly demonstrated in the election of officers as burgesses during the years after 1750, though officials from other yards, such as Martin Ware, Master Builder of Woolwich Yard, were also elected.[26] The Governor's influence counted for much at election times. Quite naturally, however, this depended not only upon his talents and attributes but also upon his propensity for interference and intrigue. Customs officials, not beyond reproach, were actively disliked on several grounds. Customs duties and payments were loathed, while some officers' high-handed methods did not endear them to the general public. For rather different reasons, many civilians resented the Corporation, its power, privileges and status. With its strong Mayor, bench of Aldermen serving for life, senior officials such as the Town Clerk, Chamberlain and Sergeants-at-Mace, and apparent legions of constables, and other officers, the Corporation appeared as a force seemingly intent upon permanent interference with everybody's lives. In some respects, however, Portsmouth's population had more reason to resent the armed forces. Although they brought prosperity to the town it was at a price. Unpaid bills, quartering, damage to property and possessions, the demand for additional land, the dreaded press gang, rape, assaults and an increased illegitimacy rate were the real price paid by Portmuthians. Embezzlement was a constant headache for the yard authorities, chiefly because of the audacity and scale. In mid-December 1772 three wherry loads of stores 'which had been stolen out of his Majesty's dock yard' were recovered. Less than three months later 2½ tons of nails were found aboard the Poole hoy. 'A great number of people have absconded on this occasion, and among them a clerk belonging to the dock'. Yard workers were discharged as a result of embezzlement, the details being tabulated below:

Table 5
Embezzlement from Portsmouth Yard
1774-1780

Year	Numbers Discharged	Materials
1774	22	Oars; Iron; Rope
1775	12	Iron; Rope; Bolts
1776	13	Rope; Pitch; Nails
1777	11	Iron; Canvas; Deals
1778	5	Rope; Iron; Mauls
1779	5	Iron; Nails
1780	8	Nails; Bolts; Rope

Source: R.J.B. Knight, 66-71.

The problem was, however, to persist. Late in October 1799 a local magistrate committed to gaol, 'six men, five of whom belong to the Dock Yard' for yard embezzlement.[27]

While the bulk of the conflict in Georgian Portsmouth was between the civilian population and the armed forces, further discord came from within the yard itself. The growing workforce, increasingly aware of their own power, became something of a law unto themselves. Proposed changes in work and pay practices led to stoppages in 1775, Sandwich being faced by angry shipwrights during his visitation that June, irate at incentive payments and the introduction of task work. Furthermore the payment system and low daily wages created a dependency upon overtime and chips to produce a decent living wage. Workmen were suspicious of proposed changes, refusing to comply with a Navy Board order of 1783 to control chips. The Naval Academy in the yard soon engendered conflict of its own. There were inter-staff disputes while the pupils, instructed to stay away from the town, refrained from doing so. Rather did they become objects of resentment and scorn as 'Academites' or 'College Volunteers'. While their uniforms provided social cohesion, they also marked them out as likely targets for attacks by local inhabitants. In January 1779 three pupils, Richard Skottowe, James Murray and James Hewitt, escaped into the town and worshipped excessively at the shrine of Bacchus, having to be carried back, rather ignominiously, to the Academy.[28]

When naval vessels were paid off at the yard or prize money was distributed mayhem was likely to ensue. Townsfolk were glad, then, that troops were available to protect them, the county newspaper observing:

Few places in England are at present more flourishing than this: the great sums of prize money spent by the sailors, added to the wages constantly laid out by the number of hands employed in the dockyard, cause a greater circulation of cash than is to be found in most parts of the kingdom.[29]

On 15 February 1788 royal marines provided a second guard at the yard during paying off operations in case of untoward 'incidents' as there were 'apprehensions that the seamen who were to be paid on that day would behave improperly'.[30] When the frigates *Apollo* and *Arethusa* were paid off in mid-April 1802 released crewmen filled the ubiquitous local hostelries and London-bound coaches which were 'now always crowded with sailors, some taking 26 at a time'.[31] Conditions were not, however, ones of total comfort. In January 1758 seventy men from the *Namur* forced their way off the ship and out of the yard, and from there set off for London to complain to their Lordships about poor food. Fifteen ringleaders seeking an audience were clapped in chains, returned to Portsmouth, court martialled aboard the *Newark* and promptly executed. That March about 200 sailors went on the rampage, practically demolished a public house on the Point, throwing the beds and furniture out into the streets, attacked the beer in the cellar and then moved into the town proper where they entered several public houses, broke windows, stove in butts of beer and caused other damage.[32] Reports from 1766 and 1783 describe vividly just how unpleasant the atmosphere in the town could become. In February 1766 it was reported that:

A riot happened at Portsmouth, in which a publican's house was almost demolished. The cause was the landlord's arresting some sailors, who had spent all their money in his house, and had at last got into his debt.

In March 1783 sailors mutinied in Portsmouth and Lord Howe was sent from London to treat with them:

The crews in many of the ships, it was said, paraded about the streets with bludgeons, in a tumultuous manner, to the great dread of the inhabitants, who were under the necessity of continuing confined to their houses, to avoid danger. His lordship and Captain Leveson Gower have been successful in appeasing the sailors, every thing remaining quiet on board and on shore on the 16th instant, when his lordship left Portsmouth.[33]

It would be misleading, however, to see all such developments as being negative. The involvement of seaborne commerce in the relationship between yard and town also needs to betaken into account, especially the role of the East India Company in Portsmouth between 1758 and 1805 and the activities of its counterpart ventures from Denmark, Sweden and the United Provinces, each of whom used yard facilities. Service in the East had certainly tempted Nelson into writing to his uncle William Suckling early in 1784 for support:

'In the India Service I understand (if it remains under the Directors) their Marine force is to be under the command of a Captain in the Royal Navy: that is a station I should like.'[34]

During Nelson's lifespan the relationship between the East India Company and the Navy underwent change, readjustment and hardening. Tensions arose over the availability of materials and the provision of repair work in dockyards, particularly at Portsmouth. The two maritime services certainly viewed each other suspiciously after 1750. Manning and wage differentials, just two of the issues, caused more than a few headaches. For repair work and replacement materials for its vessels the Company could use Portsmouth's growing yard complex. Whilst those at Chatham, Plymouth and Sheerness were also used, and whilst materials were also sent, occasionally, to Deptford, it was Portsmouth yard that handled the bulk of the Company's repair work. More often than not, co-operation was readily forthcoming so that between 1740 and 1760 some two dozen Company vessels received repairs, assistance and stores from Portsmouth's yard authorities, with guaranteed extra work for the labour force. In April 1770 when the *Cruttenden* arrived at

Spithead from China 'with a valuable Cargo' and a defective foretop mast and 'trussle trees', repairs and extra stores were provided courtesy of Portsmouth. The Indiaman *Speaker* was repaired in March 1772, having been 'run on board of by His Majesty's Sloop the Scorpion'.[35] During periods of hostility, however, attitudes and relations changed, the navy finding itself under increased strain. It was then that naval demands for payment and for replacement materials became quite manic while 'inconvenience', 'harm to the King's service' and other, similar, terms featured quite freely in correspondence between the Admiralty and the Company. Arrogance, haughtiness and a begrudging attitude became increasingly evident. When five Indiamen, protected by the *Colchester*, reached St Helens in November 1757, the Company sought cables, stores and a convoy to escort them safely to the Downs. A measured response, expressing hopes for moderation, followed:

Orders are given for their being supply'd accordingly, if the present state of the Stores will admit of it. And as the misfortunes that have lately happen'd to several of the King's Ships, require great Quantities of stores to repair them, their Lordships hope the Company's Officers will ask for no more than are absolutely necessary to carry them to the Downes, whither the Colchester is order'd to convoy them.[36]

The price of supplies certainly caused concern. When the *Hawke* was supplied with a 32-cwt anchor in March 1760 the Company was asked to pay the Navy Treasurer £66 16s. 8d. for it immediately. That June local Company agent George Huish informed the Company's Secretary in London 'there is a great Difference in the Charges for the Anchors and Cables in the late War, and those in the present', while also observing that naval suggestions that the Company acquire their own facilities in Portsmouth had cost them dearly. By 1760 the Company had acquired storage and repair facilities for itself in the Camber, Portsmouth's commercial port area., where anchor and cable storehouses were rented from two local businessmen at £20 per annum, but the premises were described that June as having an 'inconvenient situation'.[37]

Despite their location, the warehouses proved their worth in July 1760 when a yard fire, described by Horace Walpole as 'woeful' and 'occasioned by lightning', led to the Company lending the Navy two cables which it had in store.[38] Co-operation was the order of the day, too, when further yard fires broke out in 1767 and 1770. In the second case arson was suggested. Damage done was estimated at £500,000, subsequently scaled down to £150,000. Guards at all royal yards were doubled and a £1,000 reward for relevant information was posted.[39]

During the American War of Independence there was grudging co-operation. When the Indiaman *Stormont* left Gravesend late in 1776, 'in a very improper Condition', permission was given for cargo lightening at Portsmouth, with a proviso:

'… the Ship to be brought to One of the King's Moorings at the upper part of the Harbour and to afford the use of Craft from the Dock Yard to unload her, if it can be done without Inconvenience to the King's Service; but their Lordships cannot consent to the making use of His Majesty's Storehouses or Ships, Receptacles for any of her Stores or Effects.'[40]

When the Company wanted two 36-cwt anchors in January 1777 they were told 'there are but two Anchors in Store at Portsmouth of that weight', both earmarked for a fifth-rate fitting for sea. When, in the following year, a 32-cwt anchor and stock were supplied to the *Calcutta*, the Company was instructed to make sure that a full replacement was 'sent to his Majesty's yard at Deptford'. Indirect indications of naval strain during the war are that only one Company vessel – the store ship *Brilliant* – was repaired in North Dock, Portsmouth, between 15 and 23 February 1782.[41] In the last analysis, however, each service had need of the other. Thus in February 1780 the Company loaned the navy three Indiamen, *Bombay Castle, Carnatic* and *Ganges*, to assist in transatlantic trooping operations.[42] With very good reason, the naval authorities grew increasingly resentful of Company wealth and strength. And yet the Company persisted in its demands, seemingly oblivious to the impact they would have on the yard.

Significant though the East India Company was in Portsmouth, that venture was only one of several great commercial undertakings that impinged upon the thriving Georgian community's royal dockyard. Vessels of the Swedish, Danish and Dutch East India Companies also made use of Portsmouth's facilities. Between August 1789 and April 1790 the *Prince Gustavus* and the *Princess Augusta* were moored in the harbour, their stay leading to two local weddings.[43] Early in April 1790 the two craft hauled up their anchors and made ready to depart for Gothenburg. A local newspaper explained:

'The two Sweedish East Indiamen that have been laying in the harbour ever since the month of August last, have received their orders to proceed home. They have bent their sails, and are only waiting for two Sweedish frigates and a sloop of war, who are expected every hour to convey them into the Baltic.'[44]

The yard also carried out repair work on returning Danish Indiamen. In 1785 the damaged *Providentia*, skippered by Henry Kent, active in the illicit British trade under the Danish flag, over-wintered at Portsmouth while repairs were carried out to his craft.[45] In his journal for 22 April 1787 surgeon Arthur Bowes-Smith, waiting anxiously aboard the *Lady Penrhyn* for First Fleet preparations to be completed, wrote 'This day a large Danish East India Man arrived at Spithead'. The *Johanna and Maria*, skippered by Captain Andreas Belle or Balle, she was on her way back to Copenhagen from Bengal. Two days later the vessel, having sprung a leak, was reported as having 'come into harbour' at Portsmouth. Repairs completed, she set sail for Copenhagen on 2 May 1787.[46] The Danish Asiatic Company was to have more than a marginal effect upon Portsmouth life in the eighteenth century. Providing extra work for the yard and additional custom for Portsmouth's tradesmen during prolonged stays, it was also responsible for some of the tea that arrived illicitly. By comparison, however, the Dutch East India Company exerted even more additional pressure on the yard.

Between the creation of the Verenigde Oost-Indische Compagnie (VOC) in March

1602 and dissolution in 1798, the Dutch enterprise was marked by rise and gradual, then dramatic, decline. National stereotyping and other forces ensured comparative unpopularity and more than a few people shared the view articulated in the late 1750s that the Dutch were a ' People extremely Clownish ... live solely on nasty Provisions and Sea Biscuit'.[47] Activity was certainly a key feature and it was on a larger, more elaborate and extensive scale than that of the Scandinavian East India ventures. Outward-bound Dutch East Indiamen called regularly at Portsmouth, details for1750-1795 being tabulated below:

Table 6
Batavia-bound Dutch Indiamen Visiting Portsmouth 1750-1795

1750-1759	17
1760-1769	7
1770-1779	16
1780-1789	6
1790-1795	6
Total	52

Source: J.R. Bruijn, F.S. Gaastra and I. Schoffer, *Dutch-Asiatic Shipping in the 17th and 18th Centuries* II (3 vols. The Hague, 1979-87), passim.

The table, while showing steady activity after 1750, also reveals a distinct falling away during periods of war when, for obvious reasons, Dutch vessels did not call in.[48] Analysis of the outward-bound vessels reveals vital information about their impact upon Portsmouth. The size, and therefore typology, of Dutch vessels visiting Portsmouth ranged from the veritable monarchs of the sea, such as the 1300-ton *Admiraal De Suffren*, in Portsmouth for nearly a month in late November 1786, through purpose-built sleek fluits down to the seemingly meagre 136-ton packetboat *Kraai* which visited in September 1794. Some vessels were in local waters for a very short period, such as the 880-ton *Schoonderloo* which, with 24 Chinese aboard, called in for one day only on 16 October 1785. The longer the stay, moreover, the greater the risk of problems manifesting themselves. Desertion and the theft of both goods and large sums of money kept aboard some of the

vessels, given the proclivities of some Portmuthians, were just two of the issues.

Most long stays at Portsmouth by VOC vessels were occasioned by necessary repair work, increasing in consequence local employment opportunities in the yard. One such case involved the Batavia-bound 1150-ton *Voorland*, skippered by Paulus Hansen. On 24 June 1761 she arrived at Portsmouth, probably under tow having lost her rudder, for vital repair work. An old man-of-war became a temporary home for her cargo, while her powder was deposited in the magazine and her weapons were stored on the Gun Wharf. Not until 28 August, however, was she ready to leave.[49]

That visits to eighteenth-century Portsmouth by VOC vessels constituted something of a mixed blessing, causing numerous problems, led the Dutch authorities to retain consular representation in Portsmouth. And it should come as no surprise to learn that for forty years the consul, *and* the official VOC agent was none other than George Huish![50] As the East India Company agent also, he was clearly well placed to keep all parties precisely informed, while doubtless receiving handsome emoluments for so doing! His duties were probably similar for both concerns, while as Town Clerk and Coroner he could deal with officialdom at all levels. His activities and talents seemed limitless, though the latter would have been required only scantily by the VOC between 1775 and 1783. In the early 1770s official representation would have been useful, especially when visiting VOC vessels brought disease with them to Portsmouth as added cargo. While provision was made for infected vessels to perform quarantine at the Mother Bank, there were occasions when health problems could become a major issue, as happened early in November 1770. While the homeward voyage could be shortened by running up the Channel, most VOC vessels used the Ireland-Scotland route instead. Homeward-bound Dutch craft calling at Portsmouth as a result were far fewer. Plymouth was used instead and only one inward-bound VOC vessel came to Portsmouth. On 6 April 1791 the 880-ton *Schoonderloo*, skippered by Hendrik Stoete, weighed anchor at Batavia. On 27 December she arrived at Portsmouth, with 101 sailors, four passengers and a cargo valued at 109,783 guilders.

Outward-bound VOC vessels were in Portsmouth on a regular, if not to say semi-fixed, basis, with clear spin-offs for the town. Yard work, business opportunities, translation and commercial work grew, helping to iron out some of the fluctuations in the town's economic performance. The cultural intermingling and admixture, to which Portsmouth was long accustomed, received new dimensions. There was, however, a real social price to be paid – violence, social dislocation and theft – while the local poor authorities were placed under added stress. Dutch East India Company deserters, of whom there were more than a few in Portsmouth, found refuge anonymity and better pay in the ranks of Britain's navy. There may, therefore, be a connection between the departure of the 1300-ton *Admiraal De Suffren* late in December 1786 and payment of relief money to two Dutchmen by the poor authorities a month later.[51] Masters of visiting Indiamen and allied craft would have heard that Portsmouth possessed the necessary supportive infrastructure, a system that yardworkers themselves needed from time to time.

Yardworker Lifestyles in Portsmouth and Portsea.

Given the multi-faceted relationship between yard and town, what were yardworker lifestyles like in Portsmouth and Portsea between 1758 and 1805? Dockyard employees, officers and men alike, were paid on a quarterly basis. The money was despatched from the Naval Treasurer's Broad Street Pay Office in London and that for both the yard and that at Plymouth was sent down by road, 'under a proper guard' to Portsmouth. Thus dragoons arrived in Portsmouth in late March 1787 with £15,000 for the yard workforce.[52] The distribution of wages and prize money and paying off vessels meant that at times Portsmouth was veritably awash with money, especially when such operations coincided with Free Mart and Portsdown Fairs, running conterminously

each July, or the departure of the mighty West and East India fleets. But when yardworkers' hard-earned pay eventually ran short, for whatever reason, they and their families were forced to enter a complex world of debt and credit about which comparatively little is known. Tradesmen doubtless became extra accommodating. And, when times became really difficult, they would have been forced back onto local poor relief or charitable sources.

When pay was available, however, there was an impressive array of facilities in which to spend it; virtually anything and everything could be purchased. Each Tuesday, Thursday and Saturday Portsmouth market was held in the High Street. Butter, cheese, chickens, crabs, eggs, fish, lobsters, pigeons, pigs, rabbits, fruit and vegetables could be obtained there. Tea, especially that supplied by provincial merchant Edward Eagleton, could be bought in various shops, including that of bookseller and stationer James Harding whose premises were at 17, Common Hard. While directories of the 1780s and 1790s and early nineteenth century show just how sophisticated the tastes of Portsmouth's citizens were, there were also developing what might be termed 'specialised' shops. A medicine and drug warehouse opened for business in 1760. Designed to meet naval needs initially, it served those of the local populace thereafter. Jewellery, silverware, cutlery, plated and hardware goods could be obtained easily as could supplies of fashionable London hats which arrived in the town each week.[53]

One commercial establishment attracting some senior yardworkers were the town's many bookshops. Portsmouth, like other great seaport communities, boasted of the ready availability of the latest travel and exploration works, books on seamanship, naval lists, navigational manuals, poetic, religious and devotional works. John Breadhower, active in Gosport in the mid-1770s before moving to Portsmouth, carried a varied stock in his High Street premises, including local guidebooks and works on Isle of Wight rambling, accounts of courts martial and travel books. He subscribed in 1789 to *The Voyage of Governor Phillip to Botany Bay*, as did enterprising local businessman and Portsmouth 'godfather' Andrew Lindegren. Location and numbers counted for much. Furthermore, as entries in directories were by payment, bookseller numbers may well have been even greater than indicated. The spare purchasing power of some senior yard workers was certainly spent on books. Subscribers to F. Price's *A Series of Particular and Useful Observations, ... upon ... the Cathedral Church of Salisbury* (London, 1753) included Thomas Bucknell, 'Builder Assistant in his Majesty's Dock Yard at Portsmouth' and Mr Lock 'Master Shipwright of his Majesty's Dock yard at Portsmouth'. When the two-volume *Memoirs of the Late Major-General Andrew Burn R.M.* went on sale in 1815 subscribers included yard Surgeon W. Walker and Storekeeper John Allcott.

Some yard employees spent their money in other ways, living in comfort and style, as men of substance and standing. During the two decades or so before Trafalgar at least five fire insurance companies retained a Portsmouth agent. Of these, the most important was the Royal Exchange, Portsmouth being one of only four provincial agencies the Company had created by 1734.[54] Details for the 1780s are set out below.

Table 7
Fire Insurance Agents in Portsmouth, 1783 – 1805

Year	Company	Agent
1783	Sun Fire	William Baker*
1784	New Fire Office	Elias Arnaud
1784	Royal Exchange	Thomas Segeswick
1789	Phoenix	John Diaper
1805	Hants, Sussex and Dorset	Mr. Rood

* Baker was also agent for the Isle of Wight.

Source: Guildhall Library MS.14386, Sun Fire Insurance Company Agents Bond Book 1768-1841,f.91; *S.J.*, 2688, 14 December 1789; *H.C.*, 1623, 8 April 1805; J. Sadler, *The Hampshire Directory* (1784), 115; *U.B.D.*, IV, 200.

Yardworkers took out fire insurance cover on their houses, some Portsea streets being particularly favoured by them, most notably Church Row, Cumberland Street, Orange Row and Warblington Street. In some instances shipwrights, such as William Cox and Mr. Luffman, were renting from yard scavelmen John Budgen and William Inion respectively in February 1771. Shipwright Ambrose Corbin rented his Orange Street home from victualler William Cuddemore who ran the *Hat in Hand* in Camden Alley in February 1782. Portsea shipwright William Merritt insured his house 'and Kitchen adjoining' in Church Row in 1782. A sample of policy details is set out below:

'Probate, newspaper and life insurance evidence provides additional insights. Thus shipwright Thomas Damerum had a house, yard, key, wharf and outhouses in East Street in 1758, while the household goods of former Clerk of the Cheque Joseph Davis were sold off in July 1800. Some yard workers also took out life insurance, the Pelican Life Company appointing local businessman J.C. Motley as its agent in 1805.'[55]

Though attempts were made to provide the new community with identity via fortifications, street names and house numbering, and order via constables, poor law officers and others, Portsea was not problem-free. Much of the lawlessness there after 1758 bore an anti-Semitic notion to it, at least eight cases coming to court. The most dramatic involved Portsea baker Henry Fisher (junior)'s rather unpleasant antics in April 1781. Spinster Obedience Douty told magistrates how she saw him:

'throw a dead Pig into the House of Israel Abraham on the Common whilst he and his wife were sitting at supper whereby she who is big with Child was greatly terrified'.

There was a genteel element to be found in the new community. At Easter 1788 Thomas Hunt was indicted for stealing three books from the home of Portsea coal merchant Thomas Holmes.[56] The Portsea Concert Room in St George's Square had been built in 1751, the Beneficial Society's Hall in 1785 and the Green Row Rooms in 1793, were all suitable for musical performances, while in 1805 Edward Frett ran a billiard room in College Lane.[57]

Table 8
Yardworkers and Fire Insurance Cover 1760-1792

Date	Name	Occupation	Residence	Cover_Value
Mar 1761	John Bedford	Quarterman	?	£400
Nov 1770	Arthur Boulton	Shipwright	40 Warblington Street	£200
Feb 1771	John Budger	Scavelman	South side, Orange Row	£100
Feb 1771	William Inion	Scavelman	South side, Orange Row	£100
Apr 1780	Peter Martell	Shipwright	?	£200
Apr 1780	John Gooden	Quarterman	Cumberland Street	£100
Feb 1782	William Merritt	Shipwright	Church Row	
Feb 1790	John Wellstead	Foreman of Sailmakers	?	£300
Nov 1792	William Stride	Shipwright	?	£100

Sources: Guildhall Library MS. 11936/136; 203; 282; 299; 366; 390, Sun Fire Insurance Policy Registers 1761-1792, passim.

Conclusion

It is clear, therefore, that the relationship between Portsmouth yard and town in the age of Nelson was complex, fraught and multifaceted. Unpleasant though it could be, Nelson was still of the view that he would 'rather take a house in the worst part of Portsmouth' than reside in Lisbon, 'the most dirty place in Europe'.[58] Pressure of demand, particularly during periods of war, drove prices up and Portmuthians became notorious for charging highly. Local residents' complete inability to charge low prices was a constant thread running through late Georgian Portsmouth, visitors frequently commenting on it. In March 1757 India-bound Stokeham Denston, observed:

'It is now almost two months since I first arrived at this place, it is expensive dull and disagreeable the town is now so full it makes it impossible ... to get a bed at any rate, and as impossible to get victuals'.

Daniel Southwell, noted sardonically of his stay in Portsmouth in the late 1780s 'my dearly earnd Wages are flying away at a fine rate but I hope soon to be amongst Friends and not Extortioners'. 'The Innkeepers of Portsmouth seem to have all the Dispositions in the world to make out handsome Bills' observed one disillusioned visitor.[59] Local residents were similarly affected with fluctuations in yard wages and, until October 1787, no banking facilities in the town.

Major employer, but also object of dislike because of its power, the dockyard became an engine for Portsmouth's growth, though it was not the only source of development. While the farms and market gardens on Portsea Island increased output to meet naval and local population needs over time, sailors and yardworkers alike had an important role to play, not least via the injection of cash. So, too, did the great contemporary commercial ventures using Portsmouth's facilities. Within both Portsmouth and Portsea some yardworkers, particularly the senior officers, clearly enjoyed status. Master Boat Builder at Portsmouth between 1757 and 1765, Edward Hunt moved to Sheerness and Woolwich, was Master Shipwright 1772-1777, before becoming Joint Surveyor of the Navy. Sheerness Storekeeper Thomas Snell served as Portsmouth yard's Clerk of the Cheque between 1773 and his death in 1786. Navy Office clerk in November 1727 John Greenway was yard Storekeeper in Portsmouth between 1747 and his death in 1791.[60] Yard surgeon David Ramsay Kerr, in post between May 1761 and November 1794, held £1,000 worth of East India Company stock for fifteen years after 1777.[61] Status could also, however, be measured via obituaries. In February 1805 the passing was recorded of 'Mr Simmonds, a Quarter Master in the Dock Yard.'[62] This contrasted sharply with a death notice of just a few months before:

> *'Lately, at Portsea, Mr Waugh, a superannuated Shipwright, whose demise should be noticed for his open, generous and humane disposition. He subscribed £50 towards the expense of clothing the Volunteers of the town; and erected one of the monuments in Kingston Church Yard, to the memory of the unfortunate sufferers in the Royal George, which sank many years since at Spithead'.*[63]

Here, surely, was a fine example of the relationship between town and yard in the Nelsonian Age?

References

1   *H(ampshire) C(hronicle)*, 1626, 29 April 1805.

2   *HC*, 764, 14 May 1787.

3   *HC*, 1631, 3 June 1805.

4   B(ritish) L(ibrary) King's MS. 44, f.5v.

5   M. Lewis, *Spithead: An Informal History* (Allen and Unwin, 1972) 163-165; Mrs Wither Bramston to Mrs Hicks Beach, 23 June 1794: H(ampshire)R(ecord)O(ffice). 20/M64/15.

6   *C(alendar) H(ome)O(ffice)P(apers) 1773-1775*, 301; *HC*, 761, 23 April 1787; *HC*, 947, 15 November 1790; *H(ampshire)T(elegraph)*, 210,219,17 October, 19 December 1803; M.M. Cloake (ed), *A Persian at the Court of King George 1809-10* (Barrie and Jenkins 1988), 295.

7   *A(nnual)R(egister) for 1768* (6th edn. 1800), 106; *HC*, 732, 25 September 1786; *P(ortsmouth)T(elegraph)*, 52, 6 October 1800; *HT*, 206, 19 September 1803; 306, 19 August 1805; 310, 16 September 1805.

8   H.C. Robbins Landon, *Haydn: Chronicle and Works* III (5 volumes 1976-1980), 262-4.

9   J.J. Cartwright (ed.) *The Travels through England of Dr Richard Pococke*, II (2 vols. Camden Society 1888-1889), 115; James Wolfe to Mother, 11 February 1758: quoted D. Ford, *Admiral Vernon and the Navy* (1907), 191.

10   R. Wilkins, *The Borough: being a faithful, tho' humorous description of one of the strongest garrisons, and sea-port towns, in Great Britain* (1748), 1.

11   *AR for 1800* (1801), 2.

12   R J B Knight, *Portsmouth Dockyard Papers 1774-1783, The American War*, City of Portsmouth, 1987, xxxvii; P(ortsmouth) C(ity) R(ecords)O(ffice) G/ICP 1/1, *Proceedings of Portsea Improvement Commission 1764-1775*, 406b, Sir L.B. Namier and J. Brooke, *The House of Commons 1754-1790*, II (3 vols. 1964), 428.

13   *S(alisbury)J(ournal)*, 2847, 31 December 1792; 2850, 21 January 1793.

14   *SJ*, 2849, 14 January 1793. This contrasted sharply with the Jew who, in mid-November 1790, took two houses on the Hard and two on the Point 'on the prospect of a war.' On the news arriving of peace he 'put an end to his existence by cutting his throat': *HC*, 947, 15 November 1790.

15   *SJ*, 3033, 25 July 1796.

16   *SJ*, 2704, 5 April 1790; 4005, 25 December 1797. The position was advertised again in January 1804.

17   PCRO S3/182/111, Borough Sessions Papers, deposition dated 17 November 1780.

18   *HT*, 152, 6 September 1802; *SJ*, 5146, 21 June 1802; *NC*, Vol XIII (Jan-June 1805), 83.

19   Knight, xliv-xlv, Appendix III; *SJ*, 3591, 8 April 1805.

20   *HT*, 356, 4 August 1806. Numbers attending the fair that year were put at 30,000.

21   SPCK Archives, London, CS2.1 Henry Newman's Letter Book 1707-1711, 27; Lambeth Palace Library, SPG Archives, Correspondence, Vols. XII, XIII, XVII, passim.

22   S. Himsworth (ed) *Winchester College Muniments* II (3 vols Chichester 1976-1984), 712-723.

23   N(ational)A(rchive)P(ublic)R(ecord)O(ffice) Prob 11/727, f.215, Will of John Vining, dated 23 April 1740; PCRO G/ICQ 1/1 Proceedings of Portsmouth Improvement Commission 1768-1799, 139.

24   T. Wilkinson, *Memoirs* I (4 volumes 1790-1791), 214; Gilbert White, *The Natural History of Selbourne* (OUP 1937), 72.

25   *G(entleman's)M(agazine)*, LII (1782), 263; J.W. Linzee, *The History of the Linzee Family* (2 volumes Boston, Massachusetts 1917), passim; NAPRO Prob 11/1092, f.299, will dated 23 February 1782.

26   PCRO CE1/15, Book of Elections and Sessions 1776-1816, 84; CE6/2, Book of Original Entries 1751-1801, 199.

27   *GM*, XLII (1772), 594; XLIII (1773), 100; *PT*, 3, 28 October 1799.

28   J.H. Thomas, 'Officer Education in the Age of Nelson: the Contribution of Portsmouth Naval Academy' (unpublished paper 1989), 9.

29   Quoted in A. Geddes, *Portsmouth during the Great French Wars, 1770-1800*, The Portsmouth Papers, no. 9 (Portsmouth City Council 1970), 3.

30   Admiralty to Lt. General Smith, 18 February 1788 :NAPRO Adm. 2/1178. I owe this reference to the kindness of my former colleague John Lowe.

31   *SJ*,5137, 19 April 1802.

32   *GM*, XXV (1755), 234; XXVIII (1758), 42,43; *AR for 1758* (9th edn 1795), 78,81,85.

33   *AR for 1766* (6th edn 1803), 63; *AR for 1783* (2nd edn 1800), 199.

34   Horatio Nelson to William Suckling, 14 January 1784: Sir H. Nicolas (ed.), *The Dispatches and Letters of Vice Admiral Lord Viscount Nelson*, I (7 vols. 1845-1846), 93-4.

35   Philip Stephens to Peter Mitchell, 25 April 1770, 30 March 1772: BL East India Company Archive E/1/53, East India Company Miscellaneous Letters Received 1770, items 99-99a; E/1/56, Miscellaneous Letters Received 1772, f.36. The 'trussle trees' were trestle trees, for which see C. Nepean Longridge, *The Anatomy of Nelson's Ships* (1970 edn), 179-180.

36   John Clevland to Robert James, 8 November 1757: E/1/40, Miscellaneous Letters Received 1757, f.239.

37   Navy Office to East India Company, 29 March 1760; George Huish to Robert James, 5 June 1760: E/1/42, Miscellaneous Letters Received1760, items 53, 89; E/1/46, Miscellaneous Letters Received 1764, item 240; B/76 East India Company Court Minutes April 1760- April 1761, ff. 71, 100.

38   Horace Walpole to Sir Horace Mann, 7 July 1760: W.S. Lewis (ed), *The Correspondence of Horace Walpole* 21 (Yale edn 42 vols 1937-91), 419-20 and notes; *GM*, XXX (1760), 345; *AR for 1760* (7th edn 1789), 119.

39   *GM*, XL (1770), 343; *AR for 1770* (6th edn 1803), 132,133; *Cal HOP 1770-1772*, 77-8; 'An Officer of Rank', *Naval Sketch-Book* II (2 vols 1826), 262.

40   Philip Stephens to Peter Mitchell, 27 December 1776: E/1/60, Miscellaneous Letters Received 1776, item 225-a.

41   Same to same, 14 January 1777: E/1/61, Miscellaneous Letters Received 1777, item 5; J. Thomas to same, 29 May 1778: E/1/62, Miscellaneous Letters Received January – June 1778; Knight, 160.

42   Philip Stephens to Peter Mitchell, 21 February 1780: E/1/66, Miscellaneous Letters Received January-June 1780, f.170.

43   *HC*, 900, 21 December 1789; W.J.C. Moens (ed) *Allegations for Marriage Licences issued by the Bishop of Winchester 1689 to 1837*, I (2 vols Harleian Society 1893), 367.

44   *HC*, 915, 5 April 1790.

45   O. Feldbaek, *India Trade under the Danish Flag 1772-1808* (Copenhagen, 1969), 257-98. The *Providentia* was formerly the *Veteran*, a British vessel.

46   P.G. Fidlon and R.J. Ryan (eds), *The Journal of Arthur Bowes Smith: Surgeon, Lady Penrhyn 1787-1789* (Sydney 1979), 13; *Daily Universal Register*, 733, 735, 24, 26 April 1787; *Lloyd's List*, 1876, 1878, 24 April, 4 May 1787.

47   Monsieur E. Dechaulapp, Calcutta, to Brigadier Merlet, Paris, 29 January 1757: E/1/40, Miscellaneous Letters Received 1757, f.23c.

48   During the 1775-1783 struggle only 9 VOC vessels called at Portsmouth, 5 of them in 1777.

49   J.R. Bruijn, F.S. Gaastra and I. Schoffer, *Dutch-Asiatic Shipping in the 17th and 18th Centuries*, II (3 vols, The Hague, 1979-1987), 466-7, 540-1, 586-7; *Cal HOP1760-1765*, 54-5. The crew may have been lodged in Hilsea barracks while the repairs were effected.

50   G. Hampson (ed) *Portsmouth Customs Letter Books 1748-1750* (Portsmouth Record Series, 8, Winchester 1994), 64; *GM*, LVIII (1788), 1129.

51   Bruijn, Gaastra and Schoffer, III, 558-9; II, 725; PCRO PL1/27, Overseers' Accounts 1786-1789, 63.

52   *HC*, 736, 23 October 1786; 758, 2 April 1787.

53   C.R.B. Barrett, *The History of the Society of Apothecaries of London* (1905), 144; *PT*, 35, 9 June 1800.

54   H.A.L. Cockerell and E. Green, *The British Insurance Business 1547-1970* (Heinemann, 1976), 20.

55   HRO Probate Records 1759A/40, will of Thomas Damerum, dated 4 December 1758; *HT*, 42, 28 July 1800; *HT*, 280, 18 February 1805. I owe the first of these references to the kindness of Brenda Poole.

56   PCRO S3/182, deposition dated 18 April 1781; S5/2, Recorder's Notes of Evidence 1788-1789, n.p.

57F.   Warren and I. Cockman, *Music in Portsmouth 1789-1842* The Portsmouth Papers no. 69 (Portsmouth City Council 1998), 3; PCRO S13/1, Borough Gaol Rate 1805, n.p.

58   Horatio Nelson to wife, 9 January 1800: G.P.B. Naish, *Nelson's Letters to his Wife and other documents 1785-1831* (1958), 493.

59   Stokeham Denston to George Denston, 11 July 1757: Nottinghamshire Record Office DDN Denston MSS 223c/11, 12, 15, 17; Daniel Southwell to Jane Southwell, 29 April 1789, cited in Jane Southwell to Revd Charles Weedon Butler, n.d.: BL Add. MS 16381, f.120v; MS EUR E.25, Francis MSS 44, Journal of a Voyage to the East Indies begun 30th March 1774, ff.1-2.

60   Knight, 149, 154, 148.

61   Knight, 150; BL L/AG/14/5/20, 25, East India Company Stock Ledgers 1774-1783, 1791-1796.

62   *N(aval)C(hronicle)*, XIII (January-June 1805), 166.

63   *NC*, XII (July-December 1804), 342. *GM*, LXXV (1805), Pt I, 85 carried the same notice.

Dr. James Thomas *is at the School of Social, Historical and Literary Studies, University of Portsmouth.*